Strongman

Strongman

∽ THE DOUG HEPBURN STORY ∽

Tom Thurston

RONSDALE PRESS

STRONGMAN: THE DOUG HEPBURN STORY
Copyright © 2003 Tom Thurston

RONSDALE PRESS
3350 West 21st Avenue
Vancouver, B.C., Canada
V6S 1G7

Typesetting: Julie Cochrane, in New Baskerville 11 pt on 15
Cover Design: Julie Cochrane
Cover Photo: Doug Hepburn performing a dead lift, c. 1953. Courtesy Ray Beck.
Paper: Ancient Forest Friendly Rolland "Enviro" — 100% post-consumer waste, totally chlorine-free and acid-free

Ronsdale Press wishes to thank the Canada Council for the Arts, the Government of Canada through the Book Publishing Industry Development Program (BPIDP), and the Province of British Columbia through the British Columbia Arts Council for their support of its publishing program.

National Library of Canada Cataloguing in Publication Data

Thurston, Tom, 1949–
    Strongman: the Doug Hepburn story / Tom Thurston.

    Includes index.
    ISBN 1-55380-009-5

    1. Hepburn, Doug, 1926–2000. 2. Strong men — Canada — Biography.
3. Weight lifters — Canada — Biography. I. Title.
GV545.52.H46T48 2003   796.41'092   C2003-910715-9

At Ronsdale Press we are committed to protecting the environment. To this end we are working with Markets Initiative (www.oldgrowthfree.com) and printers to phase out our use of paper produced from ancient forests. This book is one step towards that goal.

Printed in Canada by Hignell Printing, Winnipeg, Manitoba

To my father,
Arthur Richard Thurston:
another strong man

Acknowledgements

To all who unselfishly donated their time, photographs and memories: Leo Aquino, Lorne Atkinson, Ray Beck, Syd Brunt, Bill Copeland, Vincent Drua, John Fraser, Ernie Fulton, Brian Getten, Stan Gibson, Guy Greavette, Bill Hadley, Phil Halley, Bobby Hindley, Dave Liddell, Gerry McGourlick, Mike McGuire, Mike Poppel, Dal Richards, Jim Taylor, Ernie Trask, Ed Vien, Barry Whittaker and Dennis Wong. A special thanks to Paul Bjarnason, who supplied his support and weightlifting expertise far beyond the normal call of duty.

CONTENTS

PREFACE

IT TOOK DOUG a few years to decide if he wanted me to write this book.

Write it for what reason? Who would care?

The questions persisted, poised before us like an unfinished Olympic press, until one wet September evening in 1994 we locked the front door of Doug's Fourth Avenue storefront living quarters in Vancouver, Canada, faced each other across his large wooden desk and attempted to convert a lifetime of exceptional experience into words, on a tape recorder.

It didn't work. Perhaps the running tape recorder made us too fact-conscious, or perhaps our close proximity to each another made us too self-conscious. Whatever the reason, we couldn't get to the root of how and why "Mighty Doug" was able to excel throughout his life.

We tried sitting in different rooms, shouting questions and answers like a couple of floor traders but this was too ludicrous. Queries and replies turned to quips and retorts, serious endeavour to snorting guffaws and not one productive word was salvaged. We tried having Doug do the note-taking while I asked questions but the pen and pad played havoc with his concentration and it wasn't long before I was back to writing and we were back to our original dilemma.

The more we struggled, the less we accomplished, until after an exasperating week or so it looked as though the book might go the way of a discarded strength routine. Then one night at about midnight, while I slept soundly in my New Westminster apartment, dreaming of a world without writer's block, it all came together. The phone rang and Doug's calm voice proclaimed, "I believe we may now proceed."

I scrambled for paper and pen and suddenly Doug's life was flowing from the receiver as sweet and tonal as one of his home-made singing tapes. Mighty Doug had found that by leaning back in his chair with the lights out and his little black cat, Cupcake, curled on his chest, he could close his eyes and experience his past as vividly as if he were back in time. Every second night or so for the next few years, my phone would ring and the words would come and I would write until writer's cramp forced me to stop.

When it was all down, hundreds of hand-written pages and notes strewn on my floors and taped to my walls, ceilings and windows, it was time to take a critical look. I was astounded. There before me was one of the most inspiring and honestly told life stories I had ever read. Every motive and act was courageously bared. As I read, I knew the first of our original two questions had been answered. A story with the potential to inspire so many *had* to be told.

I committed the first three chapters to print and read them to Doug as he sat with his eyes closed and little Cupcake curled on his chest. When I finished, he was silent for a time.

Then the second of our original questions: "Think anyone will care?"

"Everyone who reads it," I said with conviction: "anyone interested in the heights that human beings can attain through character and good athletic training."

— Tom Thurston
July 2003

CHAPTER 1

HUMBLE BEGINNINGS

Conforming is being ordinary.
But then how do you do the extraordinary?

– DOUG HEPBURN
(*National Post,* online, December 13, 2000, p. 3)

When I, Douglas Ivan Hepburn, was pulled into this world on September 16, 1926, in the Vancouver General Hospital in Vancouver, British Columbia, it was anything but smooth.

My mother Gladys, small and pretty at twenty-one with slim hips not made for childbearing, needed help, so the doctor clamped forceps on my newly-formed head and pulled, causing my pliable cranium to stretch into a high cone resembling more a rocket ship or an ice cream scoop than a braincase.

My father Ivan, tall, muscular and a year older than my mother, studied me through bleary, slightly inebriated eyes and half-jokingly voiced what everyone present was probably thinking but too polite or embarrassed to say: "My God! You're not going to make him go through life like that, are you? Can't you just put him out of his misery right now?"

The skull eventually shrank back to normal, leaving only two small scars above the temples, which I cite as proof that I never wanted to be born in the first place. However, there were other impediments that were not so easily rectified. I was born with a club foot that could be corrected only by an operation that my parents could not afford. I also had a severe alternating squint, where my eyes would lock in place if I looked either too far left or right.

My most serious setback was that my parents were on the verge of divorce after less than three years of marriage. My father's excessive drinking was the main cause, but if opposites do attract, perhaps their union was fated for failure from the outset.

My mother, born Gladys Alberta Rundle in Port Perry, Ontario on September 13, 1904, was a five-foot-four, 130-pound farmer's daughter full of the aspirations normal for women of that time and station: work hard, be happy with your lot in life, get married and have children as quickly as possible. She was strong-willed, rarely cried or showed emotion, and although she had many suitors, was more embarrassed than flattered by male attention. She made it clear that she would only marry a man who could provide the security and dependability she was searching for.

My father, born Ivan Clifford Hepburn in Hope Bay, Ontario on April 20, 1903, seemed to fit that bill. He was a six-foot one-inch, 220-pound, good looking ex-semi-pro baseball player who had a way with people that gave him a successful insurance sales career and the nick-name "Happy." He drank a bit, but this had not appeared problematic to Gladys and since his outgoing personality complemented her more reserved nature, they married in a small wedding in Edmonton, Alberta, then moved to the West Coast to set up modest housekeeping in Vancouver's West End.

For a while things went well between them. They held down good-paying sales jobs — my mother in a dress shop and my father with a life insurance company — and spent happy times together. They even made plans to have a child in the near future. It soon became apparent, however, that fun-loving Ivan had more than a passing fancy for the "dram." He would go on binges that lasted days, sometimes weeks, without so much as a thought for his job or family, and by the time I appeared, mother and father were well on their way to a breakup.

My earliest recollection of my mother is of her bouncing me on her knee and singing "Redwing" in her soft, melodic voice. To this day the memory is clear in my mind and can bring me to tears. "Sing with me, Douglas," she would prompt as she balanced me with her strong hands. I did and always felt secure.

My earliest recollection of my father is of him jack-knifing a foul-smelling and improperly applied cast from my right ankle and throwing the stinking plaster out the window. Its purpose had been to straighten the club, but the constant chafing on the top of my foot had resulted in an intense pain coupled with a large open sore, thick with infected tissue. As he sliced away the plaster he shouted, "Next things I buck off will be the heads of the idiot doctors who monkey-rigged this here! And I don't mean the heads their hats are on!"

Unhappily, he was unable to mend his failing marriage as easily. As his drinking became worse, so did the confrontations between him and my mother. They finally parted for good.

I was only three years old at the time but I remember it vividly and with extreme sadness. My mother, her face solemn but determined, was coaxing me to sleep in my bedroom crib when my father entered, quite inebriated, and they began to argue. The argument turned heated and my father shoved her. Grabbing her by the throat, he slammed her against the light switch and plunged the room into darkness. I wanted to cry but I was too afraid. I sat in shock, clinging to my pillow.

When the light finally came back on, my father had left and my mother was crying. It was one of the few times I had ever seen her break down. She cried for a long time and when she stopped, it was as though she had washed away every memory of the man who had caused her so much grief and disappointment. Standing, she lifted me from the crib — prompting my tears — and proclaimed with conviction, "Everything will be all right now, Douglas. You will see." She garbage-canned her wedding picture and everything else that reminded her of her failed marriage and set out to forge a new and better life.

Her first step was to approach Ivan for a divorce. When it became obvious that he would never agree — he would always love her though she no longer loved him — she and I moved back to Edmonton to be with her family.

The Edmonton Rundles were a tightly knit clan who lived close to one another a few miles from town. My grandparents, Bertha and Hi, shared a large house with my Uncle Fred and his family; my other two Uncles, Gordon and Clayton, occupied separate houses with their families a few miles down the road. Since my grandparents' house had the most room, my mother and I moved in with them, taking over a large bedroom on the upper floor. It was a tight squeeze but, to the Rundles, family was family, so we all made do.

For my mother it was the opportunity she needed to regain control of her life. She found a sales job in a nearby dress store, gained confidence from the support of her friends and family and looked forward to a better life without an alcoholic husband.

I also fared well. I breezed through school, excelled in art and sports despite my pretzelled eyes and twisted foot, and took great delight in exploring my new surroundings: moody streets, dark alleys and the flat, bare prairie that stretched for miles in every direction.

I also managed to get into the minor scrapes that were usual for a boy of my age. Once, when I was six and visiting a turkey farm with my mother and uncles, I was asked if I wanted to help with the feeding. Having begged to do it myself, I loaded a bucket with feed, stuffed more in my pockets and headed into the pens. When I realized how large the turkeys were and how excited they grew at the prospect of food, I suddenly changed my mind. I tossed the feed pail into the air and bolted for the house. The turkeys, aware of the feed in my pockets, chased me all the way to the front door, and it was a long time before I again ventured outside alone — even longer before I quit jumping when one of my uncles sneaked up behind me shouting, "Gobble, gobble!"

Another farm incident proved less humorous. Since the farm-house was without refrigeration, butter, cream and other perish-ables were placed in a bucket and lowered into a deep well to keep them cool. Once a day the bucket was cranked up, the re-quired rations removed and the bucket lowered again. Although I was barely seven, I loved to watch the muscular arms of the men-folk crank the bucket up and down and decided one day to try it on my own. Waiting until everyone had gone into the house, I removed the well covering and cranked. The bucket was heavier than I had anticipated, but after a good deal of time and sweat I managed to crank it to the top. Bubbling with pride, I looked for someone to show off to and lost my grip. The cream, butter and other perishables splashed down into the water, and it took months to get the water potable again. No one said too much about the incident, apparently chalking it up to the greenness of youth, but my mother made it clear that she wasn't pleased. We were guests in someone else's home and had to act the part.

A short time later, when a bed became vacant in the Shriners' Hospital for Crippled Children in Winnipeg, Manitoba, my mother immediately, and against my frantic wishes, admitted me to have my club foot straightened. Why I was so terrified to go, I'm not sure. Perhaps I was remembering the cast that gave me so much pain or feared what would happen if I acquired another infection without my father around to save me. Whatever the reason, I fought like a demon whenever doctors or nurses came near and I actually kicked the face of the operating surgeon. As it turned out, my instincts had been correct. One operation turned into many, resulting in a fused ankle, an atrophying calf and a right leg an inch shorter than my left, leaving me permanently crippled. When my cast was removed, there was more extreme pain and infection.

Upon my release from the hospital, my mother and I moved back to Vancouver where she met Bill Foster, a tall, fair-haired, no-nonsense Englishman with the striking good looks of Paul New-man. Bill had a steady job in sales and no apparent addiction to alcohol. They immediately launched a romance and, since the quickest way to the mother's heart was through the son, Bill made a point of wooing me as well as my mother. He took me to the park and to ball games on a regular basis and bought me two spectacular presents within the first two years, the first a big red wagon that I pushed and rode all over the neighbourhood, honking and hooting, the second a brand new two-wheel bicycle that I pedalled all over the city and beyond, taking great pains to make each outing more rugged than the last. On one such occasion I pedalled so hard and long that my nose bled and my legs and backside seized up. It was two full days before I could walk without wincing, and two more before I could sit on a hard bicycle seat.

Another time, while pedalling down a particularly steep street, I lost control, slid underneath a parked truck and slammed into a row of garbage cans on the other side. "You okay?" asked a couple of breathless passersby who had witnessed the near-fatal display. Nodding, I brushed myself off and offered to do it again for money. When they declined, I shrugged, hopped onto my bike and pedalled away.

After a two-year courtship, Bill and my mother decided to marry. But there was a problem: she was already married and my father, Ivan, was not about to step aside. Many times he and my mother discussed divorce — sometimes quietly, sometimes heatedly — but always his answer was no. He would always love her and that was that. Since the United States' divorce laws at that time were much more lenient than Canada's, my mother decided to move to Seattle for a year and apply for a divorce there. It was not a move that she or Bill relished — she would have to quit her job and Bill could not afford to quit *his* — but it was either that way or no way. Mother and son would move to Seattle for the required year and Bill would commute from Vancouver on weekends.

Within the month, my mother had taken a bookkeeping position with a large Seattle retail store, enrolled me into Seattle Elementary, and was doing as well as could be expected for a young woman in love and alone in a strange country. Not so for myself. Being a Canadian among Americans immediately made me distrusted by other students and my cross-eyes and club foot made me the brunt of everyone's jokes. I was christened "Gimp," Hopalong," "Cross-eyes," and "Wall-eyes." Four-letter expletives were also common, forcing me to spend my time friendless and alone.

Worse, at least to begin with, I had no one to confide in. I was too shy to approach the teachers and by the time my mother returned from her job she was in no mood to hear how unhappy I was. She'd had happier days too but we both had to tough it out. End of discussion.

As a result, I made my own fun. While the other students wrestled with school work — something I had no interest in — I spent my time staring out the window, studying picture books and waiting for the final bell to ring. At home, while my mother was at work, I explored nearby woods, collecting leaves, rocks and insects.

Left to continue in that manner, I might very well have weathered the required year without further mishap, but it was not to be. My classmates, miffed at my attempts to ignore them, started throwing rocks at me, more than once leaving me bruised and on the verge of tears. When I finally decided I'd had enough, I picked up a walnut-sized rock and, with all my pent-up frustration, bounced it off the head of the ringleader, a large and obnoxious boy named Dallas Daylen. I laid him out "carp-cold" in the middle of the school yard.

I wasn't particularly pleased with what I had done — I hated violence of any kind even then — but at least my actions had brought the matter to a head (no pun intended). Once the full facts were known I would be exonerated and the rest of my tormentors would be suitably reprimanded, or so I thought. Instead, I was hauled before the principal and expelled on the spot. No explanation, just told to go. I had been trouble from day one, and here it seemed, was the perfect opportunity to get rid of me. My mother also allowed no explanations; there *were* none for injuring another student in such a manner. Since she would have to give up her job to stay home with me, my punishment would reflect that inconvenience: I would stay in bed for one solid week without visits or entertainment of any kind. I would be allowed up only to eat, bathe and perform bodily functions. If I complained, more time would be added.

It was a fate worse than being nailed nude to the school bulletin board, for I was a boy who loved the outdoors. Running, jumping, climbing and exploring were as much a part of me as my arms, legs and bicycle. But my sentence was one week, so a week it would be. I would accept it or go mad trying to fight it. Perhaps this was what my father had meant when he had once reflected, "No matter where you go, there you are, so live with it or die."

Alone in my room, I passed the time by staring out the window, feeling sorry for myself and questioning the fairness of other aspects of my life. Why did other kids have normal eyes and legs while I didn't? Why could other kids live with both their parents while I couldn't? Why did my mother get so irritated whenever I mentioned my father's name?

When my week was up I leapt out of bed eager for answers but received few — especially concerning my father. "Never mind about things that cannot be helped and concentrate on things that can — like your homework!" my mother would say. Bill would snort in agreement.

When my mother's divorce was finalized, we returned to Vancouver, where she promptly married Bill in a private ceremony that I was not allowed to attend. She secured a job as a bookkeeper for a retail store, enrolled me into Norquay Elementary School on Vancouver's East Side and settled back to bask in the security of a happily married life.

Not so for me. Life at Norquay seemed a replay of life at Seattle Elementary. No one wanted to talk to me and the abuse and name-calling resurfaced, led by a much larger and older boy named Red Hunter, a 180–pound bully with flaming red hair and a permanent sneer who had spent the last two years in the same grade and seemed determined to take it out on me. Push eventually came to shove, but when I easily out-wrestled him in front of the entire school and held him down until he gave up, the general attitude towards me changed and everyone left me alone. Some even looked up to me, once they saw how I could run, jump, climb and play sports despite my bad leg.

And I was always willing to show off if the price were right. One time, for two ice cream cones, I scaled the high, steep roof of a nearby fire department and sat on the chimney until all the firemen rushed out. In my bid to escape, I slipped, got hung up on a rickety eavestrough and had to be rescued by the very people I was trying to trick. One fireman, a lumbering brute with a heavily waxed moustache and a mouthful of chewing tobacco, suggested that a good thrashing with the fire hose was in order, but the others felt that my fear and embarrassment were punishment enough and let me go.

Another time, for more ice cream, I jumped from the top of a towering sign-board at night and knocked myself unconscious. I leapt out into nothingness and woke up face-first on the pavement with traffic rushing past me on both sides and drivers honking and shrieking for me to get off the street!

When I reached the age of thirteen, my mother enrolled me in Kitsilano High School on Vancouver's West Side and it was there that my talent for athletics became apparent — not in weightlifting yet, but in virtually all other sports. I excelled in soccer, baseball, gymnastics, bicycling and track and field. Once, during an annual school sports day, I won almost every event in my class, including the mile run, softball throw and rope climb. My gym teacher was so impressed that he tried to steer me towards a professional sports career, but, although I enjoyed sports in general, I had not found one that I was prepared to devote my life to.

Enter schoolmate and bodybuilding enthusiast, Mike Poppel, a handsome, confident, well-proportioned athlete who gave me my first taste of "pumping iron." We trained regularly at the Vancouver YMCA and, at first, being older but slightly smaller and less muscular than Mike, I just wanted to match some of his abilities. It soon became apparent that I had natural shoulder power and could easily press above my head any weight I could get from the floor to my shoulders. Where this exceptional ability came from, I have no idea. Perhaps from my father, who had been a boxer, sprinter and all around sportsman. Perhaps from my great-grand-father, Simpson Hepburn, of Bruce County, Ontario, who was renowned for his strength and was said to have once knocked down, with a single blow of his fist, an ox which had suddenly turned on him in a field. Whatever the source, pushing heavy weights above my head was something that I could do better than most and, eager to hone this new-found ability, I would place the bar on the power rack at shoulder level, load it with weight and press it overhead as many times as my stamina would allow. I was soon able to beat Mike quite handily at this movement, as well as most other lifters my size and age, and might well have been con-tent to halt my training at that point if not for an incident that occurred shortly after my fourteenth birthday.

While attending a teen dance at the Alma Academy, a large, wooden-floored hall near the intersection of Broadway Avenue and Alma Street on Vancouver's West Side, I met Eileen Ruffel. She was a tall, lively, voluptuous girl who burst into the place look-ing larger than life and soon had every male there hounding her for a dance. I, too, was smitten, but allowed insecurity over my physical handicaps to keep me in the background — not my crip-pled foot so much, because my pant leg hid that, but my damned eyes, that had the most annoying habit of crossing and sticking at inopportune times.

Fate had other plans.

During a fast dance, the heel of Eileen's shoe broke off, flew across the packed room and hit me squarely on the kneecap. Gathering myself, I returned it to her with a bow and quipped, "A heel from a heel?" I ended up walking her home and it was the highlight of my young, hormone-charged life. We talked and joked, held hands and sang, shared a goodnight kiss that curled my toenails and answered once and for all the question of what causes erections.

As our relationship flourished with dances, parties and quiet strolls underneath the stars, it was only natural, I suppose, that I would want to impress my new love with my new abilities. I began training harder and longer and by age fifteen weighed a solid 150 pounds, a weight that I could easily press overhead. I scrimped the money together for a set of weights that allowed me the convenience of training at home in our cramped garage, and my strength and size quickly increased.

Eileen was suitably impressed and Mike pretty much took it in stride. He was the one who got me started, was he not? And for the second time in my life I might have been content to let my athletic progress take a back seat to my social life had not fate, again, stepped in.

In those days, the really massive weightlifters and bodybuilders who are common today because of steroids and other size-enhancing drugs were all but nonexistent. One starry evening while Eileen and I strolled on the beach, we happened past a man sporting the biggest muscles I had ever seen in my life. I'd seen photographs of such builds in books and magazines but these were real and "right-in-my-face," forcing me to stare. Eileen was also staring and I suddenly knew: this was what I wanted — needed — a body that big to command that kind of respect.

It was more than just impulsive desire. It was direction! After all my time, work and indecision, I finally knew what I wanted to do with my life. What I *had* to do: become strong; the stronger the better! I didn't know how or why at that point; I knew only that if I could become a strongman like this giant before me, great things would follow. Looking to the heavens, thinking perhaps there would be a sign but not really expecting one, I was shocked to see a bright falling star. My spirit soared.

After that I didn't try to explain to anyone the full significance of my decision, for who would have understood? I wasn't sure that I did myself. But at the first hint of dawn, after an all but sleepless night, I was back to the weights, training harder and with more conviction than ever before. I was no longer content to become strong, or even stronger. I had to become the strongest. That was the deal I had made with myself and that was the only way it would work.

Yet there was a problem. Since the most efficient training procedure of forcing blood into the muscles with a lot of lifting repetitions produced small results compared to the time and effort required, I needed an edge — a new training method that would make me bigger and stronger faster. Was there such a thing, or was it just wishful thinking? I spent a sleepless night tossing and wondering, then rose with the robins to find out.

Armed with a bottle of Aspirin to keep my eyeaches at bay, I scoured every strength and bodybuilding book and magazine that I could get my hands on, looking for a clue on how to speed up my progress. I particularly sought out articles written by and about my idol, John Grimek, a tall, dark, spectacularly developed professional bodybuilder from York, Pennsylvania, and by Charles A. Smith of White Plains, New York, a gifted and prolific staff writer for barbell mogul Joe Weider's *Muscle Builder* and *Muscle Power* magazines, and one of the foremost strength authorities of the time. It was gruelling work that made my eyes burn and my head pound from all the reading, but it was also invigorating because it was something that I was really passionate about. I learned quickly, and within a few months I had formed a solid training plan that I was sure would some day make me the biggest and strongest man in the world, perhaps in history.

My first step was to stop specializing in a few lifts and muscle groups and construct a routine that developed all my muscles at once. If I were to become an all around strongman I would have to have all-around body strength: bench pressing for chest, two-arm curling for biceps, French pressing for triceps, squatting for legs, deadlifting and high-pulling for the back and pressing for the shoulders — every type of movement I could come up with to make each individual muscle grow in breadth and power.

When my workout became too taxing to do all at once, I split it in half and worked my upper body one day and my lower body the next. My goal was to lift heavier weights, and my intention was to make each workout more productive and taxing than the last.

My second step was to drastically increase my daily food intake. It took food rich in protein and carbohydrates to build muscle, and I would stuff myself five to six times a day with eggs, cheese, milk, bananas, bread and potatoes — well over 8,000 calories a day while, according to dieticians, a normal calorie intake was 2,500. Soon my bewildered mother and scowling stepfather were certain I was riddled with tape worms. "If I am," I responded with pride, "they're the biggest and healthiest in the neighbourhood!"

My third step was to employ the most effective strength and size-building routine available at that time to ensure that I achieved maximum gains in the shortest time possible. The "magic formula" of that day was "5 x 8" or five sets (groups) of eight continuous repetitions, performed with a three-minute rest between each set. This was what all the strength authorities of the era advocated and what all the top lifters did: pick a weight that you could lift eight times in a row, but not nine; lift the weight eight times in a row and rest for three minutes; repeat steps one and two until you had performed the eight repetition set a total of five times. At last, when the weight became too easy to lift, increase it until eight was the limit.

I followed this four-step routine faithfully, and although I made reasonable gains in both size and strength in all muscle groups, I couldn't help feeling that there had to be a better training formula waiting to be discovered. When the search for it took precedence over everything else, my marks dropped through the floor, household tasks were left undone and visiting a public gym became my only social activity. At about this time, Mike was developing a keen interest in finance and was soon more interested in breaking into the savings and loan business than in any records that I was attempting to break. Eileen followed suit, and since they shared a common interest in business, it wasn't long before she was Mike's girl and I was "odd lifter out."

At first I was crushed. It was the first time that my "magnificent obsession" had cost me something that I had truly valued and I wasn't sure that it had been worth it. True love and true friend-ship in exchange for little more than an opportunity to pursue an ideal? What if I failed, or never had a chance in the first place?

Still, my dream remained, although only I could see it.

My poor mother could not understand how I had turned out so differently from her expectations. I had no desire to succeed in school and, from the look of it, little or no regard for anyone's feelings other than my own. All I did was eat, lift those infernal weights and give the neighbours something to gossip about, something that my proud and private mother could not abide. She tried laying down the law with me, but without success. I did-n't know why I had to follow my own path, I just did. It was the same excuse my father had offered for his alcoholism. She tried reasoning with me by explaining how I would need a good educa-tion to earn a good living, and how bad things would be for me if I failed to acquire one. Her pleas were to no avail. She even tried cleaning me out with large doses of sulphur and molasses, but that only caused her bridge club to be routed as I retaliated by breaking heavy volleys of wind into the basement heating vent.

Stepfather Bill, "old-school" to the point of fanaticism, saw my actions more as a challenge to his authority than laziness. He was the man of the house, was he not? Trying to secure a good life for mother and son at great sacrifice to himself? But the son did as he damned well pleased — presumably with the mother's blessing — and he, Bill, deserving of more respect than he was bloody-well getting, was expected to sit back and take it?

My mother and Bill argued about the situation and finally my mother agreed that I would take my meals alone in my room until my grades and attitude improved. "I'm not Ivan, is all!" Bill snorted, his blue eyes flashing as he paced the kitchen floor before us. "I want that clear from the outset."

"It is," my mother replied, her posture straight and deter-mined, her eyes never leaving him. "And I am thankful for that." She also attempted to calm the situation by borrowing enough money from her friends and savings account to have my eyes corrected, on the condition that I work harder at home, which I did. Bill was skeptical, to say the least, but since I had promised to fulfil my mother's terms he elected to give me the benefit of the doubt.

The operation was performed at the Vancouver General Hospital by Dr. Okie Smith, a thick-waisted, well-respected surgeon who had a sour bedside manner and an irritating habit of rasping through his mouth while he performed his examinations. The entire procedure, from cutting to stitching, was performed while I was awake. My face was then wrapped in bandages until I looked like Boris Karloff as "The Mummy." When the freezing wore off a few hours later, I was ready to dive out a window from the pain and required three doses of antibiotics and three hits of morphine a day to keep me sane.

When the bandages came off two weeks later, both pupils were still inside my head and I ran around screaming, "I'm blind! They've blinded me!" The pupils eventually returned to their normal positions but another problem arose: I saw double. After a week, I was back to seeing just one of everything, but I had trouble reaching out to pick up what I saw. I would sometimes miss what I reached for by six inches. That problem eventually vanished, as did the stitches, and I had normal eyes.

The feeling was incredible. Everything looked so much clearer, sharper. I could read, stare and concentrate for as long as I wanted without headaches or dizziness of any kind. I was on top of the world. Although I tried to keep my promise to become more scholarly, two consequences of the operation prevented it. First, I felt as though a river of energy had been unleashed inside me, and this made me train more and more. Second, I stumbled upon the new training formula that I had been searching for. At that time, I had no idea that it would eventually be adopted and endorsed by most world strength authorities and earn me the title of "Grandfather of Modern Powerlifting." I knew only that it felt more natural to use and afforded me a better "pump" (where the blood is forced into the muscle tissue) in less time than the traditional 5 x 8 method, which meant faster gains in size and strength. It was so simple. Instead of lifting a weight five times before taking a three-minute rest, I increased the weight and lifted it three times before resting. This allowed me to handle heavier weights during my workout and, by performing ten sets instead of five sets per workout (giving me the magic formula 10 x 3), I was able to bolt ahead of lifters using the less effective 5 x 8 method. By age seventeen I weighed 170 pounds, which I could easily military press from the power rack, had 16-inch biceps and could clean-and-press 160 pounds. I could also squat 250 pounds, bench press 220 pounds and two-hand curl 130 pounds.

Then I stumbled upon an innovation that *really* accelerated my progress — "heavy singles," where I increased my training weight yet again and rested after *each* repetition instead of after every three repetitions. This allowed me to employ the heaviest weights possible during my workout and, as a result, my lifting power soared. It was as if I had been given a secret that no one else on the planet had access to. I was so excited and motivated that I wanted only to train, train and train.

No one shared my enthusiasm. Old familiar conflicts started up at home, and, in an attempt to keep them from impeding my progress, I quit school and joined a logging camp in northern British Columbia. My job was to hook steel chokers around logs: first for a "high line" that carried logs from steep hillsides to a flat landing where they were "bucked" to size and "scaled" for board feet; later for a skidder that dragged logs to the landing. It was not a job I relished. The work was extremely taxing and left me too tired to train at night — when I had the opportunity to train at all.

My skidder operator was also far too reckless for my peace of mind. Part of my job was to crawl underneath the machine to hook and unhook chokers and the operator would barely give me time to scramble to safety before he was moving again. One morning he almost ran me over and I promptly quit and returned to Vancouver. Less than a week later, I read in the paper where the worker who had assumed my job had been killed by the same operator.

Determined to keep my life free of friction, I moved back into my parents' basement where I could train regularly. I also secured a job in a sheet metal shop that specialized in forging ship cowlings. This work also proved to be energy-draining and it wasn't long before I again found myself too tired for regular exercise. When my lifting progress began to wane, I was left with two options: get a less strenuous job, which would not have allowed me enough monthly income to survive on, or return to school.

Much to my surprise, my mother and Bill agreed to let me remain at home, rent-free, if I agreed to return to school and get good grades. Even more surprising, the principal of Kitsilano High gave me credit for my lost grade. He had faith in my ability to keep up, it seemed, even though, as he put it, "Your thinking, at times, seems to go in the back door and come out the front." Terry Banks, a reporter for the *Georgia Straight,* seemed to agree with the principal's evaluation when he wrote a few years later, "Talking with Doug Hepburn is like engaging in a game of metaphysical pinball."

Although I tried to keep my mind on my studies, the effectiveness of my heavy-singles training soon pushed them far from my mind. By age eighteen I weighed 200 pounds — a weight that I could military press from the power rack — had 16½-inch biceps and could clean-and-press 185 pounds. I could also squat 340 pounds, bench press 260 pounds and two-hand curl 140 pounds.

When I again quit school and made no attempt to look for a job, old problems resurfaced at home — only worse. There was now a monster in the basement, an eating machine that contributed nothing to the household. Bill wanted it out. It was an expense and an embarrassment and to hell with its stupid dream to become the strongest man in history. What was that likely to net anyone, except a one-way trip to the poor house? He punctuated this by slamming every door in the house and refusing to speak to me while I remained unemployed.

My mother wanted me to stay. I was her son, as irritatingly stubborn as his father, Ivan, at times, but her son all the same. She was certain that I would straighten out eventually. They just had to be patient. But Bill's patience had worn thin. One night, while I was sleeping downstairs and he and my mother were having a couple of beers upstairs in the living room, it all came to a head. They argued and Bill, drunk and shouting, "I'm sick of playing second nut to my wife's lazy lout son!", reached out and grabbed her arm as I appeared at the door.

I froze as images of my past flashed before me: my father in a drunken rage, rolling and shrieking on the backyard gravel; his slamming my mother against the light switch and plunging the room into darkness. Lifting the scowling and red-faced Bill off the floor by the front of his shirt, I hissed with a venom that I never knew I possessed, "Never do that again!" I shoved him backwards and was shocked at the result. He cart-wheeled across the room, slammed into the corner of the wall and slid to the floor semi-conscious. Unsure what to do next, I lifted my amazed and tearful mother into my arms and carried her into Kitsilano Park.

For a long time I just walked, holding her, wanting to protect her forever, and she, head on my shoulder, was apparently content to let me. I finally whispered, "Why don't you leave him?"

"And go where?" she asked.

"I'll take care of you."

"You can't take care of yourself."

"Someday I will," I heard myself say, tears welling in my eyes. "Someday I will give you everything you will ever want. I swear."

She smiled a strange, sad smile. "Don't make promises you can't keep, Douglas. That way you'll never be disappointed."

That night as I lay in my bed, the sadness of her smile wouldn't let me sleep. What had it meant? She couldn't leave because she was trapped by life or because she was trapped by love?

The next morning nothing was said of the incident, but one dark night as I returned home from a late workout, the back door opened, my suitcase and twenty dollars slid out onto the stoop and the door closed again. Bill ("Bile", as I now referred to him) had gotten the last word after all.

Not wishing to cause my mother further trouble, I accepted the decision, rented a small, ten-dollar-a-month, poorly heated east Vancouver room with a broken window and a lumpy cot, and searched for a way to get on with my dream. Food was the big thing. If I were to continue growing stronger, I would need to keep stuffing myself with protein, carbohydrates and fresh fruit — a difficult task on a near non-existent budget.

For the next few weeks, I lived aimlessly, picking up odd jobs in the morning and doing a four-hour workout in the afternoon. Then the worst news possible. I received my army draft notice. How or why I have no idea (although I was told later that it was a common occurrence to draft young men who quit school early) but the orders were clear: report to the induction centre in South Shaughnessy at the indicated date and time: 8:30 a.m. on March 8, 1944.

For a moment I contemplated running off to Bolivia or some other place where they would never find me. But since I had neither funds nor direction, I elected to keep my appointment and try to get them to change their minds, perhaps in exchange for my performing a couple of exhibition lifts for the troops somewhere.

Arriving at the appointed time, I hopped onto a suspended plate of glass to have my feet checked and heard the sweetest words ever: "You can go, the door's that way!" Fused ankles and mismatched legs, it seemed, were a military "no-no." The moment I was on the street I dropped to my knees and thanked God for blessing me with my disability. It was the only time I have ever felt that way.

After racing my bike back to my room, I received more good news. John Gunn, a kindly, middle-aged family friend and poultry farmer, had heard of my plight (probably from my mother who was still attempting to watch out for me in her own way) and wished to offer me part-time work on his large chicken ranch, Farm Boy's Poultry Services Limited, which was located in Langley, a half-hour drive from Vancouver. I was hesitant at first, perhaps remembering my Edmonton turkey melee, but soon saw it as an offer that I could not refuse. In exchange for a morning of painting, repairing, manure-shovelling or whatever, I would receive all the eggs I could eat, three dollars in wages and the rest of the day to do as I pleased.

This tickled me immensely because it not only gave me the time and energy to do my workout — as long and as heavy as I pleased — it also allowed me to hold down a second job at $1.50 a day as a lifeguard at Sunset Beach and Trout Lake in summer. The hotels loved that I was big but non-violent, and beach officials loved to watch me perform my favourite beach exercise, hand-stand push-ups on the end of a thick log, an exercise which some have called the basis of my extraordinary pressing power. At my strongest, I could push my 305-pound body up and down over forty times in a row, a sequence I would perform anywhere from thirty to forty times a day. This movement, coupled with the ten to twenty sets of heavy, military presses that I performed with weights during my gym workout, gave me incredible shoulder power that seemed to have no physical limitation.

I soon settled into a routine at the Gunn farm, which nurtured both myself and my obsession. I was eating well — dozens of eggs and bananas washed down by four to six quarts of whole milk every day — and by age nineteen I weighed 220 pounds, could military press 240 pounds from the power rack and had 17-inch bi-ceps. I could also clean-and-press 210 pounds, squat 500 pounds, bench press 310 pounds and two-hand curl 150 pounds.

As well as making huge physical gains, I made three happy acquaintances. My first was a stray black and white cat named Snuggles that snuck into my room every night through a hole in the window and slept on my chest. Since we both welcomed the extra warmth on cold nights, I adopted him and kept him well-fed with milk and bananas, even though he rarely allowed me to pet him and bolted outside whenever I awoke.

My second acquaintance was a small but intelligent strength enthusiast and concert accordionist named Leo Aquino, whom I met while working as a lifeguard on Sunset Beach. Since we both loved music, we spent many happy hours honing our talents: me doing my best to belt out Perry Como and Frank Sinatra tunes; him flawlessly performing complicated piano accordion compositions. We also spent many hours discussing religion (Leo was a practising Buddhist while I was still searching for answers), and within a short time, we had become fast friends and part-time training partners.

My third acquaintance was a tiny but powerfully built young lad of about my own age named Johnny Irving, who had a pleasant sense of humour, a "street-hustler's" way of talking and acting, and aspirations of becoming a professional acrobat. Since I also had acrobatic skills, we formed a friendship as well as a strength and hand-balancing act that we performed before beach and bar audiences at every opportunity. For spare change, beer or whatever else was offered, we would perform a series of spectacular feats: pressing Little Johnny above my head with two hands as he performed a handstand on my hands or my barbell; pressing Johnny above my head with one hand as he performed a one-handed handstand on my hand or dumbbell; hanging a ninety-pound weight on my little finger and extending my arm while Johnny performed a handstand on my other extended arm; ripping a licence plate in half with my bare hands as Johnny performed a series of flips and backflips around me.

One time, as Little Johnny was doing a one-handed handstand on my extended right arm, a drunk approached, eyed us with incredulous eyes and quipped, "Can cows fly?" Another time, as I performed one of my favourite tricks — bending a quarter against the corner of a table using just the thumb and index finger of my right hand — another spectator exclaimed, "Gives a whole new meaning to pinching pennies, don't it?"

It was also at this time, the beginning of 1948, at age twenty-two, that I began seriously entering local weightlifting meets at such places as the New Westminster YMCA, the Alma Academy, Central Park and the Marpole Community Centre. Although I knew I was strong, I surprised myself at how easily I blew away my competition. I weighed 240 pounds, could military press 290 pounds from the rack and had 20-inch biceps. I could also clean-and-press 230 pounds, squat 550 pounds, bench press 380 pounds and two-hand curl 200 pounds.

Strange to say, I received little recognition at that time from either the British Columbia Weightlifting Association (BCWA) or the Vancouver press. The BCWA recorded my wins and poundages and the papers mentioned them from time to time, but neither seemed interested in pursuing it further. I was snubbed particularly by the weightlifting division of the Canadian Amateur Athletics Union (CAAU), located in Montreal, Quebec, which was supposed to be on the lookout for new and upcoming Canadian lifting talent. The seat of Canada's strength community having always been in the East, the CAAU appeared to have an unspoken policy of "A Canadian Champion from the East or No Champion," and went out of its way to ignore my abilities even after I was regularly besting my competitors with ridiculous ease and breaking Canadian lifting records in the presence of BCWA officials and witnesses.

For example, on March 22, 1949, at a BCWA-sanctioned lifting meet at the Western Gym Club in Vancouver, I set a Canadian clean-and-press record of 300 pounds in the presence of BCWA representatives Harry Hickman and Russ Lewendon and the National Chairman of the Weightlifting Committee of the CAAU, Harry Brown. The results were sent to the CAAU in Montreal for official verification, prompting an unexpected reply. Since their best lifter could do only 220 pounds, they decided that my record lift could not have been done correctly. It was a clean-and-jerk, not a clean-and-press. That the CAAU refused to accept my lifts was verified some years later by the British Columbia Sports Hall of Fame:

> The officials in Vancouver sent details of this lift to the weightlifting headquarters in Montreal, but the national officers would not accept it. Who was Doug Hepburn? No one had even heard of him; news of the lift sounded fishy.
>
> (B.C. Sports Hall of Fame and Museum, biographical sketch of Doug Hepburn, July 7, 1966)

It was also verified by a national newspaper:

> The forms came back with a note saying: "Impossible. This man could not possibly have lifted 300 pounds. Why, the best in the east does only 220. You have made a mistake." Three times they sent that form. Three times it was sent back. It never was accepted.
>
> (Paul Rimstead, "So Strong, So What — The Sorry Life of Doug Hepburn," *Toronto Star Weekly,* March 11, 1967, p. 22)

To be fair, since my shoulder power was so far ahead of every other Canadian lifter's, Montreal may have truly believed that the press had been performed incorrectly. But when they began refusing *all* my records without bothering to send a CAAU representative to investigate, it seemed more likely that they didn't *want* to believe. Since the BCWA wasn't prepared to force the issue on my behalf (the weightlifting division of the CAAU having more power and funding than the BCWA), the situation was virtually ignored and neither the media nor the majority of the Canadian people saw my plight for what it was. Nor did they see my ability and potential for what they were. As a reporter for *Time* magazine commented:

> Most Vancouverites thought Doug was bragging when he claimed to be approaching world record lifting capability and Vancouver newspapers buried his exploits as sport-page filler-stuff, when they bothered to cover them at all.
>
> (*Time,* September 14, 1953)

At one point, I considered travelling to Montreal and performing my lifts in person, but since there was no way that I could actually *prove* that I was pressing and not jerking (at that time there were no video tapes to be slowed down and examined) I soon saw it as an unrealistic alternative. If the eastern officials wanted my lifts disqualified they would certainly find a way. What made me feel even worse was that I was now as large or larger than the body-builder who had first inspired me, but I was getting nowhere near the same respect. Even though I was performing such outstanding feats as a standing press-behind-the-neck with 330 pounds, a full squat with 600 pounds and a kneeling military press with 330 pounds, both men and women made fun of my size. I had trouble fitting into clothes and beds, required two seats at movie houses and came to see myself more as a freak than a serious athlete attempting to make a name for himself.

Then one day, while I was flipping through a copy of *Muscle Power* magazine, the answer to my dilemma leapt out at me like a startled cat: Charles A. Smith from White Plains, New York. A former war hero who earned seven decorations for meritorious service and bravery in the British Royal Navy, Smith was the weight-lifting editor for the Joe Weider magazine empire and one of the foremost strength authorities in the world. I would write this learned man for his unbiased evaluation and follow whatever advice he offered.

I hashed over my decision for a couple of days, then one dreary afternoon on February 2, 1950 at the ripe, young age of twenty-four, I penned a letter outlining my statistics and the non-recognition problem that I was having. Tossing in a couple of photographs, I signed the letter, held it to the heavens for luck and mailed it.

Since I had no idea what to expect, I did what I always did when I was nervous or struggling with a problem: I reached for my weights.

CHAPTER 2

NO RESPECT

*In the Soviet Union — I'm not talking politics —
pictures of top people always include weightlifters,
because the athlete contributes as much to society as
the nuclear scientist. They know that there.*

– DOUG HEPBURN
(as quoted by Scott Macrae, *Vancouver Sun*, December 12, 1975)

Awaiting Charles Smith's reply was the most anxious time I
have ever sweated through, including the time spent at
strength competitions awaiting my turn to lift. At competitions I
knew what to expect. If all went well, I collected my trophy, knew
that my training program was on track and prepared for the next
meet. If all went less than I expected, I ferreted out the reason
and initiated a gruelling correction procedure.

Waiting for Charles Smith's evaluation was something else.
Here was a professional in his field who had studied and evaluated
most of the strength and lifting legends of the era: from John
Davis, the World and Olympic heavyweight weightlifting champion
at that time; to Steve Stanko, Mr. America in 1944, and a former

member of the U.S. Olympic team and the first lifter in the world to total over 1000 pounds in the three Olympic lifts; to Jules Bacon, Mr. America in 1943; to my idol John Grimek, a strongman and professional bodybuilder; and to a host of others. If anyone could make Canada stand up and take notice of who I was and what I was trying to do, it was this learned professional.

Would he? Seconds turned into days and days into months. Knowing that I had to stop thinking about it or risk going insane, I threw myself into my training. Perhaps I would get the respect I was searching for without Mr. Smith's intervention.

I didn't. On May 28, 1950, I won the British Columbia Open Weightlifting Championships in Vancouver and set an unofficial *world* record clean-and-press of 339½ pounds — unofficial because the weightlifting division of the CAAU in Montreal had not yet officially recognized it. The meet was conducted under strict CAAU guidelines and again officiated by Harry Hickman, Russ Lewendon and Harry Brown. The results were sent to Montreal for official verification, prompting the familiar response from the CAAU that since their best lifter could do only 280 pounds it could not have been done correctly. "Three times the results were sent to the CAAU, accompanied by the written testimonies of the three BCWA representatives. Three times the CAAU refused to give [Doug] credit for the lift." (Paul Rimstead, "So Strong, so What — The Sorry Life of Doug Hepburn," *Toronto Star Weekly*, March 11, 1967, p. 22)

When I asked Mr. Hickman, Mr. Lewendon and Mr. Brown what they planned to do about it, their response was also familiar: "What *can* we do about it? Montreal has the final say!" I was crushed. Was I destined to be shunned by eastern Canada for my entire career, no matter how much I lifted or how many medals I was capable of winning for my country, simply because I had been born in western Canada?

At this point, in the interest of fairness, it should be pointed out that the Vancouver media might have been reluctant to become involved because they weren't sure if my record presses had been done correctly. Yes, weightlifting experts from Vancouver were certifying the lifts in writing, but, since equally credible experts in Montreal were refusing to on the grounds of bad form, who could be sure who was right?

I knew the lifts were good, however, and was fast becoming enraged at the CAAU's refusal to give me the recognition that I had clearly earned. To offset the depression that was fast flooding over me, I increased the hours I spent lifting in the gym and bouncing in bars. The less time I had to stew about my lack of recognition, the better. As it turned out, ignoring the trouble was the right thing to do. My lifting ability steadily increased and the time I spent in the bars was always more pleasure than work. Friends like Little Johnny, Leo, Mike, Eileen and many others showed up from time to time and we would joke, sing and soon be the centre of attention.

When Johnny and I felt particularly impish, we would perform our favourite gag, to the delight of the bar. Johnny and I would fake an argument, with Johnny shouting and threatening to hit me as I acted fearful. At the end of the scene, he would grab me by the scruff of the neck and run me the length of the bar. He would then roll me through the front door out onto the street, where I would lie cowering and gasping. More than one observer was shocked to the point of staring and Johnny would tuck his thumbs into his belt and snarl, "Wanna be next?" The bar would then burst into applause and it would be free beer for Johnny, myself and whoever was with us for the rest of the night. Our little skit soon became so famous that many people came to the bar for the sole purpose of watching.

I enjoyed bouncing because I rarely had problems. Everyone knew that I was non-violent and treated me more as a friend than an employee. The odd time I earned my money, however, and two instances deserve mention. Once, while I was at the Fraser Arms Hotel in Vancouver, discussing my non-recognition problem with a couple of inebriated customers, a couple of 200-pounders got into an argument that escalated into a wrestling match. Not wanting it to get out of hand, I rushed over, grabbed the top wrestler by his arm and leg and yanked up as though I was "cleaning" a heavy barbell. What happened next shocked everyone, including myself. The man flew up and over my head and landed on a table ten to fifteen feet behind me. I had been practising this movement with 400 pounds and the 200-pounder flew like Superman.

Another time at the Devonshire Hotel in Vancouver, a smallish, inebriated man with large feet and ears sitting by himself in the corner suddenly jumped up and shouted, "I'm looking for a fight!"

Wondering what had set him off, I started towards him.

"You'll do!" he shouted and charged me, swinging like a windmill.

Not wanting to hurt him, I put him in a headlock, lifted him off the floor and headed for the door. This caused him to quit swinging and to grab at anything he could get his hands and feet around to slow me down. By the time we were outside, he was attached to two chairs and a coat rack still laden with coats and hats. We sat on the chairs to catch our breath and had quite a chat before I returned to the bar and he stumbled off to find someone else to tackle.

But no matter how busy I kept myself, Charles Smith was always looming in the back of my mind. Why hadn't he written? Would he? What would he say when he did? What if there were nothing to say?

Then, in one clang of an opening mailbox, one whoop of elation on a hot, sunny May 29 in 1950, an answer was before me. The great Charles A. — the benevolent, life-giving Charles — had answered my cry for help!

Ripping the single sheet of paper from its envelope, I scanned the crisply formed, hand-penned words:

My Dear Mr. Hepburn,
Let me first say that, given your formidable dimensions and lifting ability, you have a tremendous future as a world-class weightlifter and strongman. If your fellow Canadians are reluctant to get fully behind you in this regard, rest assured that the fault lies with them and not with you. True and noble desire fortified by God-inspired faith and determination can have no fault. It can only be pure.

My eyes welled with tears of relief and admiration. Finally here was someone who understood, someone who could guide me and keep me sane among all who sought to impede and misdirect me.

The rest of Mr. Smith's letter told me exactly how to proceed: concentrate on my all around strongman feats to develop trademark capabilities that would set me apart from and above ordinary weightlifters; become adept at the Olympic snatch and the Olympic clean-and-jerk as well as the Olympic clean-and-press so that my naturally superior pressing power would make me unbeatable in any weightlifting competition; become adept at the "quick" phase of the three Olympic lifts (where the lifter drops beneath the rising bar) to ensure that my advantage of superior shoulder power was not offset by poor balance. Once I became truly unbeatable in world competition, the world (including the weightlifting division of the CAAU) would be forced to recognize my abilities. It was so simple that I wondered why I hadn't thought of it myself. I felt such a surge of renewed hope, power and determination that I rushed straight to my weights and trained with a vengeance.

Up before the roosters the following morning, I set out to master the three Olympic lifts. Each began with the bar on the floor in front of the lifter and was performed as follows:

1. Snatch. The bar is yanked upwards in *one* continuous movement to an above-the-head position; the lifter may split or squat under the bar, with the weight overhead, but must finish with the knees and elbows locked straight.
2. Clean-and-press. The bar is yanked or "cleaned" to shoulder level in one movement. The bar is then smoothly pushed or "pressed" to an above-the-head position, with the knees and elbows locked straight.
3. Clean-and-jerk. The bar is cleaned to shoulder level in one movement. The bar is then shoved or "jerked" to an above-the-head position; the lifter may split or squat under the bar, with the weight overhead, but must finish with the knees and elbows locked straight.

In all the lifts, if the bar touches any part of the body other than the hands and shoulders, the result is disqualification.

My problem with the snatch, my hardest lift, was due to my physical disability. Dropping my body beneath the rising bar was extremely difficult because my fused ankle would not bend. As a result, I had to pull the bar higher in order to compensate, which required more strength and energy during the lift. A second problem was that my fused ankle, coupled with my mismatched legs, impaired my balance while I lifted. To compensate, I had an elevated shoe built, but it did more harm than good. Through the years, my body had adjusted to the one-inch length difference, and I strained my lower back muscles whenever I used the footwear. My only solution was to practise yanking the bar as high as I could before dropping beneath it. I was never comfortable with the lift but I knew that as long as I could at least equal other lifters, my superior pressing power would keep me well ahead.

My problem with the clean-and-jerk, my second-hardest lift, was the same as with the snatch. Since my fused ankle would not bend, I had to yank the barbell higher than normal to assume the weight at shoulder height. I then had to shove it higher than normal before I could drop beneath it and lock out my elbows and knees. Poor balance was also a worry. My only solution was the same as with the snatch: pulling the weight as high as I could before attempting to drop beneath the rising bar.

My problem with my best lift, the clean-and-press, was again the result of my fused ankle and poor balance while lifting. My strong point was that I could easily press above my head any weight that I could clean to my shoulders. In fact, I could press a lot more than I could clean, as was evidenced by the world record 500-pound push-press from the shoulders that I would perform a few years later. But during a weightlifting competition, I had to first clean the weight before I could press it, so my only solution was to practise pulling the weight up as high as I could before dropping down and assuming it at shoulder height. These problems were verified by one of the foremost strength authorities of the time:

During an operation in his childhood to remedy this [club foot], some bones in his right ankle became fused together; and the mobility of that joint was thereby restricted. When Doug took up weightlifting, he found it difficult to "split" and dip under a weight because of his "tight" right ankle. This impairment resulted also in the girth of his right calf being several inches less than that of his left. Fortunately, this condition had no perceptible effect on his ability in pressing, curling, muscling-out or any other form of lifting in which he did not have to flex his right ankle. Even his ability in heavy squats with a weight on his shoulders did not seem to be affected by his ankle stiffness. However, it definitely detracted from his power and speed in lifts such as the snatch and the two hands clean-and-jerk.

(David P. Willoughby, *The Super Athletes,*
Oak Tree Publications, January 1970, p. 111)

I also started specializing in lifts and stunts that increased my reputation as a "strongman who was strong in all areas of lifting." As well as bending twelve-inch spikes, tearing licence plates and crushing cans of oil with my bare hands, I performed the following power lifts at every opportunity:

1. Press-off-the-rack — at my prime I could do 450 pounds in strict form.
2. Push press-off-the-rack — at my prime I could do 500 pounds.
3. One-arm military press — at my prime I could do one rep with 200 pounds in strict form, and 37 reps with 120 pounds in strict form.
4. Two-handed barbell curl — at my prime I could do 260 pounds in strict form.
5. Bench press — at my prime I could do 580 pounds with a wide grip.
6. Squat — at my prime I could do 800 pounds with a deep squat.
7. Deadlift — at my prime I could do 800 pounds in strict form.

8. Crucifix — at my prime I could do two 110-pound dumb-bells in strict form.
9. One-arm side hold-out — at my prime I could do 120 pounds in strict form.
10. One-arm side-press — at my prime I could do 250 pounds.
11. Hang 90 pounds from my little finger, extend it to arm's-length and hold it for ten seconds.

About this time, with the financial assistance of Bill Copeland, a young weightlifter of about my own age whom I trained with from time to time at the YMCA on Burrard Street and the Western Sports Centre on East Hastings Street (and who went on to become the Mayor of Burnaby), I moved from my old, drafty, one-room abode to an older and draftier empty store at 1108 Commercial Drive near the intersection of Venables Avenue on Vancouver's East Side. The owner, a strength enthusiast of sorts, offered it to me at a reduced rate in exchange for weightlifting advice, and pointed out that I could live in the back room and use the store area for training and setting up gym equipment. Since I really needed the extra room, I jumped at the chance and was soon training and following Charles Smith's advice with a passion. I didn't have much money and I was sleeping on a gunny-sack cot, but I was eating well — as much milk, eggs, bananas and chocolate cake as I could down a day — and I was doing what I wanted to do. The only real problem I had with my living conditions was the toilet. It had a continuous leak, despite my many attempts to repair it (or perhaps *because* of these attempts) and sounded like a bowling ball bouncing down a rain gutter every time someone flushed it.

Other lifters soon asked to move in: Ernie Fulton, a tough Irish immigrant who became the heavyweight wrestling champion of British Columbia and who participated in three world wrestling meets; the Krushnisky brothers, light-heavyweight Nick and middleweight Jake; and little Johnny Irving. In exchange for the use of their weights and gym equipment, I allowed them a couple of gunny sacks and half of my back room floor. When still other lifters, such as Stan Gibson, a wiry lightweight vegetarian; Bill Hadley, an extremely strong middleweight; Ken Lorimer, a "hard-as-nails" golden gloves boxer; and Harold Lane and Herbie Crabtree, a "Mutt and Jeff" pair of licensed electricians who had leftist political leanings (or so they wanted people to believe) began training regularly, it only made sense to start a gym where people paid for the space, equipment and training advice I'd been handing out for free. I called it the Grandview Barbell Club because it was located in the Grandview area of the city and had a grand view of lower Commercial Drive. I sold memberships for three dollars a month and soon had over seventy men, women and children training three nights a week.

I trained everyone the same way: very carefully with light weights to begin with, so that they didn't strain themselves. Once they became more experienced, I allowed them to go heavier — as long as they didn't go too heavy too fast. Training poundages should never be increased at a rate faster than the body can comfortably handle. Stimulating the muscles causes them to increase in both size and strength; overtaxing them causes all strength and size increases to stop and stay stopped until the weight is decreased and the body is allowed to recuperate.

We also had a lot of fun, especially one afternoon when a young determined middleweight lifter by the name of Bill Kelso was performing overhead presses from the power rack. He was pushing himself quite hard with my "heavy singles" program (refer to Appendix 1 for a detailed explanation) and we decided to add a little levity to the proceedings. As he struggled through his last lift, we quickly switched the light off and on and he froze.

"What happened?" he asked.

"What do you mean?" we all replied.

"Everything went black for a few seconds!"

"You must have blacked out," I fairly shouted. "You'd better get to a doctor right away!"

We waited until he was dressed and bolting for the door before we let him in on what we'd done.

"Thank God," he said, flopping into a chair. "I thought I'd busted something important."

As well as paying for the gym's rent and utilities, the membership fees were also financing my many excursions to lifting meets, as well as satisfying my gargantuan food requirement. Since I have always believed that the secret of attaining great strength is to eat a lot while performing heavy weight and low repetition exercises, I would always eat as much as I possibly could between training sessions — at times to the point of nausea. The Canadian Dietary Standards, published by the Department of National Health and Welfare, recommends 5,200 calories a day for a 200-pound man doing extremely arduous physical work all day long, and I was consuming a whopping 10,000 calories a day.

My typical daily intake was as follows:

BREAKFAST
1. Quart of whole milk.
2. Large steak.
3. Six boiled eggs.
4. Five thick pieces of buttered toast.
5. Four more glasses of milk.
6. Bowl of soup.
7. Two bowls of pudding.

MID-MORNING SNACK
1. Four quarts of whole milk.
2. Six bananas.
3. Six oranges or peaches.
4. Six tins tomato juice.

LUNCH
Fish and chips (or another steak) with all the trimmings.

MID-AFTERNOON SNACK
More milk and fruit.

DINNER
Another steak or two large tins of spaghetti.

BEDTIME SNACK

Two large hamburgers and more milk.

This heavy food intake, combined with heavy lifting, caused me to increase rapidly in muscle size and soon earned me the title, the "first of the large weightlifters." On October 17, 1950, at the Western Sports Centre, Canadian strongman and strength historian, Maurice Jones, officially recorded my measurements:

1. Height (bare feet) — 5 feet 8.5 inches.
2. Weight (stripped) — 251 pounds.
3. Neck — 18 inches.
4. Shoulder girth — 57.5 inches.
5. Bi-deltoid diameter — 23 inches.
6. Biceps (right) — 20 inches, (left) — 19.2 inches.
7. Forearm (right) — 14.5 inches, (left) — 14.1 inches.
8. Wrists (right) — 8.2 inches, (left) — 8.3 inches.
9. Chest (normal) — 52.5 inches, (expanded) — 53.2 inches.
10. Waist (relaxed) — 41.2 inches, (drawn in) — 38.5 inches.
11. Hips — 44.5 inches.
12. Thigh (right relaxed) — 28 inches, (right flexed) — 28.4 inches (left relaxed) — 28.7 inches, (left flexed) — 29 inches.
13. Knee (right) — 15.7 inches, (left) — 16 inches.
14. Calf (right atrophied) — 14.2 inches (left) — 16.2 inches
15. Ankle (right fused) — 9 inches, (left) — 9.7 inches.

My strength increased in direct proportion to my size. In late 1950, at age twenty-four, about four years before I hit my peak in both size and strength, I weighed 260 pounds, had 23-inch biceps and could easily military press 390 pounds from the power rack, clean-and-press 339 pounds, squat 580 pounds, bench press 400 pounds and two-hand curl 210 pounds.

I also performed a number of spectacular feats of strength that most people would have considered impossible at that time. The first occurred one evening outside the Western Sports Centre as a few fellow lifters and I were heading home after a workout. Feeling quite invigorated, I grabbed onto a parking meter with both hands and bent it until the money slots faced the sidewalk. It looked so out of place among the remaining straight meters on the block, that I bent them as well. The second also occurred after a workout while a few of us were on our way home. Spotting a heavy sewer cover that was sunken into the street, I lifted it out of its resting place using just the fingers of my right hand (the covers were generally removed with the help of a long, hooked, steel lever) and threw it like a frisbee across Hastings Street into a heaping garbage can that exploded on impact.

The third occurred at Lorne Atkinson's bicycle shop. I used to play around with a 110-pound anvil that Lorne had in the shop until I could finally lift it by the horn, and then press it overhead and lower it slowly into the crucifix position *and hold it there*. My fourth spectacular feat took place when I was a life guard. After working on the beach for some time I found I was able to lift overhead and carry the 425-pound life boat with its motor. Normally it took three good-sized employees to move the boat. Naturally enough, the supervisors were delighted.

As my size and abilities sky-rocketed, my association with Charles Smith evolved from a student–teacher relationship to a profound friendship between two strength enthusiasts based on mutual respect. I would read Charles' letters ten to twenty times a day and I guess it made lumbering Harold and tiny Herbie curious because it soon became apparent that they were also reading them, except that I could never catch them at it.

I tried sneaking up on them, but one always acted as guard while the other read. Whoever was watching would cough or stomp his foot and the letters would be back in place before I could obtain any clear evidence. I tried sealing the letters back in the envelopes, but I soon tired of the extra hassle. As soon as I did, they were back to their old tricks of stomping, coughing and thinking themselves quite the operators.

Then the solution. Every time I left my letters alone, I placed exactly three bread crumbs on each envelope. If the crumbs were gone when I returned, I knew that Harold and Herbie had been prying and I challenged them on it. "Into my letters again, eh boys?" Each time I did, it shocked them so much that they eventually stopped for good.

"You got a crystal ball or something?" Herbie mumbled, eyeing the room as though he was certain that it was now "bugged" with all sorts of complicated surveillance gadgets.

"No," I replied. "I bribed a couple of mice to rat on you."

"The worms!" he said.

A short time later, while I was practising some of Mr. Smith's lifting tips, I became so elated with the results that I immediately penned a letter to thank him. On a whim, I began my note, "My Dear Dipwick." Upon receiving his reply a few days later, I was delighted that he began his letter, "My Dearest Flogworthy."

From that point on it was Dipwick and Flogworthy, fast friends who discussed not just strength and weightlifting but things of all sort and description: hopes, fears, dreams, politics, philosophy, books, poems, ideals, magnificent obsessions — what it takes to make things happen, and what it takes to survive when they don't. It was as if I were back at school staring and wondering at the heavens — only this time I had someone sharing my inquisitiveness with questions and answers of his own.

"If it was easy, old boy," Charles once wrote, "everyone would be doing it!" The more I thought about that simple, obvious statement, the more I realized that struggle was the heart and soul of all athletic achievement. Yes, the training is hard and racked with pain and sacrifice at times, but the pain is as much a lure as the reward. If the athlete succeeds, he can hold his head high, knowing he has weathered all hardships and performed something that could not have been done had he not had the strength, faith and determination to see it through. Charles's final piece of advice inspired me the most:

> Do your best at all times, keep your goal clearly before you and always take time to smell the roses. It is the roses as much as anything else in life that makes what you do worth doing.

As I looked back at what my obsession had already cost me in lost love, friendship and social resources, I knew that he was right. A life is more than just one long struggle. The time between the struggles is as God-given as the time sweating in the gym, and I made a vow to make the best of every second of my existence from that moment on.

Whenever I wasn't training I was walking in the park or on the beach, singing, listening to music, reading or just plain relaxing at a coffee or movie house. When the spirit moved me I would have a quiet date with a woman I found interesting, but to be honest, at that time in my life, I considered women a threat to what I was trying to accomplish. More than once I had found myself thinking about a woman I had just met when I should have been concentrating on my workout. Knowing that I could never properly serve two masters, my choice was always my "magnificent obsession," and my promise to one day care for my mother, over love. The consequences left me hurt and lonely from time to time, but I consoled myself with the knowledge that there would be time for natural pursuits and pleasures after I made my mark on the world.

I always had time for a good laugh, however, and a "punning match" that I had with long-time friend and concert accordionist Leo Aquino one evening in downtown Vancouver's Mecca Grill comes to mind:

ME: What's up? Just loafing around?
LEO: When you have dough, you can afford to loaf.
ME: That was a crumby line.
LEO: What crust.
ME: Because I'm so well-bread.
LEO: I'll get oven with you.
ME: The yeast you can do.
LEO: That got a rise out of me.
ME: What I call half-baked humour.
LEO: I was trying to take a slice out of you.
ME: You have a very rye wit.
LEO: I hope it doesn't go against the grain.
ME: Floury too.

LEO: I call it unbleached humour.
ME: A toast! A toast!

My work always took priority over my leisure time, however, and when I became adept at the three competitive lifts, I decided to show a doubting city and country just how much I had improved. On September 30, 1950, I entered a lifting contest at Vancouver's Western Club Gym. British Columbia Weightlifting Association members Harry Hickman, Harry Brown and Russ Lewendon were again the official judges. I won the contest: clean-and-pressed 327½ pounds, clean-and-jerked 317½ pounds and snatched 255 pounds. As I attempted to clean-and-press 337½ pounds for a new world record, I lost my balance and missed the lift. I tried it a second time, but by then I was too tired.

I immediately arranged a second exhibition for November 30, 1950 (same judges and location), where I set a new world clean-and-press record of 341 pounds. To exemplify the fact that I was indeed a world-class force, I also completed a strict bench press with 400 pounds and a full squat with 504 pounds. The place erupted with cheers from both judges and spectators and a great relief washed over me.

"Finally!" I thought. "Finally they're beginning to understand!"

The BCWA forwarded the results to the CAAU in Montreal, which informed us that my lifts could not be officially accepted, this time because they had been made on a Sunday. Once again, neither the BCWA nor the press was willing to push the issue. "At least they've come up with a new excuse," Harry Brown mumbled. But I didn't find the remark the least bit humorous.

Someone in the United States was willing to take action, however. Charles A. Smith relayed news of my plight to barbell, strength and magazine mogul, Joe Weider, who immediately invited me to White Plains, New York, to give a series of lifting demonstrations. "Get him down here," Joe had apparently snorted, running a beefy hand through his thick, black hair. "Let's have a look."

It was a dream come true! Before me danced all the places and athletes I had read about all my life in strength magazines — enough history and grandeur to fuel a thousand hearts! Then reality: I didn't have enough money to make the trip, and I had no idea where I could get it. Since confessing this to such famous men was out of the question, fate seemed to have dealt me the final blow.

Enter my uncle, George Town, who owned the Quadra Club in downtown Vancouver. Well aware of the "run-around" I'd been receiving from Montreal, he fully agreed with Charles Smith that I should go to the United States to make my mark. The weightlifting division of the American AAU would have no problem officially recognizing my lifts and, once it did, the rest of the world would be forced to as well.

On December 16, 1950, ticket in hand and trademark duffel bag of milk and bananas on my shoulder, I boarded *Pacemaker,* the famous cross-country train, in Vancouver and headed for New York, and whatever destiny awaited me. My excitement mounting, I felt as though I was on the verge of something truly remarkable — a great explorer off to discover a new world.

The trip took three full days and, between gorgings of milk and bananas, gave me time and cause to become philosophical. As I watched landscape after landscape flit past, it occurred to me that life was very much like a train ride. You get on board bound for a destination and hope and pray that you get there safe and unscathed. It seems reasonable, but since you can only see as far as the next corner, you can never be sure. Only time will tell and, for the most part, it remains silent.

Arriving at New York City's busy Grand Central Station in the early evening of December 19, 1950, I was met by the very fit and distinguished Charles A. Smith, who quietly watched me exit the train. He approached me quickly.

"Mr. Flogworthy, I presume," he said with an energetic British accent, extending a hand.

"Mr. Dipwick, I presume," I replied, grasping it.

We maintained our grip as we appraised each other — both obviously impressed. As Charles was later to write:

So broad was he, so massive, so striking in appearance, that everyone around stopped, stood, stared. His very carriage spelled P O W E R!
(Osmo Kiiha, *Douglas Ivan Hepburn,*
http//www.naturalstrength.com/history/hepburn.html)

After a few pleasantries and jokes about our contrasting sizes and appetites, Charles drove us to his modest but well-maintained apartment in White Plains, where he prepared a large and tasty four-course supper. We got on well from the start and within a very short time it was as though we had been mentor and pupil our entire lives. "Don't run out into traffic unless the light is red," he warned in his characteristically opinionated tone. "They can't stop! And don't dally on the elevator. I'm not sure how long it'll hold you!"

Our conversation soon turned to Olympic weightlifting and I was amazed that he could rattle off the capabilities of every active world-class lifter, right down to the half-pound. "As far as the heavyweights go," he stated, always pacing, always full of energy, "your only competition is the current world and Olympic champion, John Davis of Brooklyn. Never underestimate him because he didn't win seven world titles on talk. Don't overestimate him because only a gorilla's got your pressing power, and he bloody isn't one. Davis's heir-apparent appears to be James Bradford of York, Pennsylvania — probably the most efficient lifter you're ever likely to lock your lookers onto — but that's still a few years off."

That night, after a good rest, we travelled by subway (Charles, a self-confessed penny-pincher, insisted that it was the fastest and cheapest form of travel in New York) to Val Pasqua's gym where I performed a powerlifting exhibition for muscular Val, shrewd and dark-haired Joe Weider and thirty or so curious onlookers: a strict two-handed curl with 200 pounds; a strict side-press with a 200-pound dumbbell; a strict, press-off-the-rack with 365 pounds; and a push press-off-the-rack (where assisting leg movement is allowed) with 385 pounds. After a brief rest and a quart of milk, I also performed my trademark lifts: hanging ninety pounds on my little finger with my arm out-stretched, and one-arm military-pressing a 200-pound dumbbell.

For a moment there was complete silence — perhaps because they weren't sure if they should applaud for a Canadian in the presence of so many American strength authorities. Then they did, singly at first, then several more, then still more, this time in unison, until they were all clapping and cheering as long and hard as they could. One by one they pumped my hand and heartily congratulated me for what I had just accomplished and for what they were certain I would accomplish in the future. I was so overwhelmed by their sincerity and their ability to place ideals and ability above nationalism that I was unable to keep my eyes from glistening with unshed tears.

"Thank you for your sportsmanship," was all I could get out. "Thank you all for your extreme sportsmanship!"

As Charles was to write:

> I have just witnessed a public demonstration in which Doug Hepburn of Canada performed ten feats of strength, not one of which could have been duplicated by any athlete in history. So far ahead of the rest of the field in his chosen sport was Hepburn that, for some of his strength feats, no one could approach within 100 pounds of his limit!
>
> (*Muscle Builder* magazine, 1951)

Val and Joe then treated Charles and me to a fantastic veal dinner with all the trimmings and assured me that I was welcome to visit at any time for as long as I chose. The gesture was so sincere that I had to blink back tears.

During our subway ride to White Plains, Charles asked, "What did you think?"

"Nice," I responded. "What did they think?"

"Nice," he responded.

Then we sat back and thought a long time about what we had each witnessed. Charles nodded to himself as he made notes in a weathered pad while I stared out the window, wondering how it would all finally end.

For the next two days, we stayed at Charles' apartment, talking strength and practising Olympic weightlifting techniques, then took a subway to Abe Goldman's gym for another exhibition. By this time, word of my Pasqua gym performance had spread and the Abe Goldman gym was crammed with famous lifters and personalities: Abe, heavyweight strongman Marvin Eder, and professional golfer Frank Stranahan, to name only a few. Fuelled by my desire to make the strongest impression possible, I repeated my Pasqua gym exhibition and added a push press-off-the-rack of 405 pounds, a strict bench press of 410 pounds and a full squat of 550 pounds. This time the place exploded with cheers and everyone charged forward to pump my hand and wish me well. "This man will be World Champion, " Charles proudly shouted, pushing his chest out as if he had just given birth to me. "If he isn't already!"

The next day we visited the Siegmund Klein gym at 717 Seventh Avenue in New York, where I performed the exhibition again and received the same enthusiastic response. Why couldn't my fellow Canadians see my feats in the same light? The more I tried to understand this, the sadder it made me, so I pushed it from my mind and made the best of being with people who did understand.

As a special treat, Charles took me to Brooklyn to meet the great World and Olympic heavyweight weightlifting Champion, John Davis. I had always held the utmost respect for this particular lifter for two reasons. First, he was an African-American who had risen to the top and stayed there for many years, despite strong racial prejudice, and I knew well how hard life can be for a person who is accepted less than others around him. Second, he was an incredibly strong lifter with a lean, muscular body that left him lighter than most heavyweight lifters. Hoisting huge weights above one's head is hard enough for any lifter, but more so for the competitor with the lightest body weight.

Before knocking on John's door, Charles offered advice that I had already given myself, "Don't do no heavy lifting in front of Davis! He'll feel bad enough when you beat him one day, without rubbing it in beforehand."

I showed the great champion only the utmost respect. He was a bit reserved, at first, probably seeing me as a threat to the crown that he had worked so hard to win and keep, and this resulted in a rather comical "ice-breaking" exchange between us:

JOHN: There are only two types of people: winners and losers.
ME: A man's reach should exceed his grasp or what's a heaven for?
JOHN: He plays best who wins.
ME: The strong man and the waterfall channel their own path.

Charles Smith eyed us, then added, "If you think chocolate-covered turds are tasteless, try them without the chocolate." John and I returned his stare, then burst out laughing. Charles joined in, and that really set us off.

The topic then turned to weightlifting, and as we discussed my non-recognition problem over coffee and upside-down cake, Davis only nodded. But the look on his handsome, sharply chiselled face said that he understood it all — and then some. When we shook hands at the end of a very pleasant evening, I made a respectful point of not gripping too hard. To my delight, he did the same.

"What did you think?" Charles asked during our trip home.

"Nice," I responded. "What did he think?"

"Nice," he replied.

We again sat back and contemplated what we had each experienced.

I spent Christmas with Charles — enjoyable, with lots of singing and good food — then, on January 6, 1951, at his urging, and after a phone call that he insisted on making to pave the way, I boarded the train to York, Pennsylvania, to meet my boyhood strength idol: famous bodybuilder John Grimek. Before leaving, I presented Charles with a coffee mug inscribed with the words: "To Charlie, my Coach — Doug Hepburn." There were tears in my eyes as I offered it, and in his as he accepted. We clasped hands and held on for a long time.

"Make me proud," he said, attempting a smile.

"I'll do my best," I replied. "If it wasn't for you, none of this would be happening."

"Oh yes it would!" Charles fairly snapped. "And don't you ever think otherwise!"

I can't put into words the excitement I felt during the one-hundred-mile train ride to York. When I was first becoming interested in strength, it was John Grimek's muscular, well-proportioned body and his ability to pose on stage that inspired me the most. He was as much the reason for my success as was Charles A. Smith, and I would soon be able to shake his hand and thank him personally. As I stared out the window of the moving train, I felt strong and vulnerable at the same time.

At York, I was met by a fit and smiling John Grimek, who was accompanied by an equally fit and smiling Ray Van Cleef, associate editor of Bob Hoffman's *Strength and Health* magazine. They immediately made me feel at ease, and I couldn't help saying to John: "I've looked up to you for years; your picture is on my wall." To my delight, he patted my shoulder and replied, "Some day you're going to be on everyone's wall." Ray heartily agreed and drove us to the sprawling Grimek residence where Mrs. Grimek and Mrs. Van Cleef, both lovely women, served us a fantastic spaghetti dinner, replete with a giant salad and a huge tray of steaming garlic bread. We spent the day talking and laughing as though we had grown up together, then travelled to Bob Hoffman's private gym in downtown York where I gave yet another lifting exhibition.

Bob was an extremely aggressive personality and businessman. Thick-necked and muscular with an intense and constant expression that bordered on a scowl, he was the owner and founder of the York Barbell Company, the editor-in-chief of *Strength and Health* magazine, the founder of American Weightlifting and the coach and unofficial sponsor of the United States weightlifting team. He was also extremely interested in my lifting ability, as were the forty or so invited lifters and strength personalities: former heavyweight lifter Steve Stanko, lightweight lifter Joe Pitman, middleweight lifter and former world champion Frank Spellman, and famous bodybuilders Jake Hitchins and Dick Bachtell, among others. John Davis had also made the trip and he greeted me with a warm smile.

"So you're he," Hoffman said, eyeing me with a sour mixture of curiosity and skepticism.

"I suppose," I replied, offering a smile.

As we shook hands, he stared into my eyes and squeezed as hard as he could. I squeezed back hard enough to let him know who had the hardest grip — by a long ways — and left it at that.

Wanting to make a grand impression without revealing my full capability to the U.S. weightlifting team, I gritted my teeth and went *almost* all out. With very little rest between exertions, I performed my trademark lifts plus a military press-off-the-rack with 350 pounds; a push press-off-the-rack with 400 pounds; a right-arm military press with a 155-pound dumbbell; and a right-hand deadlift with a replica of the famous 235-pound Louis Cyr dumbbell. Mr. Cyr was a 365-pound Canadian strongman from St. Cyprien de Napierville, Quebec, who was renowned for his strength and, in particular, his ability to lift his dumbbell from the floor with one hand. The dumbbell's extremely thick handle made the lift almost impossible for lifters with normal-sized hands such as mine.

Everyone whooped and cheered except Bob Hoffman, who remained quiet and kept looking at my hands. At the end of the night he calmly told me, "You realize you don't have the organs of a normal man." He then arranged free room and board for me for as long as I wished to stay in York, and invited me to participate in a White Plains weightlifting competition that was to take place in two days. He would pay my expenses. Assuming that it was Hoffman's way of discovering how I held up under competitive conditions, I agreed. Charles Smith and Joe Weider arranged for me to work out privately at Val Pasqua's gym, and news of the event was soon buzzing throughout the East Coast strength community.

On January 9, 1951, after spending some truly enjoyable time with the Grimeks and the Van Cleefs, I entered the U.S. Open Weightlifting Championships at White Plains, where I won the tournament, beating out a young Paul Anderson, a thick-thighed, wide-waisted, up-and-coming American lifter with stupendous squatting ability; set a world clean-and-press record of 330 pounds; and had the record officially accepted by the American AAU.

Charles Smith was there, of course, as excited as I was. "How's that for news, old boy?" he fairly bubbled. "I knew they'd invite you, but it had to be your decision!"

On the way to the change room, I passed a solemn Bob Hoffman who spoke without looking at me or stopping. "Keep coming on like that and we're gonna to have to change your nationality!" I was shocked. Was this to be my destiny? A member of the American weightlifting team competing against my own countrymen?

Needing time alone to think about the possibility of taking out U.S. citizenship, I tucked Charles's address and phone number in my coat breast pocket, slung my duffel of bananas and milk over my shoulder and headed off down an icy, snow-packed sidewalk. It was as though I had stepped into another dimension. The street was crowded, as were most New York streets in the early evening, but everything seemed alien. Looking for a quiet beach or park, I found only waves of unrecognizable streets and buildings.

It mattered little because I had already made my decision. Becoming an American citizen was not for me. Although I greatly loved their appreciation of my accomplishments, as well as their ability to place personal achievement above politics, my heart and home were in Canada. Canadians did not yet appreciate me, but that could change and I had to live and work towards that day.

Studying the unfamiliar scene unfolding around me, I suddenly realized how very much I missed the serenity of Stanley Park and its secluded beaches. Home is more than just where you come from. It is where you belong, where you can stand and breathe in memories and know that you and your recollections are one, no matter what others might think of you or try to have you think about yourself. It is the place, not the people, that you bond to, and I knew without a doubt that I was bonded to Vancouver, British Columbia, not White Plains, New York.

On January 14, 1951, after we shook hands and promised forever to remain student and mentor, I left Charles at New York's Grand Central Station and boarded the *Pacemaker* for Vancouver and an uncertain future. When I had left Vancouver for New York, my destiny had been uncertain. As I returned to Vancouver, it was still unclear, but clearer than it had been. I would return to my homeland and break records until my fellow Canadians saw me in the same light as the Americans. It wouldn't be easy, but it was something that I had to do.

As I relaxed in my train seat, I extracted a strength magazine from my duffel and perused an article about my White Plains performance:

> Less than 24 hours ago I watched Canada's Doug Hepburn give an exhibition of strength that can only be described as *fantastic* in its immensity. Hard-boiled officials and judges watched him, their mouths open, their eyes staring in amazement at the magnitude of his performance!
>
> (Joe Weider, *Muscle Builder* magazine, 1951)

I replaced the article in my duffel. What would Canadian critics have to say about that — if anything?

At the Vancouver station, I sought out a newsstand to find out: a brief blurb crammed near the bottom of the last page about my setting some sort of U.S. record — and little else. I smiled as I recalled Irish writer Brendan Behan's definition of a critic: "A critic is like a eunuch in a harem; he sees the trick performed every night but can't do it himself." So be it. If my time for national acceptance was not yet at hand, then I would "endeavour to persevere," as the saying goes, until it was.

I hopped a streetcar to my Commercial Drive gym and studied the sports section of several newspapers on the way. As I read about all the large salaries that professional athletes were earning, something that I wasn't allowed to do because I was competing as an amateur, even though amateur athletes in other countries were being paid by the state to train, I composed the following poem to Avery Brundage, the then president of the International Olympic Committee and the self-proclaimed "Protector of Amateurism":

> Dear Avery it's slavery,
> To train and strain for naught.
> I took some dough, now I'm a pro,
> What darn fool tommy-rot.
>
> To be true-blue with the AAU,
> I must be Simon-pure.
> If Simon knew what I've been through,
> He'd change his tune I'm sure.
>
> Dear Brundage, sir, may I demur,
> There's something I must say.
> I can't compete with the sports elite,
> Unless I get some pay.

Arriving at my gym, I found Herbie, Harold and a host of others (most of whom I had never seen before) passed out on the floor — as well as on top of my gunny sack bed. Reluctant to wake them, I retired to a three-dollar-a-night flop house on East Hastings. As I lay there on my lumpy mattress attempting to adjust to the noise and the train lag, I thought back to what Charles Smith had told me: "If it was easy, everyone would be doing it!" The words gave me some comfort and I fell asleep dreaming of better, more fulfilling days that I was sure were on the horizon.

Early the next morning, after stuffing myself with bananas and milk, I headed out to show my ever-supportive mother and my ever-doubting stepfather the latest fruits of my labour. To my horror, I discovered from a neighbour that they had moved to Hollywood, California, with no plans to return. They had secured jobs in a large retail store called "The Famous" — my mother in accounting and "Bile" in sales — and were embarked on a new and better life in the country that I had just left.

A great feeling of loneliness washed over me. Despite all the time I had spent alone in the last few years, it had been bearable, in part, because I knew that my mother was but a call or door-knock away. I could see or talk to her at any time, and it gave me a sense of security. Now that security had been yanked away and it made me want to talk to her even more.

She had left a forwarding address, thank God, so I immediately composed a telegram:

Dear Mother — surprised you moved — hope you are happy — I get a lift out of you — Doug

I mailed it the same day and prayed that she would respond quickly. But, as experience and my father's advice had taught me, "things happen as they happen, so live with it or die." My mother had gotten on with her life and it was time for me to get on with mine.

On March 23, 1951, I gave a weightlifting exhibition at the annual New Westminster YMCA Show in New Westminster, B.C., where I set a world clean-and-press record of 340 pounds and set a world bench press record of 420 pounds. To my dismay, both were rejected by the weightlifting division of the CAAU in Montreal, even though the American AAU had just accredited me with a world record in the clean-and-press. As usual, neither the BCWA nor the Canadian media seemed prepared to make an issue of it, so my only option was once again to force it from my mind and continue demonstrating my prowess as emphatically as I could.

On April 17, 1951, I entered a weightlifting competition at the Western Sports Centre in Vancouver. I won the competition, setting a world clean-and-press record of 345 pounds, but had my world record rejected by Montreal because it had been performed on a Sunday. By this time, I was expecting the rejection and actually laughed at how blatantly ridiculous it had all become. At least one Vancouver reporter agreed with me:

Hepburn has pressed 345 pounds, although the weightlifting coterie in the East have yet to recognize this fact. His total weight lift of 960 pounds eclipses by far the 880 pound mark of England's Alphie Knight, the current British Empire champion. However,

most of Doug's feats have been accomplished on a Sunday, a day
just not sanctionable for such things, to the AAU's way of thinking!
(Al Horton, *Vancouver News-Herald*, April 1951)

Heartened by the fact that at least one learned professional was in
my corner, I scrimped together enough money to take the train to
Los Angeles, California, and on June 19, 1952 entered the Senior
Nationals Open Weightlifting Competition where I came second
to World and Olympic Champion, John Davis, who won on total
points for the three lifts. I also set a world clean-and-press record
of 345 ½ pounds, beating Davis's 337½-pound clean-and-press by
eight pounds.

I was elated. I had entered the competition more to set a new
world clean-and-press record at a major U.S. competition than to
win, and had almost won anyway. What might have resulted, had I
trained as heavily for the snatch and the clean-and-jerk as I had
trained for the clean-and-press? I could see that my superior
pressing power was indeed pushing me towards unprecedented
achievement — just as Charles A. Smith had predicted. Once I
could consistently equal my competitors in the snatch and the
clean-and-jerk, it would be impossible for them to best me. An
eight-pound lead is huge when dealing with extremely heavy
weights and I knew that my pressing power would only increase
with time.

As usual, Charles A. Smith was ecstatic and we had a heart-
warming lunch and visit. Between mouthfuls of thick crabcake
sandwiches, he told me all the local weightlifting gossip, particularly how worried American team coach Bob Hoffman and heavyweight lifter John Davis were that they might have to face me in
Olympic competition. At the train station, he turned serious.
"This is beyond nationalism, you know," he said, gripping my
shoulder as though he were trying to squeeze that knowledge into
me. "This is bloody history!"

Before returning to Vancouver, I treated myself to a trip to California's Venice Beach — the unofficial meeting place for bodybuilders, weightlifters and strongmen of all sizes and description.

To my surprise, I found a "Best Lifts of the Beach" blackboard which listed the highest weights lifted by visitors to Venice Beach. Remaining in my street clothes, I eased my duffel from my shoulder and quickly broke all records.

Back in Vancouver, the BCWA and the press had little to say about my Los Angeles performance, of course, but not so, friends Harold and Herbie. "If you was in Russia you'd be a Master of Strength," Harold grunted in his usual gravelly monotone, his ruddy face and mannerisms conveying no more emotion than his words.

"Getting well-paid for it," Herbie continued, following me around like a hyper puppy. "Big bucks for every busted record — instead of always being busted!"

"But I'm not in Russia, am I?" I replied, barely able to control my irritation. "So why rattle on about it?"

"Just saying, that's all," Herbie replied. "It's the toilet that's rattling."

"Because you can't afford a good one," Harold concluded.

For the remainder of the year, I trained as hard as I could, and the following list outlines some of the feats that I performed during that time — officially witnessed and documented by strength expert Maurice Jones and famous bodybuilder and former Mr. U.S.A. Clarence Ross:

1. Push press of 410 lbs. — one repetition.
2. Bench press of 380 lbs. — six repetitions.
3. Olympic press of 325 lbs. — three repetitions.
4. Press-off-the-rack of 370 lbs. — one repetition.
5. Press-behind-neck with 305 lbs. — one repetition.
6. Right-hand military press of 165 lbs. — one repetition.
7. Two-arm-press-while-sitting with 157.5 lbs. — one repetition.
8. Right-arm-press-while-kneeling with 210 lbs. — one repetition.
9. One-hand-dumbbell-snatch of 180 lbs. — one repetition.
10. Right-arm-side-press of 172.5 lbs. — 10 repetitions.
11. Alternate-pressed (see-saw movement) 100 lb. dumbbells — 21 repetitions each hand.

▲ Doug at age three holding a water bucket at the Rundle farm.
(COURTESY JOHN FRASER)

Doug at six months ▶
with his father Ivan.
(COURTESY JOHN FRASER)

◀ Doug at age four
in his sailor suit.
(COURTESY
JOHN FRASER)

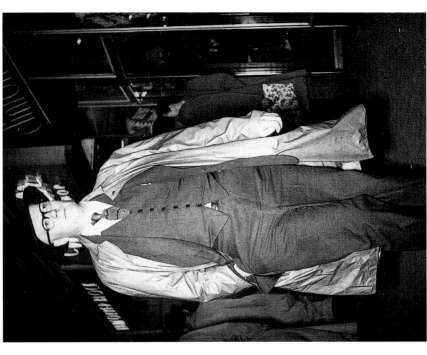

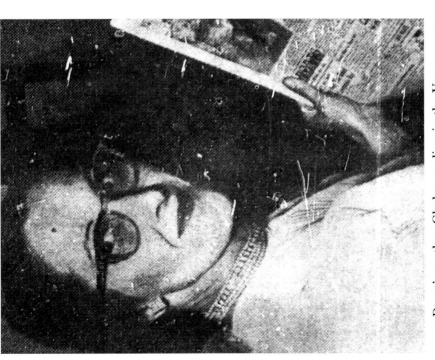

▲ Doug's mother Gladys reading in the Vancouver newspapers about Doug's winning the world championship at Stockholm. (COURTESY *THE VANCOUVER PROVINCE*, AUGUST 31, 1953)

Doug's father Ivan striding along a Vancouver street. (COURTESY JOHN FRASER) ▲

▲ Doug posing at English Bay in the early 1950s.
(COURTESY DENNIS WONG)

▲ Doug and his boyhood idol, famous strongman John Grimek, in York, Pennsylvania, January 1951. (COURTESY LEO AQUINO)

▲ Doug performing a strict curl, one of his favourite and best lifts, c. 1951. (COURTESY RAY BECK)

▲ Doug performing one of his beach acts, pressing Johnny Irving with one hand while Johnny does a one-arm hand-stand. (COURTESY RAY BECK)

Doug and Steve Stanko, the first man to total 1,000 lbs. in the three Olympic lifts, January 1951. (COURTESY LEO AQUINO) ▶

▲ Doug's enormous power came in large part from his shoulder development. Here he executes a back pose. (COURTESY RAY BECK)

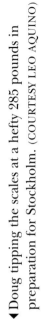

◀ Doug tipping the scales at a hefty 285 pounds in preparation for Stockholm. (COURTESY LEO AQUINO)

To Bill with best wishes
Doug

▲ Doug at the Hastings Street Gym in Vancouver, performing a snatch,
c. 1950. The photo is dedicated to Bill Copeland. Note the fused ankle
and atrophied calf of Doug's right leg. (COURTESY DENNIS WONG)

12. Olympic-pressed (cold) 250 lbs. — 10 repetitions.
13. Alternate-curled (cold and in street clothes) 75 lb. dumbbells
    — 10 repetitions each hand.
14. Crucifixed two 85 lb. dumbbells — held for three seconds.
15. Full-squatted 460 lbs. — 16 repetitions.
16. Full-squatted 500 lbs. — eight repetitions.
17. Full-squatted 560 lbs. — one repetition.
18. Cleaned a 152.5 lb. thick-handled barbell using only index
    and third fingers of right hand.
19. Cleaned-and-pressed a 110 lb. anvil — using only my right hand.
    (Leo Aquino, *Strength & Health* magazine, July 1951)

On December 5, 1951, eager to prove to Montreal once and for all who was the world's strongest Olympic presser and who deserved to represent Canada in the forthcoming 1952 Olympic Games scheduled for July 5 at Helsinki, Finland, I journeyed to New York and gave a lifting exhibition at "Manhattan's Greatest Physical Fitness Show of the Year." There, I set a world record two-handed curl of 220 pounds, a world record bench press of 465 pounds and a world record squat of 600 pounds. I also became the holder of *four* simultaneous world lifting records, including my world clean-and-press record of 345 ½ pounds.

The place exploded with cheers! Charles Smith clapped my back, as did hordes of other elated spectators, and the clamour was so great that I was certain that all of Canada would unanimously endorse me for the forthcoming 1952 Olympic Games. When it didn't happen, I was so shocked that I retreated to the alley behind my Grandview gym and shouted to the starry heavens: "Why?"

"Why not?" came a sarcastic voice from somewhere down the alley.

The question played havoc with my sleep and concentration until I remembered something that Charles Smith had once told me: "You can't make people see or understand, no matter how right you are or how much they should. You can only do what you do as well as you can and hope for the best."

So be it. I would follow Charles' sage advice and keep pursuing my ideal for the sake of the ideal alone. I would try out for the Helsinki Olympics because the facts showed that I would probably win a medal — quite possibly gold — and set a world record in the clean-and-press: Vancouver's first world record in weightlifting, and its first world record in any event since runner Percy Williams captured gold in the 1928 Olympic Games. If the weightlifting division of the CAAU in Montreal could rise above its petty discrimination to put Canada first, for once, Canada would benefit. If it couldn't, Canada would suffer. It was up to them.

On January 1, 1952, I officially began my Helsinki training. Informing the BCWA and the CAAU in Montreal so that there could be no doubt or misinterpretation as to my intentions, I settled back to await their decision. I also gave regular demonstrations at local competitions to let the Canadian people see for themselves that, as far as weightlifting was concerned, I was Canada's best and probably only hope for an Olympic gold medal. At least one Vancouver reporter agreed with me:

> Naturally, Hepburn is a cinch for the 1952 Canadian Olympic team. Or, at least, he ought to be. If he's left off, the ghost of Louis Cyr will rise out of his shrine in Trois Rivieres, hoist the selection Committee by the seat of its collective pants and dunk them in the icy waters of the St. Lawrence.
>
> (Eric Whitehead, *Vancouver Daily Province*
> *B.C. Magazine,* January 26, 1952)

When the BCWA and the CAAU both continued to turn a blind eye, I eventually bowed to their wishes and on June 15, 1952, stopped training. If Montreal would rather lose an Olympic gold medal than have it won by an athlete from the West, and the B.C. Weightlifting Association was content to let it happen, then "no medal" was what they would have. I knew that the second strongest heavyweight lifter in Canada, "Big" Dave Baillie of Noranda, Quebec, had no chance to win a medal because his lifting statistics proved it. Such information was easily available to the public. The responsibility would fall on the BCWA and the CAAU, and they were welcome to it.

But I knew that pride was also a factor. To purposely snub a lifter who held a world record in one of the three Olympic lifts was more than just bad judgment. It was an intentional slap in the face that I simply could not just stand there and take.

As I predicted, Dave Baillie did not win a medal (refer to Appendix 4 for the full results), but, to my disbelief, the press blamed me instead of Montreal! Sports columnists used such terms as "despondent" and "brooding" to explain to the reading public why I had turned my back on Helsinki, but not one gave even a hint of what my so-called despondency might have stemmed from.

On August 7, 1952, eager to prove to all Canadians that I could have won a medal at Helsinki, I gave a lifting exhibition at a local meet at the Kitsilano Pool in Vancouver where I set a world clean-and-press record of 353½ pounds; set a Canadian snatch record of 269 pounds; and set a Canadian clean-and-jerk record of 384½ pounds. As usual, all three records were rejected by the CAAU because they were performed on a Sunday. If it hadn't been that excuse, it would have been another.

But the facts remained. My three-lift total of 971 pounds was 46 pounds more than Dave Baillie's fourth place 925-pound total at the Helsinki Olympics and 8½ pounds more than American James Bradford's second place 962½-pound total. Clearly, the results prove that I probably would have won at least silver, and quite possibly gold, because my Kitsilano total had come weeks *after* I had quit my Olympic training.

Should I have turned my back on a sure medal out of principle? I didn't know.

Would Vancouver and Canada have rallied behind me if I had gone to Helsinki — perhaps as an independent lifter?

I didn't know that either. All I could do was hope that I had made the right decision, and keep demonstrating my great strength as emphatically as I could.

CHAPTER 3

STOCKHOLM

You have to really want to become the
best and be prepared to sacrifice everything to
get it — almost like a fear of failing.

— DOUG HEPBURN
(Communication with author, June 2, 1999)

One early September afternoon in 1952 while I was working out in my Grandview gym with Harold, Herbie, Leo, Little Johnny, Bill Copeland and a dozen or so other members, my future was revealed to me in a surprising manner.

I had just completed a set of heavy Olympic snatches with a 290-pound barbell and decided it was time for a mid-workout break. As was my habit, I left my barbell lying on the floor and retired with bananas, peaches and milk to the back lane to watch the birds and inhale fresh air. After remaining outside for ten minutes exactly, I went back in to complete my workout.

All appeared normal. Harold and Herbie were stacking discarded weights, Harold slow and plodding while Herbie zipped around him. Little Johnny was performing a one-armed handstand on the parallel bars while Leo and Bill "spotted" him, Leo standing with both his arms out and much larger Bill boyishly grinning. The rest were busy performing their required sets and repetitions.

Planting my feet before my barbell, I gripped it with both hands, sucked in a deep breath and smoothly snatched it above my head. It felt a little heavy, but I wrote that off to my recent rest. Once my muscles warmed, I reasoned, all would be back to normal. I turned to chalk my hands and everyone in the place was staring. "What?" I asked, wondering if I had split my pants or embarrassed myself in some other way.

"Not much," Harold monotoned, his large face red with excitement "Broke the world snatch record, is all — 320 pounds!"

"Counted the plates myself," Herbie almost stuttered, tapping the barbell for emphasis.

I tallied the poundage — including bar and collars — and they were right. While I was outside relaxing, they had upped the weight to surprise me, and had surprised themselves.

I was shocked. I had just beaten the reigning World and Olympic Heavyweight Champion John Davis — in my worst lift!

I studied the weight and tried it again.

Not quite.

No matter. I had done it once — after a heavy workout — and what I had done once I could do again.

Then the full impact of it hit me: it *had* been after a heavy workout — a grueller! How much could I have done fresh? I rested for two full days and on the morning of the third, crept from my gunny sack bed to find out.

After a few warm-up lifts, I loaded the bar to the 320-pound world record and snatched it easily — fused ankle and all. I upped the weight five pounds and snatched that for a new unofficial world record of 325 pounds!

Deciding to change lifts, I increased the barbell poundage to 363 pounds, John Davis's current world clean-and-jerk record, and the most I had ever attempted with that movement. Gripping it with both hands, I held a deep breath and cleaned it to my shoulders. It was heavy but not unmanageable. Taking a couple of breaths to replenish my supply of oxygen, I sucked in a deep one and used my arms and legs to jerk it above my head — barely. I debated adding more poundage for a new unofficial record, but decided to heed Charles Smith's advice instead: "Match them on the snatch and clean-and-jerk and no man alive can beat your press."

Reducing the weight to 345 pounds, my current world clean-and-press record, I gripped it with both hands and easily cleaned it to my shoulders. Locking my knees and hips, I smoothly pushed it above my head using just my arms and shoulders. I added five pounds for a new unofficial world clean-and-press record of 350 pounds, a whopping twenty pounds heavier than Davis's best, and up *it* went.

So there it was! I had just beaten all three of the current world weightlifting records — the snatch and the clean-and-jerk held by John Davis, and the clean-and-press held by myself. If I had competed in the 1952 Helsinki Olympics, only two months before, my total for the three lifts I had just made would have beaten John Davis's gold medal total by a hefty twenty-six pounds and would have beaten Dave Baillie by a whopping 114 pounds. The proof was in the poundages!

This did not mean that I could automatically beat Davis in an open world weightlifting competition, of course. His records were two months old as well. He'd be lifting more.

But how much more?

For a couple of weeks I contemplated my lifting opportunities. The next World Weightlifting Championships would be in Stockholm, Sweden, in September of 1953 — one year away if I decided to go. Would I still be able to break all three world records at that time? Did I *want* to get bogged down in the political mire? The CAAU's discriminatory and unfair policies *had* kept me off the Helsinki Olympic team, and *had* cost the Canadian people world recognition and the medal that I would have won for them.

But was there more? Was I hesitant to compete just because of the petty prejudices of the CAAU, or did I still possess an equally petty desire for revenge? In an attempt to find the answer, I paddled a rowboat to the centre of Vancouver's Trout Lake where I could think without distractions. Although I was sure that my absence from the competition would keep Canada from winning a medal, it would also keep me from winning one, something that I definitely didn't want to happen a second time. If I was to be hailed one day as the strongest man in history, I had to win at least one world weightlifting competition. Then came the answer: I would go to Stockholm as an independent Canadian competitor. After I won, Canada would receive the credit but the weightlifting division of the CAAU would not.

The first thing I needed to do was raise the $1,377 for my air ticket, yet I could see no way of doing it. The BCWA, through the same Harry Brown who had refused to back me against the CAAU so many times before, stated that although the association could not offer financial help, it would happily apply to the CAAU in Montreal for funding on my behalf. Given the CAAU's past treatment of me, I was immediately sceptical and received the expected response: "We will be sending no lifters to Stockholm in 1953 so we can be of no assistance." No sorrys, no good lucks — just no. Since their policy of "A Champion from the East, or No Champion" was obviously still in force, my resolve to win at Stockholm *despite* it became all the stronger.

With less than one year to prepare, I trained at the three competition lifts with a vengeance, giving special attention to the snatching and cleaning movements, as Charles Smith had so meticulously advised. I also added heavy "pull-ups" as an assistance exercise to help offset my fused ankle and impaired balance.

Since attracting independent sponsorship meant proving without a doubt that I was the strongest lifter in the world, I decided to break as many world records in as many different lifts at as many top-level competitions as I possibly could. The first was the

Canadian Junior Weightlifting Championships held on November 5, 1952, in New Westminster, British Columbia, where I showed a large audience a world clean-and-press record of 360 pounds and a world press-off-the-rack record of 430 pounds. As usual, the achievement received little notice from either the media or the BCWA, so I decided to take my quest to the United States where my talent and world records were recognized.

On November 10, 1952, I entered the Pacific Coast Championships in Portland, Oregon, determined to set a new clean-and-press record of 361 pounds — one pound greater than the world record I already held. The meet took place at the Multnoma Athletic Club in downtown Portland, a place I always enjoyed visiting because it was home to Joe Loprinzi and his six brothers: seven weightlifters who were known throughout the strength world as "the strongest family in North America." Much to my dismay, one of the three judges was Vancouverite and CAAU representative Harry Brown!

My first impulse was to refuse to lift on grounds of extreme prejudice. But since that would have been succumbing to politics, I took a deep breath, clean-and-pressed the 361-pound barbell in strict style and locked out my knees and elbows.

The packed house went crazy! Spectators whooped and leaped and the two American judges clapped my back and shook my hand — but not Harry Brown. "I didn't pass that!" he fairly scowled. "The bar touched his thigh as it went up!"

It hadn't. Everyone knew it and the place was poised to riot.

"Who disqualified him?" one fan shouted out.

"Harry Brown!" another shot back.

The stadium echoed as one. "Who the *fuck* is Harry Brown?"

I could have launched a grievance that might very well have gotten "Hapless Harry" (as I had immediately dubbed him) pop-bottled to death, but I instead repeated the lift in super-strict fashion. Three green lights flashed and it was official: I had not only set a new world clean-and-press record, I had also become one of only three lifters in history (myself, John Davis and Steve Stanko) to total over 1,000 pounds in the three Olympic lifts.

My new world press record, coupled with my new world total record, sparked a bit of interest in Vancouver, and a few weeks later the Canadian Legion set up a lifting exhibition at the Marpole Community Centre that netted $300 towards my Stockholm fund. It was a far cry from the $1,077 still needed, but it was a start and an effort that I deeply appreciated. Perhaps, I hoped, my countrymen were beginning to rally behind me after all. The press also joined in by putting out a request for mailed donations, but not one cent came in.

To my surprise, the B.C. Weightlifting Association, spearheaded by the same Harry Brown who had refused to acknowledge my world record press in Portland, also wanted to help. The Association was still penniless, of course, but seemed eager to organize three public events to raise the required amount. I wasn't sure I trusted Brown, given his history, but in order to keep the politics at bay, I accepted the Association's involvement. If it helped, fine; if it didn't, I would find another way.

Their first event was a complete washout: a jazz concert on the same evening that Spike Jones and his Madcaps were in town. Fifteen people showed, netting about fifty dollars.

Their second attempt did better. In cooperation with the Canadian Baseball League and the Vancouver Mounties baseball team, I and a few members of my Grandview gym (Roy Hilligenn, Mr. America 1951, Bill Hadley and Bill Kelso) gave a between-games lifting exhibition at Capilano Stadium during a professional "double-header" that netted about $600 and pushed the fund total to $950.

The only sour note occurred halfway through my demonstration when a disgruntled and inebriated spectator jumped to his feet and shouted "Let's get on with the game!" His equally inebriated cohort shouted, "Yeah! Want strong, get a damn bulldozer!" I didn't reply out of respect for the players and spectators who had supported me, but I was intensely disappointed. How could I expect support from people who couldn't even comprehend the significance of what I was trying to do?

I didn't give up. On May 14, 1953, I entered the Junior National Weightlifting Championships in Cleveland, Ohio, as an invited guest, where I won the tournament, setting a world bench press record of 465 pounds, a world and Junior National clean-and-press record of 366½ pounds, a Junior National snatch record of 291¼ pounds and a Junior National three-lift total record of 1,016 pounds. That last record "surpassed American Paul Anderson's second place total of 940 pounds," and the results were officially accepted by the American AAU (Jim Murray, *Iron Game History*, volume 3, no. 5, p.10).

On the way back to Canada I gave a half-time demonstration at a Seattle baseball game which, to my amazement, netted over $300 and boosted my fund total to a whopping $1,250. Both spectators and players cheered and wished me well in Stockholm even though they knew that I would be lifting against their own hero and countryman, John Davis. It was the purest example of "putting the ideal above the politics" that I had yet encountered and I was deeply moved.

In order to keep the barbell rolling, I gave a lifting exhibition at the Western Sports Centre and, in the presence of a host of witnesses and BCWA representatives, made weightlifting history by becoming the first man in history to bench press 500 pounds. Most world strength analysts and authorities considered such a feat to be impossible — which is why it was referred to as the 500-pound barrier. Yet a scant three months later, I successfully completed a 550-pound bench press and almost did 600 pounds. The strain of the 600 pounds tore my left shoulder muscle and the weight had to be removed before I was able to complete the movement. What's important, however, is that the injury had occurred after the barbell had passed the "sticking point" (the most difficult phase of the lift which is normally a few inches above the chest) and was starting back up. In other words, I made the lift, but I didn't.

Since less than one month remained until the World Championships and the fund was still $127 short, the BCWA arranged a final demonstration at the B.C. Weightlifting Championships, scheduled for August 1, 1953, at the Alma Academy in Vancouver.

It was the place where I had first met Eileen so many years before and I wondered if this was a sign of more good luck to come. I hoped so, and for a few agonizing seconds wondered how much of what I was doing was for her and us and what might have been.

In my half-time demonstration, I set a world and British Commonwealth clean-and-press record of 372 pounds; a British Commonwealth clean-and-jerk record of 372 pounds; and a British Commonwealth snatch record of 302 pounds, making a three-lift total of 1,046 pounds — a mere sixteen pounds short of John Davis's world record total of 1,062 pounds.

I was almost killed in the process.

As was the standard procedure for the Academy, its wooden lifting platform was composed of four portable sections that were slid together and bolted. Someone must have forgotten the bolts, however, because half-way through my 372-pound clean-and-jerk, the sections slid apart, throwing me into a bouncing squat with the barbell still at my shoulders. Refusing to drop the weight, I hopped until I regained my balance, then completed the lift. Everyone was so impressed, they donated the required amount to the penny. There would be no frills, not even a coach or companion, but I was heading to Stockholm in seven days.

I was elated! I was about to fulfil my lifelong dream, and determination alone had been the key. Not blind determination, where an athlete tosses a coin and hopes for the best, but an informed determination, born of facts and experience, that showed the unerring way to success. My experience proved to me that my lifting procedure was sound. The more I succeeded, the more I *knew* I would succeed in Stockholm regardless of any obstacles that remained.

For there were always obstacles, one of the worst occurring a scant few hours after I was told that I was bound for Sweden. Bursting with excitement, I rushed back to my gym, two-hand grabbed a 290-pound barbell that was lying on the floor and snatched it above my head. Since I was still wearing my street shoes, the soles slipped and I crashed to the floor, badly spraining my fused right ankle. The pain in my leg was excruciating but the pain in my mind was worse. Why had I done such a stupid thing? Rolling onto my back I screamed at the heavens through the dusty window, "How could you let this happen?"

For a few moments, I wanted to strike out at every unfair thing that had ever happened to me. But deep down I knew that it was my own fault. Forcing the rage and panic from my mind, I gathered myself as best I could and concentrated on finding a way to repair the injury in time for the competition.

Only one cure existed: staying off the injury for the remaining week, massaging it regularly and praying that it would recuperate enough to withstand the rigors of heavy lifting.

When Herbie, Harold, Leo and Little Johnny saw my dejected look and swollen ankle, they were sympathetic. "Don't worry!" Harold monotoned, scrubbing his thick neck. "You'll still win!"

"Yeah," Herbie almost stuttered, pumping my hand. "In the training bag!"

Johnny even wanted to bet me five dollars that I would bring back gold — *if* I'd spot him the initial "fin" to begin with.

I shook their hands and thanked them for their support, but I could tell by their faces that they had already written me off — especially three days later when my ankle was barely able to support my weight. Who could blame them? I had put the twist in my proverbial "lifting knickers" and it was up to me to remove it. "Get the job done or die trying," as my father had so loved to pontificate.

Resolving to do exactly that, I implemented a step-by-step program that was designed to heal my injury both physically and mentally. For the physical, I kept my injured foot elevated, massaged and rested. I regularly soaked it in hot water and salts to reduce the swelling and consumed huge doses of food supplements to help speed tendon, ligament and muscle recuperation.

For the mental, I kept imagining myself fully recovered and setting a new world record in each of the three competition lifts. Over and over I imagined it until I could actually feel the lifts go up and hear the crowd roar as I held the winning poundages above my head: no pain, no weakness, no fear of failing! I *would* win and I *would not* entertain any thoughts to the contrary!

My friends kept behind me and promised to accompany me to the airport and give me a send-off worthy of royalty. The city of Vancouver presented me with a powder blue suit so that I wouldn't have to go with holes in my clothes and I purchased a 45-rpm record of "O Canada" in case the competition officials in Sweden didn't have one.

But when the big day came — my foot still sore, my duffel crammed with milk and bananas — I limped onto the plane with not one person to see me off or wish me well. Fighting back disappointment, I searched for the bright side. Perhaps all the pain, rejection and uncertainty were necessary to increase the worth of the accomplishment. If all had gone smoothly, perhaps *I* would have been the loser. One thing I was sure of, having to continue in the face of adversity tests a man as much as anything he tries to accomplish, and at that moment I was being tested to the limit.

On the plane I sat silently in a window seat — two seats actually, the armrest between the two removed by a sympathetic stewardess — and thought about what lay ahead. My trip was in three legs: Vancouver to Quebec, Quebec to London and London to Stockholm. My mood was up and down, depending on how much my foot throbbed, but the view was fantastic and, once we reached Europe, I was particularly awed by the many war-scarred areas throughout England.

"A thin line between victory and defeat," a sixtyish female passenger with a thick English accent commented as she noticed me staring.

"Yes," I replied, feeling as though she had read my mind. As I turned away from the window, I realized that if I was to win at Stockholm, I would have to remain perfectly alert and aware from that moment on. No more impulsiveness or energy-sapping emotions of any kind. Just one all-or-nothing effort at the competition with success or failure as the result. If I kept my head, I would win. My lifting statistics were the proof. If I faltered, I would fail with no second chance to redeem myself. As if to emphasize the point, I was surprised to find that the name of my London-to-Stockholm plane was *The John Davis* — the name of the very man I would have to beat to win the title of "World's Strongest Man!"

By the time I landed in Stockholm, my foot was feeling a little better — I could walk on it without wincing, at least — but my troubles were far from over. The terminal was teeming with heavily laden travellers and when I put my duffel down beside a bustling information booth, someone must have bumped against it, for when I tucked a city map inside, I saw that my "O Canada" record had been shattered.

Instead of taking me to my accommodations at the Stockholm Sports Institute, the bus driver transported me to the Eriksdal-hallen Arena, a large Quonset hut crammed with over 5,000 spectators, where my date with destiny would take place. I spoke not a word of Swedish and the driver spoke little English, but he was letting me get a preview of the tournament before my event started in about forty-eight hours.

As I entered the arena, duffel on my shoulder, the lightweight semi-finals were in progress and a hush came over the spectator stands. "He's here," I heard someone whisper in broken English. Unlike in my home country of Canada, I was well known in Europe, with a large and loyal following. Weightlifting there was much more popular than in most other parts of the world and rumours of a giant Canadian vying for American John Davis's fifteen-year crown had sparked an intense interest.

The entire American lifting team of John Davis, Norbert Schemansky, James Bradford, Stanley Stanczyk, Tommy Kono, Dave Sheppard, Pete George and Coach Bob Hoffman was present. But not one of them acknowledged me — not even Hoffman, who made a point of turning his back on me. Beyond caring, I ignored them back and plopped myself down with the Russian lifters, who seemed a lot friendlier.

As I found out later, the Russians had two good reasons to be friendly. First, they had no heavyweight lifters competing, and thus no reason to feel threatened by my presence. Second, if I beat out American heavyweight John Davis — which I fully intended to do — the Russian team had an opportunity to beat the American team in total points for the first time in history. No wonder Hoffman wasn't smiling.

I was smiling, however.

I smiled at the crowd. I smiled at the kids who shyly asked for autographs. I smiled at the two Russian lifters beside me, a lightweight and a middleweight, who, through their interpreter, informed me that their occupations were brain surgeon and submarine commander, respectively. When asked my occupation, I replied, "I'm in the cleaning and pressing business." The Russian lifters eyed me as my words were interpreted, then laughed heartily and clapped my back. *"Velikolepno!"* they shouted. "Magnificent!"

After watching the lifting for about an hour, I had the tournament driver transport me to the Sports Institute, a large hostel composed of small compartments, a well-equipped gym and a sprawling dining room. There were also many beautiful and attentive Swedish women working as waitresses and chambermaids, but I knew better than to get romantically involved at such a crucial time. Other athletes were not so prudent. As I signed in, a young American with a compelling smile and a thick Brooklyn accent hopped around me, bubbling, "Oh boy! Look at all the broads!"

Upon depositing my duffel in my compartment, which was small and clean with a spectacular view of an alley, I examined my ankle and found it a lot less sore and swollen than when I had first stepped onto the plane. Replacing my sock and shoe, I headed for the gym to see how it held up against mild exercise. As I entered, Bob Hoffman and Norbert Schemansky were in a far corner, talking in guarded whispers and I smiled to myself as they made a point of ignoring me. Concealing my injury, I did a few light snatches to see how it felt — a little sore, but nothing that I couldn't suffer through for the brief time it would take to win the competition — and I decided to give them a glimpse of what they were up against.

Increasing my barbell poundage to 330 pounds, I cleaned it to my shoulders and pressed it to a point a few inches above my head. There, I purposely held it for three seconds — they would know how much arm and shoulder power it took to move it again. After that, I military-pressed it to a full overhead position. Their eyes stuck out like celery sticks and before Hoffman could stop himself, he blurted out, "We can't compete with a derrick!"

I left without a backward glance, content to have made my point.

That evening at the hostel dining room, I ate a solid, carbohydrate-intensive meal — sitting alone because I didn't want anything or anybody to break my concentration, not even the smiling Swedish girls, who were everywhere. Then I returned to my room to prepare for the task at hand. I began by lying on my bunk with my eyes closed and going over in my mind all the reasons that I would win gold: my sacrifices; my world records; the world class lifters I had already beaten; and my tremendous size and lifting statistics. At 270 pounds with 21-inch arms, I could press 450 pounds from the power rack, clean-and-press 368 pounds, squat 695 pounds, bench press 565 pounds and two-hand curl 252 pounds. I then envisioned myself winning: hearing the cheers of the crowd as I completed the gold medal lift; feeling the rush of my adrenalin as I was handed my gold medal and pronounced "World's Strongest Man" — clear and undeniable proof before the entire world.

Although this mental conditioning greatly increased my confidence and resolve, I knew that I needed one final re-enforcement. Moving to the window, I scanned the clear, star-spattered heavens for a falling star or some other celestial phenomenon to prove that fate was still firmly behind me. I saw nothing and was confused until it occurred to me: why did I need further re-enforcement if I truly believed? I either did or I didn't.

Did I believe?

Yes!

Was I going to win?

Yes!

Then why did I need further proof? Returning to my bunk, I closed my eyes and, before drifting off to sleep, composed the following song:

> There once was a boy, got himself a toy
> of iron and steel and lead.
> Others played, but this little boy
> lifted that toy instead.
> Just one try, it was do or die
> where that long hard road had led.
> Born to win, he steeled his chin
> and pressed that toy o'er his head.

I slept soundly and had the strangest dream. Jesus Christ and I were canoeing in the middle of Trout lake when he suddenly turned to me and asked, "Why do you think your God, my Father, chose you to be the bearer of such great strength?" What I replied, I have no idea because I immediately woke up.

My alarm clock showed 6:05 a.m., so I spent a half-hour massaging my ankle, performing light stretching exercises and inspecting my lifting gear. Experiencing very little pain or pre-event jitters, I slung my duffel over my shoulder, strolled to the dining room and was surprised to find it almost empty. I checked the wall clock and the competitors' bus schedule and, to my great relief, found that I still had plenty of time. The other competitors were either in their rooms or at the competition.

Then another stressful moment. When I tried to order breakfast — a high energy combination of pancakes and syrup with orange juice, coffee and a banana milk shake — I was unable to communicate as my breakfast waitress understood very little English, and the waitress who had taken my evening order was temporarily out of the kitchen. Words turned to gestures — a comical pantomime that would have been hilarious in any other situation — until my previous waitress appeared and translated.

After breakfast and a thorough examination of my injury —

which I found to be sore but, hopefully, not too sore — I strolled to the competition bus that was idling outside the main doors and took a rear seat. To my surprise, Humberto Selvetti, a massive Argentine heavyweight whom I would be lifting against, took a front seat. Neither of us acknowledged the other and we sat in silence throughout the ride: Humberto staring out the window, his mind who knows where; me sitting with my eyes closed, mentally listing all the reasons why I would win.

Inside the arena, I moved to a relatively isolated corner to prepare further and was once again the centre of attention to the packed house. No competitors acknowledged me, however, and I returned the snub. It was the best way. The competition first, socializing later.

I watched the lifting for a couple of hours, then changed into my lifting shoes and uniform and set about warming up for my fast-approaching event. As I performed a series of easy snatching movements, American coach Bob Hoffman happened by and casually said, without stopping or looking at me, "Winning this competition means a lot to me, what does it mean to you?"

I stared after him, quite astounded.

Was he asking me to throw the contest or was it just idle conversation?

He kept walking and it was the last time we spoke.

The only other person to approach me before the competition was the British coach, Al Murray, a fit, fiftyish ex-lifter who noticed that I was limping, despite my conscious attempt not to, and wandered over to inquire as to my intentions.

"I'll lift," I told him. "I can't win unless I do. And I fully intend to win!"

He seemed to admire my determination and said, "We can go over some poundages together, if you like. I know Davis's lifting capabilities better than he does."

This suited me for three reasons: the British had no heavyweight competitors, so they had no reason to screw me; I needed emotional support at such a stressful time (whether I wished to admit it or not); and I needed the sound advice of an experienced lifting strategist — and Al Murray was one of the best.

As important as it is for the lifter to hoist the required poundages at the required time during a competition, it is equally important for him to keep his game plan correctly matched to his opponent's strengths and weaknesses from lift to lift. If he attempts too much too soon, he can tire himself for later rounds. If he attempts too little, he can destroy his total score by missing a critical lift. Perhaps the most crucial requirement for success is for the lifter to evaluate correctly the capabilities of both himself and his competitors on the day of the meet. At this, Al Murray was a master. He quickly constructed a strategy that he was certain would make me unbeatable, with my superior pressing power, and we spent the rest of my free time discussing it in detail.

The rules of the competition were standard and simple. Each lifter was given three attempts for each of the three required lifts: the clean-and-press, the snatch and the clean-and-jerk. Once a lifter attempted a specific poundage in a specific lift, a lesser poundage could not be attempted; the poundage could only be increased. If the lifter touched the platform with any part of his body except the soles of his feet while he was lifting, or if the bar touched any part of the lifter except the hands and front of the shoulders while being cleaned, the lift would be disqualified. In the event of a tie, the lifter with the lowest body weight would win. Two green lights were required for a lift to pass. Three green lights were required for a world record.

The heavyweight division was hard-fought and filled with many surprises — particularly in the case of Humberto Selvetti, who did far better than anyone expected. In the end, it came down to three lifters: John Davis from the United States, Humberto Selvetti from Argentina, and myself.

It should be noted here that at the start of the heavyweight lifting, the Americans had needed a first and second place win in the heavyweight division to beat the Russians on total team points. Humberto and I had shattered that dream. If I beat Davis, the

Russians would win by a greater margin, which was why, I suppose, the Russian team doctor, a short, burly man by the name of Eggyaness, offered to give me a complete physical before the finals and declared me well enough to win. *"Velikolepno!"* he snorted, slapping my shoulder.

The following is an accurate compilation of the finals competition. The order of lifting has been altered for the sake of brevity, but the results and totals are exact.

The first lift was the clean-and-press. John Davis started with a 308½ pound clean-and-press and made it, jumped to 330½ pounds and made it, jumped to his final lift of 341½ pounds and made it. Humberto Selvetti started with 330½ pounds and made it, jumped to 341½ pounds and made it, jumped to his final lift of 352½ and made it. I started with 341½ pounds and made it, jumped to 363¼ and made it, jumped to my final lift of 371¼ and made it — a new world record!

An amusing incident occurred during this phase of the event. After I had succeeded with 341½ pounds, Humberto knew he could beat it and was so excited that he actually kissed me on the forehead as I came off the platform. When I pressed 371¼ with power to spare, however, he was less than enthusiastic. Both he and Davis looked extremely low.

The second lift of the event was the snatch. This was the lift that I had been dreading because I knew that it would place the most strain on my already aching and swollen right ankle. I could win, but my technique would have to be flawless — both physically and mentally. "Just match the beggars," Al whispered in my ear. "Match them and your superior pressing power will keep you well ahead."

Gritting my teeth, I told myself that I would not lose, no matter what. John Davis started with 297½ pounds and missed, tried it again and made it, jumped to his final lift of 319½ and failed. Humberto Selvetti started with 275½ pounds and made it, jumped to 297½ and missed it twice. I started with 275½ pounds and made it, then jumped to 297½ and made it.

Two events occurred during this phase of the competition, the first just after I had completed my 275½-pound lift and was preparing for my 297½-pound lift. My foot was really sore and I guess it showed because Al Murray produced a vial of smelling salts and stuck it underneath my nose. The Russian doctor, Eggyaness, bolted across the floor, yanked the vial from Al's hands and sniffed it. "Bah!" he said and immediately exchanged it for his own vial. Taking a long sniff, I immediately felt better and completed the lift. Hoffman tried to make a big deal about it, but to no avail. The judges and medical people agreed that although the vial probably contained some sort of stimulant, the power of suggestion probably had more to do with it because the Russians used it regularly but couldn't produce a champion.

The second incident occurred as I was completing the 297½-pound snatch. As previously noted, one of the grounds for lift disqualification was the lifter touching the platform with a body part other than the soles of his feet, and Bob Hoffman and Norbert Schemansky tried to make it appear as though I had. Kneeling and staring at my legs as I performed the movement, they jumped up and down and pointed, as though my left knee had touched the platform. Their ruse failed, however, when the entire arena let out a roar of disapproval that set them both back into their respective chairs, their red faces glowing like exit lights. The lifting judges declared the lift "good" and the subject was not brought up again.

The third and final lift was the clean-and-jerk, but as far as Al Murray was concerned, the fates had already spoken. "You've done it, Doug!" he shouted, clapping me on the back hard enough to make my teeth ache. "He's bloody kippered!"

"Not yet," I responded, as calmly as I could.

"Yes he is!" Al declared. "Davis would have to jerk 392 pounds to beat you, and no bloody way can he today!"

The results were as follows. John Davis started with 369¼ pounds and made it, jumped to 391¼ to tie me and missed twice for a three-lift total of 1008¼ pounds and the silver medal. Humberto Selvetti started with 352½ pounds and made it, jumped to 363¾ and missed it, tried it a second time and made it for a three-lift total of 991¾ pounds and the bronze medal. I started with 341½ pounds and made it, jumped to 363¾ and missed, tried it a second time and made it for a three-lift total of 1033 pounds and the gold medal.

I had done it — I had proved myself the world's strongest and made history at the same time! What's more, I had done it on a Sunday!

As John Davis, Humberto Selvetti and I took our places on the tri-level dais for the presentation of our medals and the playing of the National Anthem "God Save the Queen" (because my recording of "O Canada" had been broken at the airport) we all had tears in our eyes: me for what I had just done; Selvetti for what he had almost done; Davis for what he might never do again.

What I was thinking, I have no idea. Maybe it takes a while for the full magnitude of such an accomplishment to sink in. That must have been the way it was, because even though a lightweight member of the British team took me out on the town to celebrate, I remember very little — not even the lightweight's name. I was numb, talking at times but hearing very little. When the night actually ended or how I got back to the Sports Institute hostel, I have no idea. I only knew that I had won and, for that brief, incredible moment, it was the only thing that mattered.

Offering thanks to Al Murray, and a promise to give an informal lifting demonstration at his Spar Barbell Club in London, England on my way back to Vancouver, I checked out of the Sports Institute and headed into downtown Stockholm to book a flight. While having lunch at a quiet outdoor cafe, I was joined by Oscar State, the small, smiling, mid-fifties head of the British Weightlifting Association and General Secretary of the International Weightlifting Federation who was covering the World Championships for Britain's *Health & Strength* magazine (not to be confused with Bob Hoffman's *Strength & Health* magazine). He congratulated me on my victory, and handed me a personal invitation from Carl Anxt, a Zurich businessman and sausage factory owner, who wished me to give an informal lifting demonstration in Switzerland — at his full expense.

Since I was feeling quite content and in no particular hurry to end my adventure, I agreed. As we stood to leave, a middle-aged, razor-straight Swedish gentleman appeared before us with his hat in hand and addressed me in polite Swedish. "A young man here would like to twist arms with you," a bemused Oscar translated. Large posters of myself and my recent victory were plastered from one end of the city to the other, and I guess he recognized me from those. Since the contest sounded like fun I agreed to go along.

The Swedish gentleman bowed sharply, begged us to wait and abruptly left. Returning fifteen minutes later, he led us inside a nearby building, which was actually a hotel and bar that supplied food and drink on the main floor and sleeping accommodations upstairs. As we started upstairs, much to my astonishment, everyone in the establishment — well over fifty men and women — followed.

Upstairs, while spectators crowded the hall and doorway, Oscar and I were led inside a large room that was bare except for a table that was suitable for arm-wrestling, and two chairs. On one chair sat an extremely well-developed young man in his late twenties, who made no attempt to stand or acknowledge our presence. I was invited by our guide to occupy the other. As my opponent and I placed our right elbows on the table and clasped hands, not one word was spoken by anyone present and our guide made quite a production of placing and holding our arms in the "ready" position. Oscar and I were finding it all quite humorous. But my guide and opponent were deadly serious, as were most of the spectators present.

The guide made it clear that his releasing our hands would be the signal to begin. As soon as he did, the young man yanked as hard and as fast as he could, catching me off-guard and causing my elbow to momentarily leave the table: a technical loss.

You'd have thought he'd just won free food for the rest of his life! Leaping out of his chair, he hopped and cheered and the crowd cheered with him. I was getting quite a kick out of it — until Oscar said to him in Swedish, "I suppose you know that Mr. Hepburn owns the title of "World's Strongest Man."

"Not any more!" the young arm wrestler replied, quite haughtily. This initiated another explosion of cheers from the crowd, but although I felt quite insulted, I never let on.

Smiling, I indicated that I wished another round and, once again, the entire establishment went silent. We clasped arms and the starter started us — but this time I was ready. Setting my "world's strongest" shoulder, I slammed his hand against the table so hard and fast that his knuckles broke. How many, I'm not exactly sure; quite possibly all of them, as the sound made most of the spectators jump.

The young man stared at his injured hand, then left without a word. Oscar and I also left, with everyone staring silently after us. When we were outside, I asked, "What was that all about? Who was that guy?"

"The arm-wrestling champion of Sweden," Oscar replied, with a smirk. "Experiencing his first loss!"

I immediately felt regret for destroying the man's dream, but perhaps it was for the best. Along with winning comes the responsibility to remain respectful to the opponent. He had failed to do that and had forfeited his own pride as a result.

In Zurich, Switzerland, after a scenic but uneventful plane ride, we met with Mr. Anxt, a large, fortyish, physically fit man with thick eyebrows, at his sprawling and efficiently run sausage factory. Clasping my hand and appraising me as if I were 290 pounds of grade-A beef-on-the-hoof, he informed me that he wished to make me two offers. First, since he was an avid "belt-wrestler" — a popular Swiss sport similar to Japanese sumo wrestling where the belt is used to hold and throw the opponent — he wished me to become his permanent training partner. There would be a house, a car, a generous monthly salary and pretty much anything else that I wanted if I agreed. There were a lot of adept belt-wrestlers in the country and, if he expected to attain world-class status, he would require world-class strength and training.

Mr. Anxt's second offer was what Oscar had stated at the cafe: an informal lifting demonstration at a small cliff-side chalet in the small village of Le Locle. Mr. Anxt would pay all expenses, and his private car and driver would take us there within the hour. I could think over the belt-wrestling proposition on the way.

Although I was extremely flattered by both offers, I politely declined the belt-wrestling. Since I had made weightlifting history with my clean-and-press, as well as winning a gold medal for my country, I was confident that, upon my return, all Canadians would be waiting to welcome me with open arms. I did, however, agree to give the demonstration at Le Locle.

"Good!" said Mr. Anxt. He summoned his car — a lumbering Duesenberg like the ones later used on the *Hogan's Heroes* television comedy series — and its solemn, 300-pound driver raced us away as though he were attempting to out-run an avalanche. Oscar and I sat frozen in the back seat as the driver — uttering not one word the entire journey — raced along a winding, ice-caked alpine road that was flanked by rocky, snow-laden peaks on one side and bottomless cliffs on the other. At speeds exceeding 90 miles per hour, we screeched and slid, fish-tailed and spun until we finally reached our destination: a magnificent chalet restaurant overlooking some of the most breathtaking alpine scenery that I had ever beheld. Although Oscar and I were so scared we could hardly stand, we tried to hide it by pretending that it was the ice that was making us wobbly. We found out later that our driver was a member of the recently victorious Swiss Olympic bobsled team. Mr. Anxt, it seemed, liked to be associated with famous athletes.

Once my legs steadied, I gave an hour's demonstration to a packed house of whooping, cheering spectators, then sat down to a fabulous, window-side meal provided, at no charge, to Oscar and myself. As I sat sipping exceptional wine and drinking in the spectacular view, my mood was one of elation and supreme satisfaction. Everything would now be all right — of that I was certain. I had remained true to myself and my goal and with my success would come the spoils. As if to reinforce the fact, a waiter politely informed me that I was wanted on the hall telephone.

"Me?" I asked. "Who knows I'm here?"

"Mr Anxt, perhaps?" Oscar replied, taking a sip from his glass.

It made sense, so I answered the call.

"Doug Hepburn the weightlifter?" asked a polite voice. "Recently crowned 'World's Strongest Man?'"

"Yes . . ."

"This is *Time* magazine. Do you have a couple of moments?"

I was flabbergasted. Of course I did. As many as they wanted. As a celebrity, I would have to get used to such things, I surmised. And once again I felt an emotional certainty that everything would be spectacular from that moment on. The proof was a reporter from *Time* on the other end of the phone line, preparing an article that would soon be distributed across Canada and the rest of the English-speaking world.

After the interview, at Oscar's request, Mr. Anxt's driver arranged for a small, private plane to fly Oscar and me back to Zurich. Although the trip was relatively uneventful, the sky over the Alps was teeming with hundreds of gliders in all sizes, shapes and colours. It was as if the heavens were congratulating me with this explosion of brightly coloured balloons. Everything was high: my mood, the plane, the alps, the gliders — high and getting higher by the second.

At Zurich, after I thanked Mr. Anxt most kindly for his unstinting hospitality, Oscar and I parted company and I caught a flight to London, England, where I had a three-day layover before continuing to Canada and the glorious celebration that I was sure awaited me. I spent the first two days sightseeing — my hotel being within walking distance of Trafalgar Square — and on the third day gave a brief demonstration at Al Murray's Spar Barbell Club. Although I was received warmly by the lightweight lifter (who had treated me to a night on the town after my Stockholm win), the one hundred-plus spectators in attendance and Al himself, the heavyweight lifters in attendance seemed decidedly cool. Since I was there by special invitation from Al, I found their attitude surprising. But I soon wrote it off to normal social caution and set about doing what I had been asked to do: have fun and more or less show my capabilities.

I first executed my three trademark lifts: a strict 255-pound two-handed curl; a strict 200-pound one-armed press; and a strict 450-pound push-press from the rack. After gulping down a quart of milk, I performed a 365-pound clean-and-press, even though I was capable of doing over 370 pounds, as my new world press record attested. Since the demonstration was supposed to be informal and my right ankle was beginning to swell, I didn't concentrate too much on form. I received a few cheers, assumed that all was going well and retired to the changing room for a half-time break.

There, I was confused to find myself all but shunned by the heavyweight lifters. Their general comment concerning my last lift, snorted loud enough for me to hear, was: "That was no bleeding press — anyone could do it that way!"

Although I felt deeply insulted, I didn't respond. But immediately after the break I loaded the bar to my new world's record of 371½ pounds and pressed it the way I had for Hoffman and Shemansky at Stockholm. I cleaned it, pressed it a few inches above my head and held it. After a full four seconds, I completed the lift with such precision that you could have heard jaws drop. Mouths were still open as I silently returned to the dressing room, changed and left without a backward glance.

The next morning, with my gold medal tucked next to my heart, I boarded the plane for home and, hopefully, the victory celebration that I had been striving towards my entire life. I had accomplished my goal and now it was time to sit back and reap the rewards: fame, fortune, and perhaps a little gym of my own.

As I leaned back and placed my foot on the seat across from me, I took a deep, contented breath. It would be wonderful. The world was my oyster and I would savour it.

CHAPTER 4

USE, ABUSE AND THE
BRITISH EMPIRE GAMES

*When I was on top I thought I was entitled
to some license. I became self-centred.*

— DOUG HEPBURN
(Archie McDonald, "Hepburn Flexing Towards
New Goal," *Vancouver Sun,* January 22, 1974)

When I deplaned onto the Vancouver tarmac, I was immediately met by Mayor Fred Hume, the press and a police
escort, replete with flashing lights, notepads, and sharply creased
suits and uniforms. Photos were snapped and microphones were
shoved towards me as the mayor pumped my hand and asked me
how it felt to be the world's best.

I thought about it, then offered the following comment:

My victory means a certain measure of fulfilment, but I won't be
satisfied until I have reached my ultimate potential and perhaps set
a mark that will withstand all future competition.

(*Maclean's* magazine, June 1, 1954, p. 40)

Photos were snapped of my gold medal, of me with my gold medal and of my gold medal again. Then I was escorted into Mayor Hume's sparkling limo and given a siren-whining, lights-flashing tour of the city. People stared and waved, and I waved back, and I must confess that it was one of the highlights of my life. After all the rejection and loneliness I had weathered, the people of Vancouver were finally beginning to rally behind me. I wanted to climb atop the moving vehicle and whoop and whoop and whoop!

As we toured, the beaming mayor patted my shoulder as he waved to the crowd and asked me what I planned to do with my life — besides becoming history's strongest man, of course. I told him that I hoped to one day own a small gym where I could relax and perhaps teach underprivileged children how to become strong well into their later years.

"Wonderful," he kept saying. "Isn't that just wonderful!"

Then, as quickly as it had started, it was over.

The mayor informed me that he had another engagement, dropped me in front of my dark and apparently deserted Grandview gym and sped away.

As I stood alone on the sidewalk, my shouldered duffel straining my ankle and my gold medal weighing heavily against my heart, something that Little Johnny Irving had once told me popped to mind: "When you finally make it, everyone will know it and get behind you. When you're the best, why wouldn't they?"

Was this what "it" was — a brief hurrah, followed by intense loneliness? Why was I lonely? Because I had expected more than I should have and was just starting to realize it?

As I stared at my gym, I tried not to hope that it was full of food, drinks and crouching people waiting to hoist me onto their shoulders and sing, "For he's a jolly good champion!"

"Right, Doug," I mumbled to myself as I started for the front door. "And later, Peter Pan will swoop down from a falling star and fly you to Never Never Land, where you'll never grow old or feel pain again."

Unlocking the front door, I clicked on the lights and found the floor covered with scattered newspapers, empty liquor bottles and snoring people. They had apparently been planning a party, but had not lasted until my homecoming.

To my dismay, my gunny sack bed was again occupied. Too exhausted to argue, I crammed a few newspapers into my duffel and retreated to a place that I knew all too well: the East Hastings flop house where I had ended up after my victorious return from White Plains.

Too tense to sleep, I scanned the newspapers, hoping to find something to alleviate the depression that was fast flooding over me. The first item that caught my eye was a front page headline: HEPBURN WORLD'S STRONGEST MAN! (Vancouver *News-Herald*, August 31, 1953).

Big deal, I grunted. Where is he now?

The next item was a same-day article from a different newspaper:

HEPBURN'S MIGHTY HEART EARNS PLAUDITS OF WORLD!
A twenty-six-year-old man with a club foot and a partially withered leg is the toast of Europe today. Doug Hepburn, who has worked at his chosen sport for eight long years, virtually unrecognized in his home town, has brought Vancouver its first world record and first world championship of any kind since Percy Williams won in the 1928 Olympic Games. Harry Brown, head of the Canadian Weight-lifting Association, said Sunday, "Hepburn hasn't begun to show what he can do." Harry predicts he will shatter all existing world records — and soon! All Vancouver can do is humbly welcome home a great champion and take pride in the fact that this is his home.

(*Vancouver Sun*, August 31, 1953)

A second article echoed much of the same:

MIGHTY SPIRIT WINS!
The magnificent muscles which hoisted Vancouver's Doug Hepburn to world champion weightlifter status are not nearly so impressive as the spirit that built them. He's a lesson to all of us what self-confidence and unflagging determination can do.

(*Vancouver Sun*, September 2, 1953)

I sat back and took a deep breath. Perhaps there *was* a change taking place. I hoped so, because I knew that my accomplishment could inspire a lot of people to realize their own hopes and dreams if it was just given the chance.

A third article made me immediately apprehensive:

> It now appears that the dramatic victory in Stockholm of Doug Hepburn, the strong man, has been greeted in Vancouver, his home town, with an unprecedented wave of torpor. Rarely has a world champion inspired such ennui. Efforts are now being made to provide the champion with a hero's homecoming and I trust that suitable hosannas will ring out when the big boy returns.
>
> (*Vancouver Sun*, September 10, 1953)

I put the papers aside. Was that why Mayor Hume had shown up with his victory ride through the city? Because he was shamed into it? Just enough "going through the motions" to pacify his voting public? Still unable to sleep, I implemented a technique that I had developed as a child. I imagined myself in a locked and burning building with only minutes to live. What would I do? How could I free myself in time? My real problems quickly gave way to my imaginary ones, and I was soon soundly in the land of "Nod."

Early the next morning, I hit the nearest newsstand and found the following article:

GIVE HEPBURN HIS DUE!

We're amazed that Vancouver has no plans to give Douglas Hepburn the real civic honours earned at Stockholm. The first world champion the city has produced since Percy Williams and Jimmie McLarin is back home with little more recognition than he might get for winning a horseshoe pitching contest at Calgary. Mayor Hume met him with an official handshake at the airport and the newspaper photographers were there. Since then the only attempt at honouring the world champion weightlifter is that City Council is "considering" entering his name on the city's civic honour roll. While Aldermen will undoubtedly come up with the necessary unanimous vote, Vancouver will still be neglecting Hepburn shockingly. Any man good enough to top the world's best in sport or any field deserves full recognition from the city where he was born and where he trained himself to be champion. In all ways Doug Hepburn has earned full civic honours from Vancouver. Let's see that he gets them.

(*Vancouver Sun*, September 24, 1953)

I crumpled the article and tossed it into a corner. Did I want honours that no one really wanted to give me? Taking a deep breath, I tried to force the disappointment from my mind by exploring the bright side. Mayor Hume *had* met me at the airport, and the city, according to the papers, *was* exploring ways to honour my achievement. So why not give them the benefit of the doubt and see how it all worked out? Nothing worthwhile ever comes easily, so why was I expecting this to?

As this line of thinking made me feel somewhat better, I set off to find my mother, who had returned to Vancouver in my absence. A recent newspaper article had identified her new address as 3617 West Twelfth Avenue, Vancouver, so I rushed over to welcome her home and show her the spoils of my most recent victory.

When we met on her front porch, we were both genuinely happy to see each other. She looked quite attractive in a stylish, black dress, her hair tied back in a loose bun, but, as usual for us, there was no hugging or kissing. It had never been her way to express emotion openly and, as a consequence, I had always been forced to respond in kind. Inviting me inside for tea and biscuits, she nodded and smiled at my medal (although she wouldn't hold it or have her picture taken with it) and matter-of-factly related how stepfather Bill had died suddenly of natural causes in California. "His passing was a shock," she said, carefully pouring tea from a dainty porcelain pot. "It is the way of the world, however, so I will weather it. There is no need for you to worry."

As I watched her sip her tea, her back razor straight and her grim determination evident, I felt intense respect and wonder at her unwavering resolve. She faced her problems with little complaint or emotion and simply continued in the face of them, digging in her heels when necessary — but only when necessary — thereby attaining an inner strength and focus that I could only dream of. Since there was little more to say between us at that point, I patted her hand and invited her to contact me if she needed anything — a small, sincere offer of which she would be too proud to avail herself — and headed back to my Grandview gym.

When I arrived, everyone was awake and eager to give me the welcome that they had been unable to extend the night before and, I must admit, I truly relished the laughter and companionship. They clapped my back, hefted my medal and even tried hoisting my 290 pounds onto their shoulders. Their effort was cut short, however, when a couple of them bolted for the aspirin bottle and a couple more to vomit in the alley.

Then, as quickly as it had started, *that* welcome was also over. They all returned to their own lives and homes, and I was left with the familiar problem of finding a way to keep the wolf from my door.

Eventually, the city of Vancouver came through with a string of awards and honours for me (refer to Appendix 3 for a complete list), which I deeply appreciated, but which did little to help me financially. Like it or not, becoming and remaining a world champion athlete is not a cheap endeavour. At a minimum, it takes food, lodging, clothing, equipment, travelling expenses and a stress-free environment where the athlete can concentrate on developing his or her skills. Moving to the United States would have placed me in such an environment, but at the expense of my Canadian citizenship. Moving to Switzerland would have given me financial stability, but at the cost of my pride.

To make matters worse, Mayor Hume and the council immediately publicized my Stockholm win to their full advantage. They flaunted my name and photograph at every opportunity, and invited me to every social function, from fundraisings to ribbon-cuttings to sports events. Food, drink and hearty pats on my back were always there, but financial help was never offered — even though everyone who invited me knew that I was just barely eking out an existence. At the end of the day or evening, they all returned to their fancy homes and happy lives, while I returned to my drafty gym and gunny sack bed to wonder what the next day would bring.

Harold and Herbie also took full advantage of the situation by constantly haranguing me about how different everything would be if I were living in Russia where they respected athletes. "No use — no abuse!" Harold would monotone, plodding through his gym chores like a robot in low gear. And Herbie, flitting around us like a nervous fly, would agree. "Never make it here 'cause you ain't got them sneaky, ratty brains."

Although I was close to agreeing, I refused to give them the satisfaction. I still wanted to believe that my home city of Vancouver and the people who ran it would eventually see my achievement for what it was — a level of human excellence that had never been reached before in the field of weightlifting — and come up with some sort of financial help that would have allowed me to achieve even more.

It never happened. The city of Vancouver kept cashing in on me without the vaguest thought for my financial welfare until, one day, I simply stopped attending their social functions for free. Once I did, the invitations stopped and it was as if I had never existed. The mayor and his council went on about their business of running Vancouver, and I was left to fulfil my dream of owning a gym for underprivileged kids the best way that I could — no small feat for a man with no trade other than the ability to hoist weight above his head.

In the meantime, I had to be constantly on guard for con artists looking to turn an unholy dollar at my expense. Once, as I was signing a long line of autographs, I noticed that one of the many open pages being thrust at me was covering a blank check. Another time, while I was having tea at the home of a middle-aged gym member, he called in a very well-endowed and scantily clad young lady of about eighteen, whom he referred to as his daughter, and invited me to feel her extremely hard stomach.

"Go ahead," he coaxed. "Brick washboard!"

When I turned to decline his offer, I saw that he was holding a camera.

Since it was clear that my new-found honours weren't going to change my life to any great degree, I went back to doing what I had always done: teaching classes in advanced weightlifting, giving lifting demonstrations and setting strength records. Although I was convinced that I deserved some sort of financial compensation for the time and effort that I had expended, I knew that I couldn't make others agree. If my fellow Vancouverites wanted to rally behind me in the form of regular sponsorship that would have allowed me to continue as an amateur or by advertising endorsements or lecture tours that would have allowed me to turn professional, they would. If they didn't, they wouldn't.

On November 2, 1953, I gave a lifting demonstration at the B.C. Senior Weightlifting Championships in Vancouver where I set a world push-press record of 440 pounds and a world two-handed curl record of 225 pounds, with both records *accepted* by the weightlifting division of the CAAU. Having the CAAU finally accept my records was a small victory, but a victory none the less. Now, at last, everyone in the world, including my countrymen, agreed that I was a true world champion. My next step was to become the strongest man in history.

Less than a week later, as though it were fated, I received an all-expense-paid invitation from Big Ed Yarick, an Oakland, California gym owner, to give a demonstration at his annual "Big Show." Less than two days later, I also received an all-expense-paid invitation to appear on *Art Linkletter's Houseparty,* a popular afternoon television show from Hollywood, California. Whether the two windfalls were somehow connected, I have no idea. But I accepted.

On November 4, 1953, I strict-pressed Art, who weighed over 200 pounds, on his own program, prompting a standing ovation from a packed house consisting mostly of women.

On November 11, 1953, I deep-squatted 665 pounds, breaking Paul Anderson's world record of 660 pounds, at the "Big Show," where I also strict-pressed a pair of 160-pound dumbbells, right hand military-pressed a 170-pound dumbbell, strict-pressed 260-pound Ed Yarick, cleaned 90 pounds with my little finger and performed a pedestal handstand at a body weight of 280 pounds. Although the "Big Show" spectators gave me a standing ovation that lasted well over three minutes, Canadian papers barely mentioned it.

Undaunted, on December 10, 1953, I gave a demonstration at the second Annual Strength and Health Show in Vancouver, Canada, and became the first man in history *officially* to bench press 502 pounds. First man in history! I was realizing my dream faster than I had thought possible.

Although this feat went unnoticed in Canada, something came of it in the United States. Joe Malcewicz, a well-known California wrestling promoter, who had been keeping a careful eye on my progress, invited me to Los Angeles, all expenses paid, to sign a professional wrestling contract. Since I am not violent by nature, the offer at first left me cold. But since it was a way to salt away a few dollars, perhaps even enough for a gym, I travelled to hear his proposal.

I took off my shirt and his eyes bulged. "Get pictures!" he shouted, all but shoving his photographer towards me. "We got us another Yukon Eric!"

Yukon, whose real name was Eric Holmback, was a six-foot one-inch, 285-pound wrestler with a 66-inch chest who drew a huge crowd wherever he went. Mr. Malcewicz, a keen judge of "wrestler flesh," could see the same drawing power in my size and my strongman reputation.

A contract guaranteeing me five figures a year to start (six figures within the following three years) was immediately thrust towards me, but I was still unsure. The money was enough to purchase a chain of gyms and keep my mother in style for the rest of her life, but what would happen to my dream of becoming the strongest man in history? Could a man participating in phony wrestling matches be a true advocate of physical excellence?

Not about to lose 290 pounds of "walking money" without a

fight, Mr. Malcewicz talked me into a trial period. For two weeks straight — three hours a day, seven days a week — he had wrestlers Yukon Eric and Pat Frayley take me into the ring and show me how it all went: from the holds, to the falls, to the politics. Although I paid strict attention and gave it my best shot, I knew after the first session that it wasn't for me. It was largely showmanship, with the bouts choreographed and the winners picked ahead of time. But it still required a tremendous amount of skill, strength and stamina. Sprains, broken noses and dislocated joints were common. Fall the right way and you could wind up on a hospital bed. Fall the wrong way and you could end up on a slab.

The worst part was my requirement to "put the slug" on my opponents — and get slugged in return. This "violence for the sake of violence" I could neither stand nor comprehend. What sort of people (writer Phillip Wylie called them "the screeching, orgiastic onlookers") needed to watch two athletes hurting each other in public to attain gratification? Wouldn't the world be a better place if people just treated each other with respect and tried to get along?

While I wrestled with this contradiction in the solitude of my Los Angeles hotel room, the phone rang. Mayor Hume asked me to return to Canada as soon as possible. He had caught wind of Mr. Malcewicz's offer and was afraid that a professional wrestling career would nullify my status as an amateur athlete. The British Empire Games were scheduled for Vancouver in August of 1954 and he wanted his city to win at least one gold medal. "Provide that victory," he promised, "and the city of Vancouver — *your* city — will make it well worth your while."

Given the way that the city had recently used, then abused me, I was immediately leery. What's the saying: screw me once, shame on you; screw me twice, shame on me? But I was a weightlifter, not a politician. Maybe this was how politics worked.

The calls from the mayor continued — three to five a day — until I finally said, "Enough! I'll do it! What exactly will I receive in return?"

"Win us the gold medal and we will give you your gym!" he promised.

Back in Vancouver, Mayor Hume and I sealed our agreement with a handshake. His aide, Charles Southerland, a humourless man with a black patch covering one eye, asked me how much I would require a month for training expenses. "Two, three hundred a month?"

"One hundred and fifty will do," I said, not wishing to take advantage. "Just enough to eat and pay the bills."

The mayor agreed and immediately hired me as his personal bodyguard, a function that I would never have to perform. As he confided to me that he would pay me from his own pocket to ensure that my amateur status remained intact, he also informed me that Harry Brown had been appointed "weightlifting coordinator" for the Canadian weightlifting team, and that Lionel St. Jean, a gruff, supposedly experienced lifting trainer from Montreal, had been hired as coach. I, of course, was free to train in any manner that I chose, which I had fully intended to do anyway.

Deal made, I placed my wrestling career on hold, notified all my friends and students of my intention and set about constructing a schedule that would allow me to train to my fullest potential with the least amount of distraction. As I had learned from my Stockholm training, mental preparation was as important as physical readiness in lifting world record poundages. And I was determined once again to break as many records during the competition as I could.

Training for the British Empire Games should have been easier than training for Stockholm, but it was a great deal harder. While training for Stockholm I was still under the "great illusion" that winning would automatically make me an international hero who would become rich and famous and live happily ever after. Whenever I had grown tired or depressed in the past, I had revitalized my enthusiasm with this illusion, but while training for the British Empire Games, I no longer had it to fall back on. If I won, I *might* get my own gym *if* the mayor was a man of his word. The people of Vancouver and the rest of Canada *might* finally get behind me *if* they felt that my performance warranted it. But there were no guarantees.

Since my Stockholm program had won me gold, I used Stockholm as the basis of my British Empire Games program as well, with one exception. While training for the World Championships, I had experimented with a squat-style "cleaning" movement, but my fused ankle and mismatched legs had always left me feeling off-balance with this method. For my British Empire Games training, therefore, I employed only a split-style "clean", where I slid one foot ahead of my body and one foot behind as I yanked the weight to my shoulders. This method considerably improved my balance and made me more relaxed and confident while working out. (Refer to Appendix 6 for my exact BEG training program.)

Once the media and my fellow Vancouverites were notified that I would be representing them in the forthcoming Games, they rallied behind me with a passion. My name and photograph were plastered everywhere and the media touted my potential for a gold medal on a daily basis. Harry Brown — the same Harry Brown who had refused my world press record in Portland — swelled his chest as though he had single-handedly discovered me and predicted:

> Canadian weightlifters will carry off more points than any of the other eight Canadian teams entered in the nine British Empire Games events. Canada will place first and second in the heavyweight class.
>
> (*Vancouver Sun*, "Canada's Lifters Are Strongest Yet," June 4, 1954)

This time, the weightlifting division of the CAAU had no problem nominating me for the Canadian weightlifting team; Canadian British Empire Games President, Major John Davies, quickly ratified the choices (consisting of seven members and one alternative) in order of merit:

1. Doug Hepburn — world heavyweight champion, Vancouver, British Columbia.
2. Gerald Gratton — light-heavyweight, Verdun, Quebec.
3. Dave Baillie — heavyweight, Noranda, Quebec.

4. Jules Sylvain — featherweight, Quebec City, Quebec.
5. Keevil Daly — middle-heavyweight, St. John's, Newfoundland.
6. Stan Gibson — lightweight, Vancouver, British Columbia.
7. Jean Dubé — middleweight, Quebec City, Quebec.
8. Rosaire Smith (alternate) — bantamweight, Drummondville, Quebec.

Although I desperately wanted to win gold for my city and country, the tensions of my demanding training schedule soon made the distractions of my busy gym a weight around my neck. Enter, again, Mr. John Gunn from Farm Boy's Poultry Services Limited, who invited me to stay at his Langley farm while I trained for the games, free of charge and with no strings attached. I accepted with much appreciation and my time spent there was perhaps the happiest and most productive of my life. As well as proving himself a true friend who cared about me as a person as well as an athlete, he helped me convert his large tool shed into a fully equipped gym where I was soon lifting more weight than ever in all three of the Olympic lifts. The more I trained, the more I knew that I would not only win gold, but I would also set a new world record in the press and the three-lift total as well.

There are no sure things in life or lifting, however, as an event that occurred shortly before the commencement of the Games made clear. The entire Canadian team was invited to a celebration dinner at the prestigious Vancouver Hotel, and to my disgust, many of the Games executives seated at the head of the table were drunk. I don't look down on a person who takes the odd drink, but there is a time and place for it and this occasion was neither the time nor the place. Here we all were, serious athletes, and most of the people in charge were drunk to the point of slurring their words. They even had a few of the young female athletes up doing the cancan for them.

Although it might not have bothered either the athletes or the executives, it bothered me. It sullied an event that should have been solemn. They wouldn't have been drunk at their board meeting, so why were they drunk here? Eventually retreating into a back room, I stumbled upon a daughter of one of the executives necking with her boyfriend.

"Why aren't you with the others?" she asked with a trace of annoyance.

"Not a chance," I said. "I'm here to lift weights and that's all I'll do. If they want to turn it into a clown show, they can do it without me!"

As I turned to leave, I heard her whisper to her boyfriend: "Big fat pig!"

I tried to ignore the comment, but I couldn't help thinking that the Canadian team management board should be reprimanded. As if in response to my misgivings, I severely injured my right thigh the next day while training — almost a mirror-image of my pre-Stockholm setback. As I performed a series of heavy snatches, my front foot twisted during the quick portion of the lift and tore my right thigh muscle to the point that I was forced to drop the weight and fall to the floor to avoid further injury. It wasn't a matter of gritting my teeth and ignoring the pain. The injury was so critical that another slip would have ended my career.

For a few agonizing moments, I wondered if the injury really was a form of divine retribution: a punishment to the team as a whole by taking away their only chance for a gold medal. Too pained to think about it further, I steeled myself and set about constructing a training program to cure the injury. To strengthen myself physically, I employed a regimen of rest, massage and light stretching. Anything more vigorous would have only added to the injury and forced me to withdraw from the competition. I also took large and regular doses of food supplements to help speed muscle, tendon and ligament recuperation.

To strengthen myself mentally, I focused on the facts that my injury had not been severe enough to put me out of the competition (not at the moment, at least) and that my split style of cleaning (which did not put as much stress on the thigh muscle as the squat style of cleaning) would allow me to keep training while the healing process took place. This positive thinking enabled me to keep myself motivated on both a conscious and subconscious level, a balance that I would need to maintain if I were to exert maximum efforts when I needed them. I spent most of my free time visualizing myself fully recovered and lifting more world record poundages than ever.

If there is a secret to maintaining a winning state of mind, it is to always remain confident, but not *too* confident. Overconfidence can impede your performance by preventing your body from secreting enough adrenaline. Your mind will tell you: why bother if it isn't necessary? Underconfidence can do the same thing, but for a different reason. It asks you: why bother if I can't win?

The preferred state of mind for ensuring maximum performance during a competitive event is to be *99 percent certain that you can win, but one percent afraid that something could go wrong at the last minute to cause you to lose!* It is this fear factor, almost a panic, that most often makes the difference in a hard fought competition. Given two lifters of equal talent, it will usually be the one who is most afraid of losing his dream who will be able to secrete the most amount of adrenaline into his system when the need arises.

Since my entire future hinged on my winning gold at the British Empire Games, I had no doubt that my thigh injury would keep my fear factor well above the required level. But I couldn't help feeling that I also needed a spiritual boost — something to show me that the fates were still with me.

To my surprise, I received it sooner than I expected. One of the conditions of eligibility for every BEG lifter was the successful completion of a set of qualifying lifts for each division. Under normal circumstances the completion of the three required lifts — one clean-and-press, one snatch and one clean-and-jerk totalling no less than 870 pounds — would have been a snap because it was nowhere near my full lifting potential. But these circumstances were far from ordinary. My thigh injury was still critical and, as I took my place on the qualifying platform, I was certain that one slip or over-exertion on my part would end my lifting career.

My first lift was a 300-pound clean-and-press. It went up easily because I made a point of performing the lift with very little knee bending while cleaning, and made a further point of locking the knee completely before pressing.

My second lift was a 270-pound snatch, and that's when the trouble started. Forced to bend my knee to perform the lift properly, I felt such pain and fear of further injury that I missed my first two attempts. Since three lifts per event were all that were allowed, I had to succeed with my third attempt or I was off the team and out of the Games. My "fear of failure" indicator shot through the roof and I prayed for a miracle. Since I knew that my knee could not withstand more bending, my only option was to complete the lift using arm and shoulder strength alone. But could I? It seemed like an impossible task and most strength authorities of the era would have bet against it. Grasping the 270-pound barbell with both hands, I locked my knees straight and "arm-and-shouldered" the bar upwards as hard and as fast as I could.

To everyone's amazement, including my own, the bar fairly flew to the overhead position and was declared "good" by the qualifying judges. Everyone clapped and cheered, including the judges, and for that brief moment, I was certain that I could have snatched any weight that was placed before me. I still had one more qualifying lift to complete, a 300-pound clean-and-jerk, but I knew that it was just a formality. Experiencing the miracle of the 270-pound arm and shoulder snatch had given me the confidence to tell myself: yes you will qualify because you won't allow it to happen any other way.

I made my final lift without a hitch and that night, as I stood in the stillness of John Gunn's farm, staring up at the clear night sky, I knew without a doubt that I would also win gold at the British Empire Games. I had already risen to the most critical occasion I was likely to face, so any problems that I encountered at the Games would be child's play. What had first appeared as a physical setback had turned out to be a spiritual and emotional godsend.

The British Empire Games was scheduled for July 30, 1954 to August 7, 1954. In its honour, the city of Vancouver had con-

structed a $1.5 million stadium capable of seating 25,000 specta-
tors. Local Boy Scouts acted as pages and Lord Alexander of Tunis,
a former war hero and Governor General of Canada, was the
guest of honour. Come Games time, the stadium was packed and
expectations were sky-high that Vancouver would not only come
away with at least one gold medal, but probably a world record
as well.

Although I also felt that I had an excellent chance of winning,
injured thigh or not, I made it clear to everyone — BEG executives, spectators and members of the media alike — that I would
do only as much as my injury would safely allow. I would win gold
and perhaps set a new Games clean-and-press record, but I would
not risk going for a new world record unless I was certain that my
torn thigh muscle could withstand the strain. As I was quoted by a
major magazine reporter:

> I'm not trying any fancy stuff.
> I'm only here to win.
>   (*Life* magazine, July 1954)

Which is what I did. The only British Columbia athlete to win gold
in any event, I set a new BEG clean-and-press record of 370
pounds, 30 pounds more than silver medallist Dave Baillie of Quebec and 60 pounds more than bronze medallist Harold Cleghorn
of New Zealand. I also set a new Games total of 1040 pounds with
a 370-pound clean-and-jerk, a 370-pound clean-and-press and a
300-pound snatch.

Mayor Hume and the people of Vancouver had their gold, and
I had set two British Empire Games records without further injury
to my thigh. It should have been a magnificent victory for all concerned.

It wasn't. Instead of celebrating our mutual victory, the media
belittled my accomplishments with inferences that I could have
set a world record if I had *wanted* to. I was irritated as well as confused. Had I not made the extent of the danger clear? What
would they have preferred, a little more for them at the expense

of my health? The belittlement did not stop there. Shortly before the medals presentation, while I was relaxing near the top of the bleachers, the loudspeaker requested me to proceed to the victory podium located in the middle of the stadium infield. Although I complied as quickly as I could, the stadium was packed and I was so disoriented by all the doors and halls that I became lost. By the time I arrived at the podium, everyone was waiting and a bored Alexander of Tunis was looking at his watch.

"You're quite a man!" he smiled, pinning my medal.

"You're quite a fellow yourself!" I replied, returning his smile.

We warmly exchanged handshakes and I felt the incident forgotten. The next morning, the papers dubbed me "The Man Who Kept Alexander Waiting!" and made it sound as though I had done it on purpose. That same morning a tiny Englishman with thick eyebrows and a heavy moustache stopped me on the street, tapped my chest with his cane butt and snorted, "Look here, Hepburn! The next time Lord Alexander waits to meet with you, you nip down there smartly!" Turning on his heel, he strutted away as though he had just flattened Jack Dempsey.

The entire situation amazed me. Why would intelligent people prefer to dwell on inconsequential matters rather than the fact that I had just made weightlifting history while injured?

Since I had no idea why such a public backlash might be occurring, I returned to the solace of my old ambitions: a gym of my own where I could teach children, and my promise to care for my mother in her declining years. Mayor Hume had promised the gym to me if I won. I had held up my end of the bargain and it was time that he and council did the same.

Two days later, I met with Mayor Hume and Charles Southerland in the Mayor's City Hall office. We chatted for a while, and when the subject of my gym came up, Mayor Hume nodded and reached for the phone.

"Hold on, Mr. Mayor," Southerland said, stopping him. "Let's think about this a little longer!"

What that meant, exactly, I have no idea. The meeting ended

shortly after with, "We'll get back to you as soon as we have something concrete," and from that moment on, neither the mayor nor Charles Southerland would meet with me or accept my calls.

I was shocked. Were they breaking their word?

My training allowance of $150 per month stopped the moment I won the medal, of course, and I knew my gym was a lost cause once rumours began circulating that I had ignored meetings with the mayor and city — even though such rumours made no sense. Since owning my own gym free and clear had been a dream that I had worked towards for most of my adult life, was it rational to believe that I would have discarded it at a whim?

A lot of Canadians did believe, however. Why wouldn't they? Since not one newspaper ever printed the complete story, the general public was given only the information that the good mayor and his council wished them to be given: Mayor Hume had magnanimously paid $150 a month from his own pocket to allow greedy and money-starved Doug Hepburn to compete in the British Empire Games. In other words, it was the weightlifter who should be grateful to the mayor for his generosity and not the other way around:

> Mayor Fred Hume has denied that he ever promised to purchase a gymnasium for world weightlifting champion Doug Hepburn, or committed the city [Vancouver] to such an action. "I can't understand Hepburn making statements like that," the mayor said.
> (Vancouver *News-Herald*, November 23, 1954, p. 31)

In an attempt to inform the public of what had happened, I tried to buy space in the local newspapers, but to no avail. To be fair, it was probably because I didn't have a contract to prove my allegations. Friend and Vancouver lawyer, Harry Rankin, refused to become involved for the same reason, and the problem remained. Almost twenty years after the fact, the story was still being reported as follows:

> He came back from his remarkable one-man sally into Sweden a little arrogant, very broke and much disgruntled, flailing his home

town for its alleged lack of appreciation. He was then hired for a liberal stipend by Mayor Fred Hume, a gentle, generous man who needed a bodyguard like he needed a second heart.

(Eric Whitehead, Vancouver *Province*,
"Big Hepburn," December 2, 1975)

With no deal and no gym in which to pursue my ideal, I was truly perplexed and uncertain about my life. My BEG victory had drawn a few new members to my Grandview gym, as had my Stockholm win, but not enough to make any great financial difference. The 1954 World Weightlifting Championships were scheduled to be held in Germany, but I couldn't afford to travel there to defend my title. Even though I had devoted all my time, money and energy to training for the BEG, not one person or organization in Canada thought enough of my effort to sponsor me, even though I was heavily favoured to win another gold medal and set another world clean-and-press record.

A few years later, while visiting Harry Rankin at his home, I was approached by a former coach of the Russian Weightlifting team who asked why I had never defended my World Weightlifting title. When I replied that it was because I lacked the funds, he could not comprehend my response. Although I explained it to him at least a dozen times during the evening, he never fully understood. He just kept patting my arm and shoulder, saying, *"Velikolepno! Velikolepno!"*

While I struggled to find direction for my life, I found myself spending more time drinking. I'm not sure why, exactly — probably because I no longer had a reason not to. Before, when I was training with a definable goal before me, I drank very little because I didn't want to jeopardize my chances for success. I didn't mind training instead of socializing because I saw what I was working towards as something infinitely more important.

As more of my dreams failed to materialize, I found it harder, if not impossible, to continue depriving myself, and began seeking compensation for the sacrifices I had made. I was still training hard, but I was drinking hard too — only beer, thank God, but sometimes as many as thirty to forty glasses at a sitting.

Rumours must have circulated that I was heading down the same path as my father because one dank spring afternoon as I sat outside my Grandview gym, resting from my workout, he appeared out of nowhere. He was drunk and scowling, and held his hat with both hands. Although I'd seen little of him since my childhood, we recognized each other immediately.

"What do you think you're doing?" he hissed with enough venom to heart-stop an elephant. "Don't you know a Hepburn can't quit drinking once he starts?"

He'd been hiding his right hand behind his hat and before I could answer, he threw a hook at my head. Although he had boxed in his younger days, the alcohol had eroded his reflexes and I was able to push him backwards onto his behind.

"Wait'll I catch my breath," he said, glaring up at me. "We'll try that again!"

I retreated into my gym and locked the door. He didn't attempt to follow.

The next day, he turned up at my watering hole, sober and with a more hospitable attitude. He politely asked to join me and, when I agreed, he sat across from me and bought a tray of beers. The alcohol loosened his tongue and he got down to why he had really showed up — to give me a detailed explanation of how a man loses himself to alcohol. As best I can recall, here is what he told me:

> Alcohol dulls your mind and your capacity to reason. It gets you off on a side street and the more you drink, the farther down this side street you go until you can't find your way back. The alcohol has screwed up your thinking patterns. The way you think now doesn't mesh with how you thought before so no matter how hard you try or how badly you want to, you can never get yourself back to the way you were in the beginning — even if you quit cold-turkey and never take another drop — which damn few alcoholics are able to do. And damn few Hepburns — because as far as booze is concerned, we're cursed. Once John Barley-Corn, the demon of alcohol, starts a Hepburn drinking, he can never quit!

I'm sure he was serious and perhaps trying to make up for past mistakes. But the whole situation was so absurd that I couldn't take it seriously. Here he was, a confirmed, hopeless alcoholic, already half in the bag, giving me, the son he had deserted years ago and at whom he had taken a drunken swing, a lecture on the evils of drink.

Thanking him for his concern, I assured him that I wasn't in danger of becoming an alcoholic because I had far too much willpower to allow myself to fall victim to it, and invited him to visit whenever he wished. He seemed eager to form a belated relationship with me and, since I saw no harm in it — as long as he didn't try running my life — I was content to let him. Maybe it was my subconscious telling me that I wanted to know the father I never had. Whatever the reason, it felt right and I went with it.

Nodding sadly, he shook my hand and left. He showed up from time to time, both at bars and at my gym, but he seldom again lectured me on the subject of alcoholism. He had warned me; how I responded to his warning was up to me.

Whenever I felt particularly dejected, I would wonder if I *was* heading down a side road with no return. At those times, I guess I needed a way to escape more than I needed advice, because the thoughts were always fleeting. "What now?" I would end up wondering. "Two golds, kept your word while all around you were breaking theirs — and still nothing."

One morning in early September 1954, as if in answer, a tall, handsome, heavily-muscled man in his early thirties appeared at my gym: famous Toronto wrestler and wrestling promoter, Whipper Billy Watson. His business partner, the equally famous Canadian wrestling promoter Frank Tunney, had heard of American Joe Malcewicz's wrestling offer and had sent Whipper Billy with an offer of his own.

"Hundred grand a year!" Whipper Billy stated, quite matter-of-factly. "Not right off the turn-buckle — you'll need to learn the ropes. But within three to four years. Guaranteed starting salary of twenty grand a year, with regular increases as you start pulling in a crowd. It'll happen because we'll damn well see to it!"

Although the lure of big money combined with a way to finally rid myself of my indecision was tempting, I still had little desire to become a professional "pretender." A man who despised hurting and being hurt participating in a profession where inflicting and receiving pain was a daily occurrence: how could that possibly work out?

"No," I finally said. "I'll stick with what has always been my passion."

"Okay" Whipper Billy replied. "Then show up at our wrestling matches as a special attraction. Spectators will pour in!"

Since this proposal appealed to me, I agreed. I sold my gym to Nick and Jake Krushnisky, bid my parents and friends a fond adieu and set off by bus to seek my fortune as a travelling strongman. As I sat watching the city of Vancouver shrink behind me, my elation was swelling by the moment.

Within a few weeks, my arrangement with Frank and Billy was in full swing and was working out better than I could have imagined. My attachment to the wrestling circuit did indeed increase the "draw" substantially and my percentage of the nightly proceeds increased as a result. After twenty shows at a rate of two to three a week, I had earned just over $3,000 and was becoming more popular by the day. In larger cities like Toronto, Ottawa, Cleveland and Buffalo, I made between $200 and $300 a night. Best of all, my principles remained uncompromised and my goal to inspire as many people as possible was closer to fulfilment.

I always performed my demonstrations in the same order. First, my trademark feat of ripping licence plates and crushing cans of oil with my bare hands to show spectators that I was more than just a barbell-orientated strongman. Next I went on to cleaning and lifting heavy weights with my little finger to show that even my smallest digit had tremendous tendon and ligament power. Finally, I performed a series of world record shoulder presses, squats, bench presses and two-handed curls to prove that I was a world champion power lifter as well as world champion Olympic lifter. Touring most of Canada and the northern United States, we always received a standing ovation, followed by a stampede of autograph-hungry fans.

Then, on November 21, 1954, a rainy night in Quebec, it all turned sour. A large wrestling card was scheduled for the Montreal Forum. I was heavily advertised as the featured strongman and during the afternoon preceding the meet, the city had rolled out the red carpet for me. I was given an honourary key to the city and chauffeured through Montreal in a limo (much as I had been in Vancouver by Mayor Hume). Later, I was congratulated by an assistant coach of the Canadian Olympic Weightlifting team who placed his hand on my shoulder and boldly proclaimed: "Let me shake the hand of the only world weightlifting champion that Canada will *ever* have!"

On the night of the card the arena was packed and I was placed in a seat of honour at ringside where everyone strained to see who all the "hoopla" was about. Halfway through the wrestling matches, I began my demonstration and, to my surprise, received little applause. As I concluded a series of world record lifts, including a 500-pound bench press, a 460-pound push-press-off-the-rack and a one-armed 167-pound dumbbell press, the ring announcer, a tall, fit man who spoke mostly French to the audience, suddenly ordered a replica of French-Canadian strongman Louis Cyr's famous 235-pound dumbbell to be brought onto the stage. He then challenged me to "one-hand-deadlift" the dumbbell (deadlift meaning to lift it from the floor until the legs, back and arm are straight) the way the great Louis apparently had on many occasions.

Since Montreal was the home of the Weightlifting Division of the CAAU which had never shown my abilities much respect, it irked me that I was not forewarned about the challenge. But since I had already lifted a replica in New York a few years earlier (refer back to Chapter 2) I went along.

As in New York, I found it quite difficult to secure a proper grip on its exceptionally thick handle with my relatively small hands. My extreme hand and finger strength enabled me to perform the feat with a semi-grip, but it must have appeared awkward to the crowd because I received little applause. Taking this in stride, I started for the microphone to explain the situation to the spectators, but before I was able to, the announcer called out for volunteers from the audience to come onto the stage and also try. One by one they came, all with big hands, and every time the dumbbell left the floor the entire forum exploded with cheers and applause.

Feeling quite insulted, I waited patiently for the volunteers to finish their attempts, then placed a 450-pound bar on the squat rack and military-pressed it above my head. Politely plucking the microphone from the open-mouthed announcer's hand, I calmly asked the audience, "Would any of you care to come down on stage and try this?"

Dead silence.

I removed twenty pounds. "How about now?"

No response.

Another twenty pounds and another.

No one in the audience moved, spoke or smiled.

Content to have made my point, I completed my demonstration and left both the stage and the forum.

I suppose that I should have felt a little satisfaction at finally getting back at the city that had given me so much grief and rejection throughout my career but I didn't. I felt sad and embarrassed for allowing my emotions to rule me. Was this the way a man of principle should be acting? I knew that it wasn't and I contemplated giving up the wrestling circuit because of it.

At that point, Whipper Billy Watson again approached me with a wrestling contract — one with more years, money and perks attached to it due to my widening reputation as a travelling strongman. "They really want you, Doug," he said.

"But do I want them?" I replied.

"Trust me," Whipper Billy said, giving me a smile that he must have stolen from a used car salesman. "Have I ever steered you wrong so far?"

I returned his smile. Although I had never met him before he had strode into my Vancouver gym, I had heard of him. He was as famous in the wrestling game as I was in the strength world, and well known for his ring antics and showmanship. Since he was also a rich and shrewd businessman, I knew that his promises were probably sound.

Suddenly everyone I knew was involved.

"Go wrestling!" said my father and mother.

"Go wrestling!" echoed my friends.

"Got to do something," philosophized former employer, John Gunn.

Taking a deep breath, I gritted my teeth and on January 3, 1955, at the age of twenty-nine, signed a five-year contract. I didn't particularly want to, but if nothing else, it would enable me to purchase my own gym and, at that dark time, something seemed better than nothing.

True to their contract, Frank and Billy rolled up their sleeves and set about turning me into a star attraction: "Mighty Doug Hepburn — World's Strongest Man!" They had me grow a moustache to make me appear more virile and every day for two months, Billy and fellow wrestler, Pat Frayley ("Pat the Ears" as he was known to the other wrestlers — although not to his face) took me into a private gym in the basement of Toronto's Maple Leaf Gardens and taught me the ropes. I didn't learn a lot because there wasn't time — just the basics of falling and throwing, and finally the submission hold that would become my wrestling trademark: the inverted bear-hug. When it came time for me to end a match, I would press my opponent into the air with both hands, spin him upside down and hug him until he quit.

With my superior strength and lifting ability, wrestling should have been easy for me. It wasn't. While weightlifting, for the most part, is composed of well-balanced, straight-line pushing and pulling movements, wrestling is more to do with off-balance twisting and rolling movements. The skills that I was strong at and the skills that my wrestling opponents were strong at were often so at odds that it left me confused enough to scream. Add to this my less than enthusiastic desire to learn or be associated with the wrestling "game" and I soon realized that my five-year stint would be a living hell — if I was lucky enough to remain alive for that long. Under a starry, Toronto sky, I vowed to quit the circuit the moment that my contract was up, buy myself a little gym in Vancouver's East Side and have nothing more to do with wrestling in any form for the rest of my years — amen!

As previously mentioned, what pained me the most about my matches was having to contend with the "violence for the sake of violence," both while training and performing. Hits, slams, bruises, dislocations and breaks were common occurrences that I abhorred — the giving, worse than the receiving. As I once explained to a local magazine:

> I'm a gentle giant who doesn't get bellicose with anyone. While wrestling I had to put the slug on people. I'm a poet inside, not a wrestler outside.
>
> (Doug Hepburn, as told to Dick Beddoes,
> <i>Liberty</i> magazine, 1956, p. 38)</div>

My first professional wrestling bout took place on March 22, 1955, at Toronto's Maple Leaf Gardens and was a semi-final "tomato can" match with an unknown by the name of Frank Marconi. His job was to lose quickly and decisively and that is exactly what he did. We grappled for a couple of seconds to give the crowd the impression that we were feeling each other out, then I flipped him into the air and squeezed him until he was counted out. I ended by strutting around the ring flexing my "strongest-in-the-world" muscles. My fame as the world's strongest combined with my perceived invincibility in the ring made me an instant money-maker.

Frank and Billy ran me through this act a couple more times with different opponents, then decided it was time for a main event. Who better as my opponent than the popular, flannel-shirted, barrel-chested Yukon Eric? We were about the same size and weight and each of us used a bearhug as a submission hold — his, the conventional version. The idea captured the imagination of the paying public and they came out in droves.

Our first match, which took place on November 2, 1955 in Edmonton, Alberta, drew a crowd of 7,500 people in forty-below-zero weather. We wrestled to a draw to test the public's reaction. When it became evident that the match-up definitely had what it took to be a top draw, Frank and Billy paired us twice more. During the first of these contests, on November 7, 1955 in Niagara Falls, we again wrestled to a draw. But during the second match, on November 8, 1955 at Hamilton, I was allowed to beat Yukon by butting him into the corner with my huge chest and finishing him off with my trademark submission hold. This cemented my status as a credible and popular wrestler and, from then on, I was committed by my contract to go along with whatever it took to make me even more popular.

Once I wrestled a 400-plus pound monster called "the Blimp," who was so fat that he had to be lifted into the ring with a crane. The worst part was his extreme body odour, which was so intense that it almost made me vomit. Not wanting to be subjected to it any longer than necessary, I sucked in a deep breath, "drop-kicked" him onto his back and sought refuge at the far end of the ring holding my nose while he was counted out.

At other times, I was made to wrestle two average-sized opponents at once. The fans really loved this because I could usually toss them around like rag dolls. I would invariably win by squeezing each of them unconscious (or so it would appear to the audience) — sometimes both with the same squeeze.

From then on, I was travelling the southern Canadian/northern United States circuit with the likes of Yukon Eric, Pat Frayley, Whipper Billy, Ski Hi Lee, Sandor Kovacs, Farmer Don Marlin, Dick the Bruiser, Angelo Poffo, Bobby Managoff and a host of others. We wrestled three to four bouts a week. In larger cities, I earned $500 to $900 a night while in smaller locations I earned about $35 a night. For my first year, I grossed $25,000 and netted about $15,000 — which wasn't bad for 1955. Frank and Whipper Billy estimated that I would earn between $50,000 and $60,000 a year during the next two years and about $100,000 a year after that. It would be more than enough to buy a gym when the time came — perhaps even a chain of them.

Along with the money and fame came another benefit — women. As Whipper Billy whispered to me the first time I stepped into the ring: "Your women troubles are now over!" He was right. After each card, every wrestler was besieged by waves of "ring-following" women, eager for autographs, kisses and whatever else they could glom onto with their souvenir-hunting hands and bodies. I must admit that I succumbed to the temptation from time to time, but only with someone whom I found desirable in ways besides sexual.

One such person was a tall, voluptuous woman of about my own age who I shall refer to only as Colleen. She began showing up at wrestling cards in more than one town and city and we spent some truly enjoyable times walking, singing or frequenting late night movies or coffee shops. I liked her relaxed personality — confident, rather than loud and pushy like most of the other women who followed the circuit — and I particularly liked the fact that she was intelligent and easy to talk to. Sharing a common love for music and animals, we spent many nights just talking, and more than once, I was struck by how much she and my mother seemed to possess the same strength of character. "Life is what we make of it," she would say, whenever the subject of my disgust for wrestling came up. "Better to make a good living than a poor one."

After a time, she made it clear that she wished our relationship to become something more lasting. Since I was not ready for commitment and did not want to take advantage of her feelings for me, I broke it off. It saddened me for quite a while because I truly enjoyed her company, but all things considered, I was certain that it was the right thing to do.

Many of the other wrestlers were not as fair as I was. They would seduce these star-struck women as fast as they showed up — sometimes two and three a night — then dump them as quickly, without a thought for their feelings. A couple of the more unscrupulous wrestlers carried cots in their vehicles and dressing rooms.

Although the violence and exploitation wore away at me daily, not all my time spent as a travelling gladiator was bad. For the most part, the wrestlers were a jovial, fun-loving group who shared a strong kinship and loved to party during their off-hours. Practical jokes were common. Once, while Pat Frayley, Yukon Eric and I were drinking beer with a six-foot-six, 330-pound Russian wrestler known as "Ivan the Terrible," in a small bar in Hamilton, Ontario, we began feeding him bars of laxative and telling him that they were chocolate. To our amazement, he washed down three entire bars with no apparent ill effects. That evening must have been a different story, however, because the next day Ivan, appearing quite pale and gaunt, wagged a long finger at the bemused bartender and said in a thick Russian accent, "Something wrong with beer here! All night long I fart and fart!"

Another time, Yukon, Pat Frayley and I were driving to a Cleveland meet with a huge African-American named "Coco Bonk," who let it slip that he was deathly afraid of graveyards. We immediately fed him beer until he passed out, drove him to the middle of the largest, spookiest graveyard we could find and stretched him out on the hood of our rented 1952 Cadillac. Giggling like school kids, we crouched behind gothic headstones with the remainder of the beer and waited for the fun to start. About midnight he stirred, looked around and froze. "Oh oh," was all he said. He then scrambled behind the wheel, started the engine and sped off as if Satan himself were chasing him. In our drunken states, we had neglected to remove the keys from the ignition and had to walk fifteen miles to the motel, with everyone blaming everyone else for the screw-up.

Even stranger was what occurred while Pat Frayley and I were driving back to Canada after a meet in Yakima. We ran out of money and gas, in that order, and were quite stumped for alternatives. I've been known to sing a little and Pat strummed the ukulele from time to time, so we approached a nearby bar and offered songs for gas. The owner, a sour, pug-nosed type, who looked as though he'd been on the losing end of more than a few alley brawls, was hesitant at first. But when the packed house booed, thumped their glasses and stomped their boots, he agreed: beer for the night and enough gas to get us home in exchange for ten songs. It must have been something to watch — 600 plus pounds of tipsy wrestlers singing, dancing and plunking — because by the end of our ten songs, the entire establishment was whooping, clapping and dancing along, and the bartender offered us steady employment. I was sick enough of wrestling to accept but Pat wasn't, so it was back to the ring for another four years, six months, thirteen days and seven and one-quarter hours.

Bad times far outweighed the good times, however, and by my eighth month I truly despised what I was doing. Depression sometimes struck me two to three times a day and I would sit for hours alone in my hotel room trying to make sense out of what I was doing. Worse, what was becoming of my gym for underprivileged kids? I was making good money, but I was spending it all on beer. Alcohol was the only thing that seemed to block out the pain, panic and depression of what I was doing.

The more I gave into my vice, the worse I felt, and the more I could hear my father's admonishing voice. "See how quickly you get lost? Who's the loser now?" The words slammed me like a forearm strike across my windpipe every time I heard them. Was this what I had degenerated into? The strongest man in the world, now its biggest loser?

My depression eventually caused me to start missing matches that I was under contract to attend. Knowing that I would have to parade and prostitute myself and my abilities in a phony and degrading manner caused me such emotional pain and dread that I would lie on my hotel bed, unable to move.

"Okay, time to go!" I would tell myself. "They're waiting for me and the clock's ticking. I made a deal and my word is good!"

Except that it wasn't good. Once it was too late for me to attend my match, I was immediately overcome with remorse. My drinking was out of control, my life was out of control, and I knew that if I didn't find help soon I might very well die.

Hoping to break my depression with familiar surroundings, Frank and Whipper Billy booked me for a match in New Westminster, British Columbia. Although I probably should have been looking forward to it, I took in very little — not even the name of my opponent. I had no desire to see friends or family and went through my match as though I was a spectator myself: watching it all take place but experiencing very little, not even the whoops and cheers of the crowd as I inverted my hapless opponent, squeezed him into submission and slammed him to the mat. When it was over, I collected my money, retreated to a secluded bar near Preston Beach and began knocking back beers with a vengeance.

A few loggers recognized me and we were soon all drinking together — laughing, singing and having a grand old time. At closing time, one of the loggers coaxed me into his old Ford half-ton and drove me home to meet his family. Although it was almost three in the morning when we arrived, no one minded. His wife cooked us a huge breakfast and his children sat on my knee, and everyone was so nice to me that I suddenly broke down. Here was this simple man and his family who had everything, and here I was, with all my fame and strength and ideals, who had nothing!

Fighting back tears, I retreated to the backyard. Why can't I be happy too, I felt like shouting. How can I turn myself around? But the heavens remained silent — no falling stars, godly interventions or indications that I had been heard at all. Perhaps I hadn't been. Perhaps my belief in fate and the importance of achieving and maintaining a world title was nothing more than an illusion — the pathetic pretenses of an insecure cripple looking to bring meaning to his empty and miserable life.

In an attempt to counteract my remorse, I travelled to Toronto and purchased a sparkling new Cadillac Eldorado: silver with gold wheels. Since I had always wanted one, I slapped $4,500 cash against the $9,300 price tag and took a tour of the city, just as Mayor Hume and I had done after my return from Europe. I picked up Pat Frayley, who puffed a thick cigar as we drove, and quipped, "I wonder what the poor people are doing?"

As we drove, people stared and waved, and we honked and waved back. But deep down I knew that it was all a sham. My car meant little to me compared to my two gold lifting medals. My medals were a symbol of victory while the car was a symbol of defeat.

Returning to the wrestling circuit, I fell back into an energy-sapping depression — this time only worse. My drinking was completely out of control, and I blew so many matches that Frank and Billy made me put up my new Cadillac as a bond. They also sent me to a psychiatrist, at their expense, but it did little good: I hated wrestling and always would.

Other wrestlers, already resentful at having to take a back seat to someone with less wrestling experience, saw what was going on and became still more upset. If I was so unhappy, why didn't I just quit and give the opportunity to someone who wanted it? This didn't go unheard and a few even tried to force me out. Once, after being notified by Whipper Billy that I was to wrestle two opponents at once during the evening's performance, I made the mistake of shaking my head and mumbling, "Same old shit!" After my match, I opened my locker to find it crammed with freshly soiled toilet paper.

With each practice and performance I received more "cheap shots" to the face, throat, kidneys and ribs, and once, as I stepped soaking wet from the shower, a 300-pound wrestler named "Mighty Ursus" laughingly choked me with a towel from behind until I almost passed out. Whether these incidents were random or an orchestrated attempt by Frank and Billy to make me more aggressive, I have no idea. I only knew that I could no longer remain a quitter and a phony in my own eyes. One bleak November night in 1955, while driving back to Toronto after a U.S. wrestling tour, I told Pat Frayley and Yukon Eric that I was quitting.

Yukon sort of understood, having a family from whom he hated to be separated, but Pat just scowled and shook his head. "You know, Hepburn," he snorted in his gravelly voice, "I've just spent the better part of eleven months with you — travelling, rooming, drinking and talking. And I still don't understand a damn thing about you!"

"Join the club," I replied.

Frank and Billy tried to talk me into staying, of course. There was still a little over four years left on my contract but we all knew that it was no use. My drinking was out of control and I was suffering from a sort of severe battle-fatigue. Whatever I was searching for or being steered towards, if anything, had nothing to do with wrestling. Although I tried my best to explain that to Frank and Billy, I'm sure they never understood.

"We pushed him too hard!" they told clamouring reporters when word leaked out. "He got here too fast!"

Although I owed Frank and Billy $800 for their share of my most recent earnings, when I offered it to them, they just shook their heads and my hand. "Keep it, Doug. You're gonna need it!" As I stuffed my luggage into my Caddy a resentful wrestler shouted out, "What's it like to be all brawn and no brain?"

"What's it like to be neither?" I said, without the least trace of malice or regret, and sped away.

As I hit the open road with the cold winter wind on my face, a new feeling of strength and satisfaction washed over me. I had been temporarily ensnared by the lure of materialism, but I was now free and bound for the home I should never have strayed from in the first place. Raising my eyes to the clear blue sky, I composed the following couplet:

> Forgive me, Lord, and take me back,
> I sold my soul for a Cadillac!

As Toronto shrank in my rearview mirror, I sensed that my soul had been returned to me, and that I had been taught a valuable lesson in the process: better to make little and be happy, than to make millions and be miserable. I would return to my home city, rekindle my dream and never judge happiness in terms of materialism again. I wasn't sure how I'd achieve my goal, I just knew that I would as long as I didn't falter along the way.

CHAPTER 5

INTO THE DEPTHS

No one feels enlightened unless
he struggles. If people feel sorry for me,
I feel sorry for them.

— DOUG HEPBURN
(Archie McDonald, "Hepburn's Legend Lives On,"
Vancouver Sun, December 7, 1994)

When I arrived in Vancouver on a cold, rainy December evening, ten months after I had first set out on my wrestling tour, everything had changed. Most of my friends and training partners had left in search of their own lives and futures. The city seemed considerably colder, both the weather and the people. I missed the feeling of security and belonging that placing my feet down on my native soil had always afforded me.

As I stopped my Caddy in front of my Grandview gym, it was immediately evident that it too had changed. The Krushnisky brothers, it seemed, had been unable to keep it going and it was now a sales outlet for a bedding company specializing in low-end mattresses and box springs.

Unsure how to proceed without my gym to fall back on, I spent the night in a familiar East Hastings rooming house (the nightly rate had increased from three dollars to four) and rose before the robins the next morning to seek my life's direction. Reluctant to face my mother and father until I had found it, I stopped in at the Waldorf Hotel for a beer and ended up knocking them back as fast as the waiter could deliver them. Had I been right to give up what some men would have probably considered a dream come true? Deep down, I knew that the answer was yes. But it did little to alleviate my immediate problems. My wrestling money would soon be gone and then what — back to bouncing in the bars? The absurdity of it made me laugh. Had I thrown away huge money to get away from wrestling, only to end up wrestling drunks for peanuts?

Opening the morning paper during a breakfast of scrambled eggs and toast, I found the "whole story" of my quitting wrestling told by reporters who had no idea what the whole story was: Hepburn the brooder; Hepburn the quitter; but not a word about Hepburn the sincere athlete who hated violence and only wanted to help people. "If you're going to assassinate a man's character," my father had said, "never try to balance it with facts. What fun would that be?"

In the same breath, the article went on to herald the good news: yes, Hepburn was a screw-up, but he did have a knack for lifting heavy poundages and if he played his cards right, his city and country just *might* allow him to represent them in the forthcoming 1956 Olympic Games, *if* he could just get over that damned despondency of his. I exchanged the paper for a magazine and there it was again:

> Barring accident or injury or the onset of one of his sieges of melancholia, he is an overwhelming favourite and already has ardent supporters who are visualizing him as the Olympic Games Champion at Melbourne Australia in 1956.
>
> (*Maclean's* magazine, June 1, 1954, p. 26)

The article failed to address how I was supposed to get to Australia with little funds and no sponsorship. The time and money that I had spent training for the British Empire Games had left me too broke to travel to the 1954 World Weightlifting Championships, even though I had again been the overwhelming favourite to win gold and set a world clean-and-press record. My wrestling obligations had left me unable to attend the 1955 World Weightlifting Championships, even though I had been favoured to win gold and set a world record at *that* time. Now the push was on again for "Mighty Doug" to go out and give his all for his city and country — at his own expense, of course.

I thought about Melbourne for all of a few seconds and erased it from my mind. If winning one World Championship had caused little change in my life, why bother with the hassle and expense of trying to win a second one.

Enter Ray Beck, a tall, well-built friend and fellow weight-enthusiast, who was in and out of the gym business and who chanced to have a cache of gym equipment from a previous venture. My Grandview gym had kept the wolf away while I had pursued my goal and ideal *before* wrestling, so why not a second gym after the fact — especially while my notoriety was still fresh in the minds of most Vancouverites? Remembering my pledge never again to place materialism above happiness, I was at first hesitant. But since I would have to make a living one way or another, opening another gym seemed to be the most sensible route.

As luck would have it, we found a vacant store at 1130 Commercial Drive, a stone's throw from my original Grandview location, and I took it as a sign of good luck. Ray and I signed a monthly lease, placed a six-foot picture of "Doug Hepburn, former World Weightlifting Champion and World's Strongest Man" on the roof directly above the front door and immediately drew a large attendance. Many of my former students returned, as well as a steady stream of new members. Ray and I were soon making ends meet every month, and earning a little extra for our effort.

As the Melbourne Olympics neared, the clamour for my participation increased, but it was unnecessary. I made it clear that I was not interested. I also detailed the reasons to my students and, as I look back on it, the times shared with them were some of the fondest and most satisfying that I have spent in a gym. After our regular workouts, we would all have long, relaxed discussions about super strength and what it took to build and maintain it. As they listened attentively, nodding in agreement, I would feel at peace with who I was and what I was attempting to accomplish with my life.

Other well-meaning acquaintances, however, like Ray, my father, and a host of friends, members and fellow lifters felt that I should expand my business. If I were doing a lot of good with one gym, I could do a lot more with many — and I could also help myself a little more as a consequence.

It seemed logical, so I opened a second gym on downtown Seymour Street for business people and a third in New Westminster for people of all ages. The Commercial Drive gym evolved into a women-only club, and for the next couple of years or so, all three endeavours went extremely well. I was still physically large, with world-class lifting capability and, as I rotated from gym to gym, lecturing and instructing, I felt satisfied, my students felt satisfied and my desire for alcohol all but disappeared.

Then, for no apparent reason, my feeling of contentment slowly began to erode. From some dark place deep within me came this nagging doubt (almost an apprehension) that all was not as perfect and self-fulfilling as I was leading myself to believe. What I was doing *was* important. I knew that without a doubt. But I also knew that there was something more important that I should have been doing — something that I couldn't define in word or concept, but which could help people far more than the gym and which could help them throughout the world.

Day by day the feeling became stronger, but not one iota clearer. And I found myself spending more time and effort trying to sort it out — time spent mostly in bars. Workouts, which had once left me invigorated, fulfilled and focused, now left me with a growing apprehension that time was running out. I risked becoming an also-ran — a "settler," as my mother had termed it so many years ago — while my true destiny passed by.

I remembered my mother's first use of the term, when she had warned me of the importance of sound schooling and a good living. "Do not be a settler, Douglas! The cost is too high and painful!" I knew that she had been talking about herself and her lost opportunities; the sadness in her eyes made me want to heed her warning, but I had no idea how to go about it. How do you fight something as indefinable as an "inkling," a sensation that comes and goes so quickly, without rhyme or reason, that makes you wonder if it exists at all?

I saw friends from time to time: Mike and Eileen, who were still together and working towards a career in the savings and loan business; Little Johnny who was still intent on becoming a professional acrobat; and Leo Aquino, who was already a professional piano accordion player. But those meetings only made me feel worse. Here they all were, knowing their goals and well on their way to fulfilling them. And here I was, aching to succeed as well, but with my face against a blank, unscaleable wall, still living alone in the back of my gym.

My determination dwindled and I soon sank into a confusion that bordered on depression. The more I struggled to overcome it, the worse it got, leaving me, at times, so depleted of energy and desire that all I wanted to do was sit — not even think, just sit — because everything I had worked towards had lost its meaning. The 1957 and 1958 World Weightlifting Championships came and went but I barely noticed. From time to time my father showed up with his slurred opinions of what he felt was happening to me, but I had heard it all before: beware the evils of drink; beware the Hepburn curse; beware, beware, beware.

I kept attending my classes and workouts, but it became clear to both myself and my students that I had lost my passion. Attendance rates soon dropped through the floor, I got behind in my financial obligations (despite my own best efforts) and one cold November day in 1958, I was forced to close all three schools and sell my Eldorado for $2,500 to settle my debts.

To my surprise, I found myself more relieved than deflated.

Since I hadn't belonged where I had been, I was now free to go out and discover where I did belong.

Bill Copeland, always the smiling, supportive friend, invited me to join the fire department with him, but I knew that I would never fit in. Whatever destiny held in store for me, it was not working nine to five for someone else — no matter how important fire prevention was to the city.

Ray suggested co-owning a sports equipment store but I declined that offer as well. I saw little future in it and hated the thought of having to keep regular hours. When an opportunity to try out for the B.C. Lions football team came up, I went in as lineman, but was quickly cut. As I told a reporter a few years later, "I just had no understanding of the game" (Clancy Loranger, Vancouver *Province,* June 16, 1965).

I must have been the talk of the town at that time, because no sooner had I been dumped from football, than I was ferreted out at my Waldorf Hotel watering hole by Cliff Parker, a flashy Vancouver wrestling promoter, who offered me one more crack at the lucrative world of professional wrestling. The smug way that he emphasized the word "lucrative," made me immediately decline his offer. As he stood to leave, he snorted at me, "To do what?" Having no answer, I motioned him back down into his seat.

"One match here in Vancouver to begin with," he said. "If I decide there's no future in it, there'll be no more."

"What if *I* decide there's no future in it?" I asked, knowing that only a miracle could make me want to stay in a sport that I abhorred.

He shrugged and offered me his hand. I took it and a match was set up for November 30, 1959, at the Garden's Auditorium in New Westminster before a packed house. My opponent was a local grappler named Luther Lindsay, who was about my size but possessed neither my strength nor wrestling prowess. His main worry seemed to be getting through the match in one piece and, as things turned out, it was a valid concern. Although the match was choreographed with "Mighty Doug" to be the eventual winner, this particular match, for some reason, produced a drastic change in my character. As soon as the crowd started screaming for blood, something snapped inside me and I heard myself shouting back, "You want it, I'll give it to you!" With that, I snatched poor Lindsay into the air and body-slammed him so hard that he bounced a good foot from the canvas. As the crowd roared its approval, I slammed him again and again, then ended the match by dropping my full 305 pounds on his chest for the "pin."

As they carried poor Lindsay back to his dressing room, he managed to wheeze, "Never match me with Hepburn again." But I knew that it would never happen. My temporary loss of control had both scared and sickened me. I pocketed my $300 cash earnings for the night and informed Cliff that I was quitting and would never again step into a wrestling ring. As I exited the main doors, he shouted something about having another match arranged for the following week at Exhibition Park at twice the money because of my fabulous performance. But I had already erased it from my memory and was looking for a quiet place to relax.

Too tense to sleep, I ended up at east Vancouver's Trout Lake park. As I sat there, staring out across the calm, still water, a young jogger happened by with two of the most impressive husky dogs that I had ever seen. I had always loved dogs, huskies in particular. As I watched them disappear into the darkness, I remembered Calgary wrestling promoter, Al Oeming, describing a particularly strong and rugged breed called a freight husky, that he was raising in his backyard. He had purchased his first male and female at a small settlement near Alaska's Porcupine River, and had found the dogs to have an average weight of 180 pounds.

On impulse, I contacted Bill Copeland and asked him if he had enough spare space on his large Burnaby lot to accommodate such a venture. Bill offered not only space for the animals in his back yard but a spare room for me in his basement. When I discussed the idea of the dogs with friend and fellow British Empire Games lifting competitor Stan Gibson, he agreed and offered to drive me to the Vancouver bus depot as soon as I was packed to go.

Shortly before Stan arrived to pick me up at my East Hastings rooming house, I received a phone call from Cliff Parker, who curtly informed me that if I didn't show up for the Vancouver wrestling match that he had arranged for me, I would be out of the business for good. He would pick up the phone and damn-well see to it. Thanking him for his concern, I politely suggested that he book someone else in my place, perhaps Mr. Lindsay if he wasn't too shaken up from our last encounter, and hung up the phone. I then took the Greyhound to Calgary, bought a pair of pups from Mr. Oeming — a large male, that I named Buck, and a larger female, that I named Chinook — and promptly transported them to their new home in Burnaby.

When Bill saw the pups, so tiny he could hold each one of them in the palm of his hand, he smiled, and commented, "Bum-holes no bigger than shirt buttons!" But as they quickly grew, consuming a gargantuan amount of food in the process, it became apparent that I would need a lot more space.

After conferring with a few real estate companies, to no avail, I rented a large, old three-level house on an acre of land in the Woodland Hills area of Whalley, B.C. (three blocks east of the intersection of the King George Highway and the No. 10 Highway) from a former dog breeder by the name of Don Loveless. A former POW in a German prison camp during the Second World War, he had raised mastiffs because they were much larger and stronger than the German shepherds he had grown to hate, and, as a result, had plenty of kennels and runs. I was certain that my future had taken a giant dog-leap for the better. I also set up a private gym in the basement and, to supplement my breeding income, wrote strength-building courses, which I printed on an old Gestetner mimeograph machine and sold mail-order for two to three dollars apiece. Since I had simultaneously held world records in the two-handed press, the two-handed curl, the bench press and the squat (as well as a host of other, more unconventional lifts and feats of strength), my intention was to write a detailed training course on each and see what kind of a response I received. To my delight, they sold well and I was soon netting ten to fifteen dollars on an average day, and twenty to fifty dollars on a good day.

Since I was back to doing what I wanted to do, this success gave me emotional as well as financial satisfaction and every afternoon after my writing, training and dog-tending, I strolled down to the Clova Inn in downtown Cloverdale and celebrated with a couple of beers — just a couple. Its atmosphere was friendly, as was its mostly blue-collar clientele, and I spent many happy times laughing, joking and telling weightlifting and dog stories.

During this time, a rather comical thing occurred while I was riding a street car down Commercial Drive enroute to a dog food wholesaler. As we neared the building where Ray Beck and I had once operated our gym, I made two disturbing observations. First, that the gym had been turned into a bright and busy underground "cat house." Second, that my large picture was still on the roof. Exiting the vehicle to get a better look, I was immediately approached by a large, Louisville Slugger-armed house manager, who recognized me and all but dragged me inside for a grand tour. He led me from room to room, from woman to woman, like a proud street-vendor hawking his wares and assured me that I was welcome to sample any or all of them at any time for half price. When I politely asked for the return of my sign, he refused. The picture had been an integral part of the bargaining price and had turned out to be a huge boon for business.

Back at my Woodland Hills kennels, my dogs bred and sold well, and I was soon the proud owner of over twenty canines and a growing reputation as the man to see when it came to freight huskies. As I watched these magnificent animals grow and flourish, I couldn't help sensing that I had been led to them for a reason other than simple association; it seemed the work of fate and I spent many hours trying to decipher its meaning. The huskies had great physical strength and the breed was known for its ability to survive for long periods on very little food and water, but I was sure that the message had to be something more profound.

Then, as I watched them interact — particularly Buck and Chinook leading the pack, Buck strong and Chinook even stronger — I realized that their greatest attribute was their indomitable heart and spirit. They weathered hardships such as sickness and injury without faltering and expected nothing in return — not even human companionship or approval. Did I need to develop a similar attitude in my own life?

As it turned out, my lesson was something quite different, and it haunts me to this day. While at the Clova Inn one quiet afternoon, I was approached by a kindly, elderly man named Brian Powell, who had a problem. His wife had just taken sick and he could no longer afford to care for their dog, a giant St. Bernard that they had aptly dubbed Bernard. Assuring me that Bernard was an extremely gentle creature, loving and loyal, Brian asked me if I would adopt him. I had the room and means, and Brian and his wife would be forever grateful, since the alternative was to have the dog electrocuted at the local pound.

Since I was raising huskies instead of St. Bernards, I was hesitant. But the man's pleading eyes made me agree. Assuming that the other dogs would also adopt Bernard, I took him back to my kennels, fed him, groomed him and placed him inside the run. Within seconds, the huskies turned on him and would have torn him to shreds if I hadn't yanked him to safety.

Feeling sorry for the animal and not wishing to break my word to Mr. Powell, I built Bernard a separate run and kennel, but it soon became apparent that, while the huskies could function quite happily without human intervention, this loving St. Bernard could not. He howled all night and day until I petted or walked him and, while I was away from the house, he flopped onto his side and panted as though his breathing was restricted.

Perhaps, if I hadn't tried to harden myself against him, I would have seen what was happening and taken steps to remedy the situation. Instead, certain that it was in the dog's best interest, I adopted my father's philosophy on survival: "Get tough or die — life don't make no allowances for also-rans!"

One overcast September afternoon in 1960 as I returned from town, a group of neighbourhood kids, who had been playing with Bernard inside his run, rushed up to me and asked me if they could take him home to keep. They could see that he was unhappy and promised to give him a good home with lots of food, love and exercise. They had no money but they would gladly do chores in exchange because they really loved Bernard and Bernard loved them.

Since I, too, had developed a fondness for the dog's gentleness and felt certain that he would eventually adapt, I declined their offer, but I assured them that they were welcome to visit Bernard any time they wanted for as long as they wanted. The children were perhaps too disappointed to visit an unhappy animal that they knew they could never possess; whatever the cause, they never returned. Bernard, in response, became more depressed and spent more time on his side. One morning, as I approached the pens for the morning feeding, I found him dead in his run. As far as I could tell, he had died of a broken heart.

The message that I had been seeking from my interaction with the dogs was now perfectly clear: I could no more survive with my heart hardened against the world than this poor animal had been able to survive in a place and manner both contrary to his nature. And my refusal to see this and remedy it had cost him his life. Eager to get into something that I liked after spending so much time at something that I despised, I had jumped at the chance, oblivious of the possible consequences.

Wrapping Bernard in a thick blanket, I buried him in the back yard beneath a cross of sticks and twine that I could see from my bedroom window. Every night before I slept, I would stare out at it and cry for a long time. I tried to get on with my life by rationalizing it all away — things will happen the way they will happen — but since I couldn't escape my feelings of guilt, I found myself turning more and more to the solace of the Clova Inn. My father would join me from time to time, warning me that I was well on my way down a Hepburn side road, but I paid him little heed, refusing to believe that a father who had all but deserted his family could understand guilt or moral obligation.

As dogs and bills piled up, I soon realized that I was well on my way to a second bankruptcy, but I paid that little mind as well. I was prepared to accept it without complaint. I welcomed it, in fact. About this time I made the acquaintance of Roger Williams, a gaunt, ash-skinned, fast-talking but good-hearted sign writer and painter, who had a pretty wife named Ida, a nine-year-old daughter named Melissa and a passion for passing bum cheques. His fraud was so blatant that it was almost inconceivable that he could keep getting away with it. But he did — regularly. He would bounce a cheque on Monday to get himself and his family through the week, obtain church absolution on Sunday and bounce another one on the way home. He was always generous with his ill-gotten gain, however, and never saw it as theft. When there was painting to be done, he painted. When there wasn't, he did what was necessary to provide for his family.

Since Roger and his family needed a place to live and I needed a way to cut expenses, I invited them to move in. In hindsight, it might seem a goofy idea, given Roger's apparent addiction to "walking the crooked line," but he promised to be straight with me, and I took him at his word.

As it turned out, the arrangement was a godsend for all of us. Ida cooked and sewed, Melissa helped me with my canine chores and I helped Roger with his sign-painting in exchange for his teaching me the trade. They were never late with their rent, allowed me both privacy and companionship when I needed them and went out of their way to help me come to terms with Bernard's unfortunate death.

As a result, the tension in my life slowly began to dissipate. My breeding business stabilized, I wrote and sold more courses and I returned to regular training. Little Melissa delighted in working out with me and I delighted in teaching her. I made her a set of wooden barbells that she lifted while I performed my workout, and we had good times together.

The more I saw how happy Roger and his family were, poor but deeply committed to one another, the more I wondered if our association had also been fated. Perhaps it was time for me to start my own family.

But with whom? I had lost my only true love years ago to my "magnificent obsession," and there had really been no one since.

Re-enter Colleen, the tall, buxom woman with the long auburn hair whom I had spent time with while wrestling. Walking into a Cloverdale butcher shop one hot July afternoon in 1960, I found her wrapping meat behind the counter. She recognized me, struck up a conversation, and within a very short time it was as if we had never parted. Still attractive with a keen interest in music, she made a point of telling me that she was divorced with a five-year-old daughter named Brianna. She also tried to talk me back into wrestling, but when I made it clear that wrestling was no longer an option, she agreed to drop the subject for good.

We began dating — nothing expensive because I couldn't afford it — and spent the first few weeks trying to discover as much as we could about each other. She liked the dogs and the idea of breeding them for a living, but once she got a taste of my spartan lifestyle, coupled with my obvious reluctance to change, she made it clear that she wished our relationship to remain casual, at least for a while. She had a daughter to raise, which couldn't be done properly on hopes alone — especially ones that seemed to have as little foundation or direction as mine.

Brianna was an endearing child whose hair and facial features reminded me of her mother, but whose moody personality reminded me of myself. Although she appeared to be happy and energetic most of the time, she also spent a lot of time by herself thinking. When I asked her what was on her mind, she would just shrug and say, "Things, I guess." But she never took me into her confidence.

Although I truly liked both mother and daughter, I knew that before I could think of parenthood I would first have to be absolutely certain I wanted it. My own upbringing had shown me how important a happy, stable home was to a child, and the last thing I wanted was to follow in my father's footsteps.

Slowly, a feeling of certainty began to form. Colleen and Brianna persuaded me to go out more, and it wasn't long before I truly looked forward to these excursions. We took long, leisurely walks with Buck and Chinook, attended the odd movie and restaurant and shared barbecues with Roger and his family at the beach or in our large Cloverdale backyard, where we sang, laughed and joked well into the wee hours of the morning. Melissa and Brianna got along well and I took great delight in making up stories for them — their favourite being the adventures of Mighty Matt, a strongman with a tender heart who toured the country doing good deeds.

One night, as Colleen, Brianna and I sat having a checkers tournament on the kitchen table, I was struck by how closely my relationship with Brianna and her mother paralleled my stepfather Bill's relationship with my mother and me. As I sat watching the little girl laugh and clap her hands in excitement, I silently vowed never to make her feel the way Bill had often made me feel — a burden rather than a blessing. As this feeling increased, I again wondered if I was meant to take Colleen and Brianna for my own.

As usual, I couldn't make up my mind and everyone I knew offered advice. My mother liked both Colleen and Brianna and felt that I should marry immediately. Although my father also liked them, he was adamant that I shouldn't get married until I quit drinking for good — something that he was positive the Hepburn curse would never allow. Both Roger and Ida told me to follow my heart. But since my heart was as confused as the rest of me, I decided to wait for some sort of a sign, which I received a short time later.

Buck and Chinook produced a female offspring that I named Aklavik, after a small town in Alaska. From the outset, Chinook was always punishing the pup. As I found out later from Al Oeming, Aklavik had been a "diabolo" or devil dog, and Chinook had sensed it from the beginning. When Aklavik had her own pups, she killed them all and she and Chinook fought to the death over it. When I saw what was happening I tried to pull them apart, but, with all my strength, I was unable to. Chinook finally took the devil dog by the throat and held on until the fight was over. At Aklavik's death, Chinook immediately calmed and allowed me to remove the carcass for burial.

For some reason, this incident haunted me, and left me almost fearful of marriage. Brianna sensed it and soon everything became less emotional and personal between us. Although I tried to get her to do things that I knew made her happy, like caring for the dogs, going for walks and listening to stories of Mighty Matt, she took less and less interest. Colleen became so concerned that she suggested we break up for good. Then, just I was ready to agree, a series of events occurred that made it unnecessary.

One windy morning while Colleen was at work, Brianna agreed to help me feed the dogs and we went to the cages with two large buckets of dog meal laced with meat and fish scraps. Begging to do the feeding herself, the way I had begged to feed the turkeys myself at the Rundle farm, Brianna doled out the food while I held the buckets and the dogs became so excited that they fought one another. This frightened poor Brianna half to death and she jumped back from the cages the way I had bolted from the turkeys and stood wide-eyed and shaking. Trying to explain to her that it was nothing personal, that the dogs were just anxious to get at their food, I placed my hand on her shoulder, but she pulled away. Things were no longer the same between us and she was going to make sure that I remembered whose fault it was.

On the way back to the house, we happened upon an injured bird that was lying in the middle of the path. It had been badly mauled by a hawk or some other predator, but it was alive and little Brianna begged to adopt it. Although I gave the bird little chance to recover, we placed it in a makeshift cage with some food and water and sat back to see if miracles still happened.

"Please, God," she prayed, in a way that brought tears to my eyes, "let him fly high in the sky again!"

We spent the remainder of the day and half the night keeping a strict vigil to no avail. It died and I had the near-impossible job of explaining that death was just a part of life and that the little bird had gone to a happier place where it could fly as long and as high as it wanted. Wrapping it in a soft cloth, we placed it in a small box and buried it atop a hill beneath a tree home to a flock of birds. We bowed our heads, said a short prayer and sang the chorus of "Redwing" — perhaps because my mother had always sang it to comfort me.

She stood trying to be strong, her lower lip quivering, then fell into my arms crying. I can't explain how that felt. All my life I had wanted to have that kind of connection with my mother, but I had never been able to initiate it. Yet there, under a blanket of stars, over a dead bird's grave, this little girl had mustered courage that I had never been capable of, and had given me one of the most profound emotional experiences of my life: complete trust and forgiveness.

From that moment, everything became better with the three of us. Colleen and I formed a more complete understanding of who we were and what each of us needed to be happy, and Brianna and I once again became fast friends. We would play games, exercise and care for the dogs. And each night before Brianna and Colleen returned to their Cloverdale apartment, I would tell her and Melissa a bedtime story about Robbie the Robin, a little bird that had dreamed of becoming an eagle, but had instead become an angel that flew around the forest helping other birds.

Left to proceed in that manner, Colleen and I might very well have married and set up housekeeping on our own, but life is full of wild cards. In the middle of a painting job, Roger Williams was arrested for passing bad cheques and was sentenced to six months in jail. Ida and Melissa moved out of the house to be near him and I was left with the problem of having to scrounge enough monthly income from my dogs and courses to make ends meet. This, of course, resurrected a former problem: deciding if I wanted Colleen and Brianna to move in with me. I had grown to care deeply for both of them, perhaps even to the point of love. But was I capable of maintaining a long-term commitment when my mind, emotions and finances were in such a haphazard state? The more I struggled with the problem, the more confused I became and the more I looked for solace in the Clova Inn. I continued training, selling courses and caring for my dogs because it kept me somewhat anchored, but I laughed at the absurdity of it. I drank to keep from making a decision, yet the more I drank, the more I needed to decide.

One rainy night, as I returned from the bar, singing at the top of my lungs, I found Chinook lying in her run with Buck whimpering beside her. She was barely breathing and, for a few horrid seconds, I wasn't sure what had happened. Easing her jaws open, I saw that something was choking her: a long strip of cheese cloth. How she had gotten it, or when, I had no idea, but she had swallowed a lot of it and was so bloated that she could barely breathe. Scooping her into my arms, I ran for the house, but, by the time I got there, she was dead.

Wanting to give her a special funeral, I wrapped her in my best blanket and carried her to a small bridge that spanned the rushing Serpentine River. Lifting her to the heavens, I spoke of how much she had meant to me: her strength in ruling the pack and her ability to persevere against all odds, the way I had never been able to. I dropped her into the current so that she could be carried out to sea — a Viking funeral for a Viking heart — then headed to the Clova Inn where I drank with a vengeance.

When Colleen saw what was happening, she reluctantly stopped coming around. If I chose to be a hopeless alcoholic who refused help, she couldn't prevent it, but the cost would be the love and company of her and her daughter. They had faced enough pain and disappointment in their lives without a lot of my unnecessary self-pity.

It made little difference to me at that point, since in my own mind I had no future anyhow. And by late August of 1961, I had lost my house and business. I kept Buck, gave the rest of the dogs away for their own good (as I should have done with poor Bernard) and set out to spend the rest of my days in solitude.

After storing my weights and equipment in a small, unheated

enclosure that was owned by Brett Pine, an assistant pharmacist at the Cloverdale drug store, I rented a tiny, roach-infested room near the Clova Inn for Buck and myself and did cleaning and sweeping to make ends meet. All my spare time was spent either drinking or walking Buck — the latter after the former — and slowly but surely I sank towards the muddy bottom of my existence. My guilt remained, requiring its daily fix of alcohol to make it bearable, but every day I found myself caring less and less about what the next day would bring. I had become a loser and a drunk.

In the Clova Inn I was still famous, to a degree, with many patrons eager to buy me beer, so I easily downed forty to fifty a night for little expense. In exchange, I would sing, tell lifting and wrestling stories and be the life of the party. It all became a little sordid. Once I even performed a one-armed handstand on a bar stool for two free hotdogs — on the condition that I ate them while remaining in the handstand.

This went on, minute by hour, day by week until it suddenly occurred to me that people were no longer laughing with me — they were laughing at me. The respect that I had worked so hard to earn throughout my life had gone the way of stale beer and it was as if my entire world had collapsed around me. Stumbling into the cramped washroom, I stared into the filthy mirror and was shocked by what stared back: eyes bloodshot and sunken; face ashen and trembling. Where was the strongman who had walked proudly, breaking world strength records and inspiring everyone in his wake?

By the time I had stumbled back to my corner table, my mood had changed. I was no longer "Good Old Doug — everyone's pal and buddy." I recognized that the people I thought were my friends had turned on me, and I wanted nothing more to do with them. To drink until I couldn't drink any more, was all I wanted. During that bleak and painful time, that's all there was.

The consequences were horrendous: blackouts that lasted days, sometimes weeks; hangovers that left me pleading for death; a marked decrease in both my strength and my body weight; and an inability to look at myself in the mirror. "If you want something to laugh at," I reasoned through my drug-induced fog, "I'll give it to you. I'll become the biggest laughing stock in history and get the last laugh on *you!*" Although it made no rational sense, it made little difference, because rationality no longer had anything to do with it.

In my more lucid moments I dreamed of an existence with no depression or haunting regrets, but the fantasies were rare and short-lived. Life was what it was, I was what I was, so to hell with it all.

About this time I met a sour and grizzled hermit whose last name was Peden. He never used his first name and had rejected the world by moving to a dilapidated shack a few miles up the Serpentine River. He returned to civilization from time to time for dry goods, trapping equipment and as much beer as he could carry. But he stayed no longer than absolutely necessary. He was a confirmed alcoholic with no desire to quit and a personality that was either one step above or below the freight husky — depending on your point of view. While the husky could survive with little human intervention, Peden would have been elated with none. He hated people, seeing them only as irritants.

In the bar he sat in the farthest, darkest corner and sourly drank beer until either the bar closed or he ran out of money. He scowled at me from time to time as I went through my similar ritual. But there was no communication. His business was his and the rest of the world's was theirs and that was the way it had better stay — or else.

Still, I could sense that we both felt some sort of connection. For months this continued until one day, without warning or provocation, he turned to me and rasped, "Oughta take a damn flame-thrower to it all!" Before I could respond, he leapt up and launched into a seething, damning oration on life in general: politics, religion, taxes, sex, unemployment, immigration, inflation, greed and the fluctuating prices of gasoline. He downed more beer, and began pacing in front of my table, unleashing oceans of pent-up frustration and hatred.

In my dank state of mind, I couldn't disagree with him, so I listened, nodding occasionally, until one day he invited me to his Serpentine shack to live and share expenses. Each would buy his own beer and we would split the rest of the expenses down the middle. We would trap food in winter, grow it in summer and do as we damn well pleased in between.

Even though completely drunk, I could see that life with Peden would be no picnic, but feeling wholly without direction, I agreed — providing that Buck agreed as well. Leading Peden outside to where the big husky was tied beside a couple of well-gnawed bones, I motioned for Peden to pet him. If Buck allowed it, we moved up the Serpentine. If he didn't, all bets were off.

To my astonishment, Buck took to Peden right away. Perhaps he sensed Peden's emotional toughness or his "husky" misanthropy. Whatever the reason, Buck allowed Peden to place a hand on him and, as far as I was concerned, that was as good as a handshake. We pooled our first month's expenses and Peden weaved off to purchase supplies while I stumbled down to the Cloverdale pharmacy to tell Brett Pine of my intentions.

Although Brett wasn't at all sure that my moving in with Peden was a good idea, or even a rational one, he agreed to store my possessions until my return. When I offered to pay him, he replied the way Frank Tunney and Whipper Billy Watson had replied the afternoon that I had left wrestling. "Keep it, Doug — you're going to need it."

The next stop was the government liquor store, where we purchased as much beer as we could tie onto two large packboards. Strapping the supplies onto a third packboard (which Peden informed me I would have to carry with my "beer board") we were soon roaring and back-firing along in Peden's unmuffled, unlicensed Studebaker truck. Pedestrians pointed, shouted and ran for their lives.

Sucking on a couple of "warm ones," we soon left civilization and steered up a rarely used track that followed the twisting, rushing Serpentine River. A couple of miles upstream, the track ended and we donned the pack-boards and proceeded on foot. The cabin was another four miles upstream and Peden, weaving and cursing under the weight of his pack, checked a string of muskrat traps along the way.

As the numbing effect of the alcohol wore off and I saw just how mean and cranky Peden could be, I had serious doubts about what I was doing. I felt as though I had rejected all that was good and right in the world and was heading up a river that was named after a snake with Satan himself breaking trail. When Peden began stuffing dead, wet muskrats onto the pack right next to the food, I started into the beer full force, as did he, and by the time we reached our destination we were barely able to keep our legs under us.

Peden's cabin was far worse than he had described. There was a rusty pot-bellied stove for heat, holes in the roof for catching rain water, wooden crates for furniture and filthy blankets for bedding. Recently skinned muskrat pelts and carcasses hung from every log rafter and everything smelled of death and decay.

Upon entering the kitchen, I wished that I had paid more attention to the shopping. Everything was either canned or dried and everything that wasn't sealed was riddled with bugs and worms, which Peden ate like candy. According to him, if they didn't hurt the many animals who survived on them, they wouldn't hurt us. In winter we'd trade pelts for beer and in summer we'd trade berries and mushrooms for beer so there would be no problem. Everything was geared to keeping the alcohol flowing because at that place and time, alcohol was the only thing that mattered to us.

When we became sober enough to eat, we consumed porridge soaked with a bubbling mixture of powdered milk and beer, followed by cold peas from the can for dessert. Buck tore into the many animal carcasses lying about — both inside and outside the cabin — and seemed quite content.

When it came time to use the toilet, I was in for another surprise. The outhouse consisted of an unsteady log platform jutting out over the rushing Serpentine. The theory was sound, I suppose — do your business and have the rapids wash it away — but the practicality of it left a lot to be desired. The rusty, upside-down toilet paper pail was devoid of paper and I was extremely doubtful that the platform would support even Buck's weight, let alone mine. Since late September was no time of year to be experimenting, I decided to do my business behind trees and bushes — always humming or singing loudly so that Peden wouldn't mistake me for something shootable.

The more time I spent with Peden, the more I realized the extent of our emotional differences, especially during the time we were drinking. I was a passive drunk. I stayed awake as long as I could, singing and playing with Buck, then slipped into a deep sleep haunted by past hurts and disappointments. I kept my pain inside me.

Peden was the opposite. He ranted, raved and foamed at the mouth about every wrong that had ever been perpetrated against him. He swore, threw things and called down death and destruction upon humanity in a thousand forms. At the height of his rage, he hauled out a weathered, double-barrelled Greener shotgun and blew holes in everything within range, both inside and outside the cabin. Once, he blew the toilet paper pail and most of the wooden platform from the outhouse. Another time, he blew apart a giant porcupine, ate a portion of it raw and picked his teeth with a quill.

I soon felt trapped between heaven and hell. On one side, was the solitude of nature and on the other, the unholy tirades of Satan himself. Which would claim me?

Not all my time at Peden's cabin was surreal, however. Although my feelings of pain and regret remained and required a constant fix of alcohol to keep them manageable, slowly, with just myself, Buck and the solitude of nature to contend with, I began to touch upon the questions I needed to ask to re-enter the world of the living. Did I truly want to give up for good, or was it all just a vain attempt to save myself from more failure and rejection? More to the point, what would it take to get me "back into the game" again?

Looking for insight and perhaps a bit of companionship, I made the mistake of asking Peden why he drank. Unleashing a barrage of four-letter expletives, he leapt to his feet and shouted that it was none of my damn business. He had chosen me because he thought we shared a common state of mind — contempt for the human race — but if we didn't, I could pack up and get out.

"You're a gutless coward who's spent your whole life whining and snivelling about how the world let you down!" he snarled. "But you're the one let it happen so why don't you just admit it and shut the hell up! You might be strong but tough is what it takes and you haven't the toughness God gave a gulled gopher!"

As his rage intensified, the room spun and it was as if his admonitions were a witch's brew of every hurt and disappointment that I had experienced in my life: my mother begging me not to become a "settler" — which I had; Colleen begging me not be become a quitter — which I had; little Brianna begging me to fly high in the sky again — something I couldn't seem to manage. But the worst was my father's voice, pleading and menacing: "See how easy it happens? Who's the gutless loser now?"

Clamping my hands over my ears, I wanted to die. It was time, I deserved it and I set out to make it happen. Peden and I had just packed in another load of beer and I flew into it, determined to drink myself to death. Yanking bottle caps off with my bare hands, I guzzled until my lungs gasped and my stomach churned. Peden joined in, ranting and firing his Greener, and suddenly something snapped inside me. With a rage that I never knew I was capable of, I grabbed the shotgun from Peden's hands, shoved him to the dirt floor and fired both barrels into the ground a few feet from his head.

The dual explosion shocked me back to reality. I tried to speak but couldn't. Dropping the Greener, I stumbled outside, threw up out of fear and disgust and passed out on the cold, wet snow.

When I awoke, hours later, Buck was lying beside me keeping

me warm. One thing was mirror-clear inside my pounding head: I no longer wanted to die. I wanted to live, make peace with my friends and my family and salvage whatever was left of my life and destiny. My brief display of senseless violence had shown me what was at the bottom of my downward spiral, and I wanted to stop it while I still could.

Packing my meagre belongings into a paper shopping bag, I hugged Buck goodbye, made Peden promise to care for him until I returned — I knew that all the carcasses would keep him well fed with a minimum of care — and set my sights for Cloverdale: no more excuses; no more hiding. I would make up for all the mistakes I had made in my life and all the pain I had caused. It wouldn't be quick or easy, but I would succeed or die trying.

As I began my long journey back to civilization and the man that I once was, I prayed to God to show me what to do.

CHAPTER 6

DEATH, DEMONS AND LSD

My success is in spiritual terms.

— DOUG HEPBURN
(Archie McDonald, "Hepburn's Riches Are
Strictly Spiritual," *Vancouver Sun,* 1990)

Reaching Cloverdale shortly before dawn, I wandered its deserted streets and ended up resting on the wooden steps in front of the post office. Too weary to sleep, I studied the serenity that surrounded me. A snow bird stirring in a nearby fir tree inspired me to compose the following poem:

> A robin's joyous singing
> of its song to dawn's first light.
> A morning star still clinging
> to the vestiges of night.
> Soon gray turns to gold as shadows fade and die.
> Dewed petals each unfold as azure fills the sky.

Feeling better in spirit, if not body and mind, I napped until the drugstore opened, then sought out silver-haired Brett Pine, who loaned me a few dollars and offered me free lodging in the shed where he had stored my weights and possessions. He made a point of stating that it wasn't charity. The accommodation would be in exchange for a bit of sweeping up from time to time — an exchange which I gratefully accepted.

It was a combination of sweet and sour luck. It was sweet because it showed that at least one human on the planet still cared about what happened to me — something that I really needed to know at that dark time. It was sour because I was within walking distance of the Clova Inn, which to my amazement, I considered frequenting. It was a thought short-lived, however, because on February 18, 1962, at the age of thirty-six, I steeled my back, gritted my teeth and checked myself into the Hollywood Hospital, a well-known alternative treatment medical facility for alcoholics, located near the corner of Sixth Avenue and Sixth Street in New Westminster.

Actually, the Hollywood was much more than a medical clinic. It was owned and operated by Dr. Ian Maclean, Canada's foremost authority on LSD (short for lysergic acid diethylamide, an organic compound that induces psychotic symptoms similar to those of schizophrenia). He only took in patients whose addiction could be cured by this drug. The treatments were extremely expensive and controversial, but since Dr. Maclean had experienced success with those patients who truly wanted to be cured, I felt that he was my best chance. As conventional cures had never worked for my father, I had little faith that they would work for me and I was ready to try Dr. Maclean's controversial treatments.

I couldn't afford the cost, of course, but Dr. Maclean offered me a deal that I could not refuse: free treatments in exchange for my services as a paid orderly. Although most of the patients who entered the facility were weak and sickly, others were completely "off the wall" and could become extremely violent at times, a danger to themselves as well as others.

The Hollywood Hospital was actually two hospitals in one. The first half of the building, where I and the non-violent patients resided, was much like the average hotel. It was clean, quiet and composed of small rooms equipped with cots, tables, chairs, lamps and closets. Crisp, clean bedding covered the cots and sharply pleated curtains adorned windows that afforded a relaxing view of flowers, trees and blue sky.

The second half — sardonically referred to as "East Berlin" — was less appealing. It was separated from the first half by a steel door that was always locked and guarded. The rooms, also with steel doors, were stripped of everything that could be used for a suicide attempt, including the patients' clothes. Once a patient was locked inside, he or she could only be released by a signed order from Dr. Maclean, and guards and orderlies were required to keep a regular and documented watch.

"The patients are generally out of their minds with addiction at this point," Dr. John Holloway, a rather short, reserved psychologist and first assistant to Dr. Maclean, explained, "and they will take any opportunity to end the pain. One unfortunate strangled himself with a lamp cord, after pleading for the lamp for a week and swearing to God that he would do himself no harm with it. Another choked herself to death by swallowing her underwear. Still another tore a mattress apart, fashioned a spear from one of the springs and plunged it through his heart."

After checking in and touring the facilities, I spent the next few days describing my life to Dr. Maclean in terms of what I had expected, what had resulted and who or what I felt was to blame. His sombre, piercing eyes seemed as though they were penetrating my innermost thoughts and fears, yet his face remained composed as though his being aware of my problem and keeping it from me was an integral part of the treatment. I began to understand that the success of my treatment hinged on my realizing *exactly* what was required of me, and then having the courage to see it through to its full and final completion.

On the eve of my LSD treatment, Dr. Maclean came to my room and prepared me for what was to come. The session would last anywhere from four to fourteen hours and I would receive no food or drink until it was over. According to Dr. Maclean, my problem stemmed from deep-seated emotional regret that had resulted in my subconscious mind wanting me dead. Since I could never have cured myself, I was extremely lucky that I had sought help.

"As some people go through life," Dr. Maclean explained, "they inevitably screw up and fail — as all humans do — but find it impossible to accept and become their own judge and jury. In some cases, they become so hard on themselves that they start a conflict between their conscious and unconscious minds. The conscious mind attempts to reason the mistake away in a normal manner: 'Oh well, I gave it my best shot but it didn't work, that's life.' The unconscious mind, however, refuses to let it go. The body has screwed up and must be punished — no other way. Since the conscious mind also acts as the body's first line of defence, the unconscious must find a way to block out the conscious mind so that it can begin punishing the body. In the case of Doug Hepburn, the manner employed is excessive use of alcohol and the punishment is death. Why? Because *this* body really screwed up. It had everything, then lost everything and let everyone down in the process.

"So, slowly but surely, the unconscious mind sets out to disable the protective conscious mind with false promises: 'Let's go for just one beer, all your friends will be there and you'll have fun — That's what you really want, isn't it?' So the body drinks and, as the conscious mind is numbed, the unconscious mind is given free reign to really start punishing. The more the body drinks, the happier it feels until it either doesn't realize or doesn't care that other things are suffering: health, family, career, determination, self respect, to name only a few — until it finally pays the ultimate price of death."

As I sat listening to Dr. Maclean, I was stunned. The same giant, indomitable will that had made me a world champion was now trying to kill me. "But how does a person protect himself from himself?" I asked.

"You must allow yourself to be killed," Dr. Maclean continued.

"When the LSD enters your system you will embark on a "trip" inside your mind where someone or something will try to kill you in a manner that you will find too horrible and terrifying to face. But face it you must. If you have the courage, you will break your addiction stone-cold and never wish to drink again. If you do not, you will make yourself more despicable to your subconscious and your problem will become infinitely worse. Allowing yourself to be killed will erase the guilt from your subconscious mind and allow you to start a new life.

"But be forewarned: even if you are successful, you will need to be careful for the rest of your life because if you fall back to being too hard on yourself, which it is your nature to do, the problem will resurface with a vengeance. I must also tell you that, based on my experience in this hospital, only one person in one thousand has been able to submit to his or her death. And those who believe in a higher power are the most likely to succeed. Good luck."

After Dr. Maclean left, I thought briefly about praying to God for help, but found myself, instead, contemplating what my father had once told me about the danger of alcohol. "It dulls your mind and your capacity to reason," he had said as we sat consuming beer in the Waldorf Hotel bar. "It gets you off on a side street, and the more you drink, the farther down this street you go until you can't find your way back because the alcohol has screwed up your thinking patterns. The way you think now doesn't mesh with the way you thought before, so no matter how hard you try you can never ever get back to the way you were in the beginning — even if you quit cold-turkey and never took another drop, which few alcoholics, and no Hepburns, are able to do. As far as booze is concerned, we're cursed. Once a Hepburn starts drinking, he can never quit."

As I sat silently, becoming more scared and confused by the second, I wondered what would happen to me if I did beat my addiction. If I couldn't go back to who I was in the beginning, then who would I become? Would it be worse or better than before? I again contemplated praying, but couldn't bring myself to do it. Maybe I was trying to punish God for deserting me and allowing me to sink to rock bottom. That thought made me remember what Dr. Maclean had said about my subconscious trying to kill me and I froze: what if my subconscious was after my soul as well as my life and was initiating these feelings of bitterness towards God to weaken my faith during the session?

Needing to reach out to something, I closed my eyes and spoke the Alcoholic's Prayer:

God grant me the serenity to accept the things I cannot change, the courage to change the things that I can and the wisdom to know the difference.

I don't know why I chose that particular prayer, since it seemed a bit impersonal under the circumstances, but it made me feel better and allowed me to fall into a deep sleep. My dream was familiar: Jesus Christ and me paddling a canoe in the middle of Trout Lake. "Why did God, your father, give me this great gift of strength?" I asked.

"Why did He give Samson his?" Christ replied.

"So that Samson could help people. But then God took it back."

"Took or Samson gave?"

The next morning, nervous and clad in a loose sweat suit, I was led by a smiling and very beautiful female orderly to the room where my confrontation with myself would take place. Aptly named the Psychedelic Unit, it was set up to resemble the average living room: three easy chairs facing one long sofa, thick window curtains that allowed only a sliver of light into the room and a state-of-the-art record player attached by long wires to two large speakers.

Dr. Maclean and his colleague, Dr. Holloway, were seated in two of the easy chairs and I was invited to occupy the third. After a brief discussion designed to reduce my anxiety, a solemn male orderly entered with a glass tumbler containing a clear liquid that

I was told was a "fifty-fifty" solution of LSD and mescaline — the latter being a hallucination-inducing alkaloid used to intensify the LSD experience.

I took a deep breath and studied the mixture as Dr. Maclean prepared me for what was to come. I would swallow all the liquid in the tumbler and lie on the sofa with a dry, folded towel covering my eyes. I would not leave the sofa or remove the towel for *any* reason until I was instructed to do so by Dr. Maclean. Failure to comply with any step of the procedure would result in failure. It was up to me.

Placing a reassuring hand on my shoulder, Dr. Maclean repeated what he had told me the previous afternoon. "Only one in one thousand has the strength and courage to remain on the couch for the entire session and to submit to his own death when the time comes. Will you, Doug Hepburn, be that one?"

I contemplated the question for a few seconds, then swallowed the tasteless liquid and waited for something to happen. Nothing.

More waiting.

Suddenly, the room went completely dark for a couple of seconds. Then it returned to normal. I mentioned this to Dr. Holloway who explained that a cloud had passed in front of the sun and only I had noticed.

I was then positioned prone on the sofa with a folded towel over my eyes. Suddenly music was playing — harsh, symphonic music that wove itself over and around me, poking and prodding into my every pore and fibre as it struggled to control me.

The music was accompanied by a regular, echoing thumping that sounded like a steel wrench against a hollow pipe: the record player needle against the record.

As the music became harsher and louder, it seemed to wash the inside of my mind with thick, billowing swirls of purple. The shades and thicknesses changed — like lapping water against a shore — but always there were swirls, and always the swirls were purple.

As the music crashed and pounded, I began to move.

Up.

Down.

I couldn't tell.

Down. Slowly at first, then as quickly as a runaway elevator.

I wanted to escape, jump off while I still could, but I was frozen.

Down through swirling purple I dropped — deeper and deeper. Flashes of rock and mud appeared through the swirls and I knew that I was plummeting down a deep crevice.

No. It was a pit, stinking of slime, filth and rotten garbage. A mixture of every putrid stench I had ever known. I ached to cover my nose and mouth but still I could not move.

Faster and faster I dropped.

The stench became worse, intensified by heat that seared my flesh and scorched my lungs. I struggled to cry out but no sound would form. From the swirling, stinking walls I caught glimpses of skulls and bones dripping with flies and maggots, and then the echoes of voices shrieking in despair. Serpents struck at me from all sides but still I could not move or cry out.

I dropped into a high, wide cavern thick with sulphurous lava smoke and was suddenly chained naked atop a high rock altar — my hands and ankles blistering from the shackles and my lungs so congested with sulphur that I couldn't breathe. Thrashing and choking, I felt more lost and alone than I had ever felt before and I was certain that everything was against me: the smoke, the fire, the pain and the blaring, demonic music that was mutilating my eardrums.

A vision of Christ on the cross flashed inside my mind and for an instant I felt his pain: heavy nails driving into my hands and feet; whips slashing across my back; thorns digging into my head; a spear tip thrusting into my side. Then I began to fall within myself, as though my body had become a bottomless, suffocating tunnel that could no longer support my mind. I had to escape but I couldn't. I wanted to beg for my life, shriek out in terror. But I couldn't. I was lost, alone and so terrified that my heart felt ready to pound through my chest.

In an explosion of deep purple, my life passed before me in reverse. Or maybe I plummeted past it. I couldn't tell. I knew only that my time on earth was being yanked back from me and when I reached the end of my fall it would be as though I had never existed. Panicking, I tried to slow myself with will alone. My temples pounded and my stomach knotted and burned from the strain, but I eventually became motionless. Praying for strength, I was bombarded by familiar faces and voices: my sad mother saying, "Don't be a settler, Douglas, the cost is too high; my inebriated father snarling, "It is what it is, so live with it or die; soft-spoken Dr. Maclean whispering, "To live, you must first die."

I allowed myself to drop and was immediately exploded up out of the tunnel into purple, billowing clouds. As I flew upwards, faster and faster, I felt that I was being offered a rare opportunity to learn great things, perhaps all there was to learn about my mortal existence — if I chose to. To my surprise, my answer was: not yet. I needed more time to contemplate what had happened, to remain who and what I was for a while longer until I had fulfilled all of my earthly goals.

I started back down and suddenly I was back on the hospital couch with the cloth being removed from my eyes. As the drapes were thrown open to expose a flood of gorgeous sunlight and a view of trees and flowers, I was struck with such an overwhelming sense of peace, love and relief that I broke down and cried aloud for several minutes. Everything had changed. Every negative emotion that I had ever been plagued with was gone. I had been reborn and I felt elated!

But there was more to come. As I smiled at Dr. Maclean and Dr. Holloway, their happy, supportive faces were transformed. Before my eyes the flesh rotted and dripped from their skulls and their eyes and teeth yellowed and turned into squirming maggots. "Although you *feel* reborn," Dr. Maclean explained, "you still have deep-rooted hate for the way you were shunned, belittled and rejected. And this hate has now taken form."

I attempted to will the ugliness away but I couldn't. My stomach knotted and I felt my elation souring into extreme depression. There was a light knock on the door and the male orderly entered with a mirror placed face down on a tray. It was an ordinary mirror, yet it filled me with dread. I didn't want to look at it, touch it or have it in the room with me.

Removing his hand from my shoulder, Dr. Maclean told me to lift the mirror and stare directly into it. I tried, but was unable to make my body respond. He warned that if I didn't, I would never be completely cured, and that most patients lacked the strength to perform this simple act.

Summoning all the determination that I possessed, I snatched up the mirror and stared at the most hideous face that I had yet encountered. My face was rotting, dripping and worm-infested. The longer I stared, the more grotesque I became. As I began to sweat and shake, Dr. Maclean explained that what I beheld was the hate I held for myself, and before I could be truly free of my addiction, I would have to find a way to expel this feeling of self-hatred from my life.

I tried to will this image away, but I couldn't. How does a man overcome himself? Gritting my teeth, I concentrated with all my might and, for a few seconds, the ugliness went away: the skin healed, the worms disappeared and the eyes, ears and nose returned to their normal shapes and locations. The grotesqueness quickly returned, however — only worse — and I knew that I could never succeed on my own. Dropping to my knees, I prayed for strength and was immediately infused with a surge of energy so strong that it left me momentarily breathless. I stared into the mirror and laughed aloud at how easily I was able to will my ugliness away.

I looked at Dr. Maclean and Dr. Holloway and their faces were normal too — smiling, supportive and completely respectful of what I had been able to achieve. As they each shook my hand and congratulated me for my courage, faith and determination, Dr. Maclean faced me and very solemnly said, "You, Mr. Hepburn, can do anything that you wish to do!"

Staring at my image in the mirror, I knew that it was true.

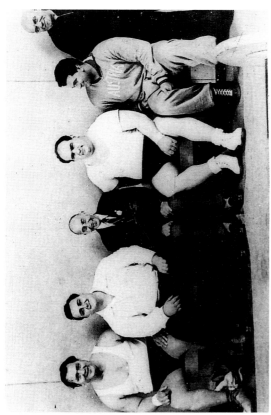
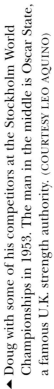

▲ Doug with some of his competitors at the Stockholm World Championships in 1953. The man in the middle is Oscar State, a famous U.K. strength authority. (COURTESY LEO AQUINO)

▼ Doug in Sweden, in 1953, showing off his muscles. (COURTESY LEO AQUINO)

▶ Doug on the winner's podium at the 1953 World Championships along with John Davis (seven times world champion), second place; and Humberto Selvetti, third. (COURTESY LEO AQUINO)

▶ Doug meeting with then Vancouver Mayor Fred Hume after Stockholm. (COURTESY RAY BECK)

▲ 1954 BEG Weightlifting Team: Kneeling, left to right: – David Baillie, Douglas Hepburn. Standing, left to right: – Lionel St. Jean (Coach), Gerald Gratton, Jules Sylvain, Charlie Walker (Manager), Stan Gibson, Guy Dubé, Keevil Daly. (COURTESY STAN GIBSON)

▶ Doug preparing for the 1954 Vancouver British Empire Games in Vancouver. (COURTESY RAY BECK)

▶ Doug with his friend and fellow Vancouver lifter Stan Gibson in their BEG blazers. (COURTESY STAN GIBSON)

▲ Doug Hepburn, the winner of the 1954 Vancouver British Empire Games with a total lifting weight of 1,040 pounds. In second place was Dave Baillie of Quebec; in third place was Harold Cleghorn of New Zealand. At this time Doug was at his heaviest weight ever — 315 pounds. (COURTESY DENNIS WONG)

▶ Doug snapping a chain, one of a wide variety of strength feats he enjoyed performing. (COURTESY RAY BECK)

▶ 305-pound Doug Hepburn completing a handstand pushup, one of his favourite training exercises. (COURTESY LEO AQUINO)

▲ Doug in a classic pose. (COURTESY RAY BECK)

▲ This "relaxed" pose
shows just how
massive Doug was.
(COURTESY LEO
AQUINO)

Doug lifting six
Vancouver Canuck
players standing on
a platform during
an appearance at
the Kerrisdale
Arena in 1953.
(PHOTO: ROY LEBLANC,
VANCOUVER SUN)

Dr. Maclean then instructed me to rest on the couch for a while before returning to my room. As I complied, he and Dr. Holloway put on some peaceful music and left. While I relaxed on the soft cushions, completely contented with myself and the world, another strange thing happened. An impish apparition that, from my father's descriptions and warnings, I identified as the demon of drink, John Barley-Corn, floated up out of my body and rotated in front of me — slowly at first, then faster and faster. He was dressed as an Irish leprechaun, replete with a top hat, gold shoe buckles and a silver-tipped cane. As I stared, he stopped spinning, gave me a wink and cane-salute as if to say, "See you, Dougie-boy, it's been a hoot!" and disappeared into the ceiling.

As I stared after him I couldn't help wondering: was this impish creature the root of the Hepburn curse or was I still under the influence of the LSD? Whatever the answer, I had expelled him from my body, hopefully for good, and I felt such pride and relief that I wanted to leap up and shout Hallelujah!

There was a light knock on the door and the attractive nurse from earlier that day entered and sat beside me on the couch.

"How are you?" she asked, patting my hand. "Is there anything that I can do for you?"

I barely heard. She was so soft and sweet-smelling that I just wanted to reach out, and make love to her to share my elation. She politely pulled away and said, "Now Doug, I'm a married woman."

With those words, I immediately stopped and had no further urge to proceed. Even in my heaviest drinking days I would never have forced myself on any woman, no matter how strongly I might have wished to.

As I found out later, the nurse's presence had been the final test to ensure that I was sufficiently recovered to be released. An emotionally out-of-control man of normal strength amid an unsuspecting public would have been dangerous; a man of my strength in such a state would have been the equivalent of a wounded King Kong running amok in a teacup factory.

When Dr. Maclean and Dr. Holloway returned, they told me

that my "discarded baggage" would only remain discarded for as long as I could avoid my old habit of excessive self-blame. Expressing confidence that my exceptional courage, faith and determination would see me through, they again shook my hand.

I knew that I would never touch alcohol again in any form from that day forward, but for a different reason. What I had experienced in that filth-infested pit had been something much more than a drug-induced hallucination. I had come face to face with the power, perhaps even the destiny, that had been influencing me all of my life. And it had changed me forever.

When I was fully rested and cleared by Dr. Maclean to leave the hospital, my first thought was how much I wanted to take Colleen into my arms and tell her all the wonderful things that had happened. When I rushed to the Cloverdale butcher shop, I found her still working and retreated to a park bench near the rear of the building to wait.

As I sat watching the world unfold around me, still captivated by how intricately everything was tied to everything else, I was suddenly flooded with confidence. I would one day be known as the strongest man in history. I didn't know how, I knew only that now I had the faith to see it through.

CHAPTER 7

SAVED BY THE BARBELL

A lot of idols crash around a man,
but a man keeps going.

— DOUG HEPBURN
(Al Hooper, "Doug Hepburn," Vancouver *Province*, April 18, 1963)

After my LSD-induced confrontation with myself, I remained at the Hollywood Hospital, as per my agreement with Dr. Maclean, in the capacity of paid orderly. To appear less threatening to the patients, I was referred to as the Athletic Director, a title with which I also felt more at ease. I was given a salary of fifty dollars a month, food and lodging and the freedom to come and go as I pleased. I was also given exclusive access to a large, covered enclosure at the far end of the grounds, which I converted to an indoor gym.

When I felt fully recovered from my LSD session, I retrieved my weights from Brett Pine's shed and prepared to make good on my promise to become the strongest man in history. Loading my barbell with a mere fifty pounds, I placed it in the middle of my new gym's wooden floor and studied it. What a strange obsession to be tied to. Why, of all the pursuits under God's heaven, did I choose to spend my time defying gravity?

Or did it choose me?

Taking a deep breath, I easily cleaned the barbell to my shoulders, military-pressed it overhead and felt an "off-the-chart" certainty that I could accomplish any strength goal that I set my mind to.

As I repeated the movement, I closed my eyes and visualized what it would take. Above all, I would need an unwavering determination to succeed without tricks, shortcuts or unfair advantage of any kind because it is the competitor's *knowledge that he competes fairly* that gives him his edge. He feels not only pride in his ability to resist cheating but a certainty that he deserves to win because of it. Since his mind is never in conflict with itself (his conscious saying "Yes I can win because I deserve to," and his unconscious saying, "No I can't win because I don't deserve to") he is always able to give his best effort.

While a cheater may be devoid of conscious guilt, he may have considerable subconscious misgivings which, after a time, will hinder his ability to give a maximum performance. The more the cheater receives praise and glory for his feats that he accomplished through the use of drugs, modified gear or equipment or other illegal means, the greater his psychological disadvantage becomes. As my life has shown, unconscious guilt can be a formidable adversary.

I also needed to remain absolutely certain that I had done nothing in thought, word or deed to disqualify myself on a spiritual level, thereby tuning myself into the power of the universe instead of away from it. Once again, the need is to prevent conflict between the conscious and unconscious minds because the competitor who is *certain* that he deserves to win on all levels of his existence has a distinct advantage over the competitor who is not. In order to expect a miracle, the lifter must be able to reach into that mystical realm where miracles occur, and they occur on a spiritual level.

Had I always shown complete honesty in my training and competing? Yes. I wore only swimming trunks, loose-fitting clothes or regulation lifting apparel. I employed no wraps, artificial aids or tricks of any kind. I took no drugs or stimulants and had no desire to do so. My intent was always to best myself rather than my opponents, because a fair competition is nothing more than a group of competitors attempting their personal bests at the same time. The cheater cheats himself more than anyone else because he never allows himself to experience his true capabilities, thereby making all his time, effort and determination meaningless.

Had I always exercised moral faith? Unfortunately, no. Many times I had given into depression that had resulted in alcoholism, self-pity and violence. Although I had always believed in a universal power capable of granting miracles, I had not always been able to keep myself spiritually worthy, and this had to change if I was to one day achieve my goals.

Yet miracles had occurred regularly in my life. They hadn't always been immediately recognizable but they had happened just the same: as a confused teenager, I had prayed to the stars for a way to set myself apart from other people and had become the strongest in the world — perhaps in history; I had competed at Stockholm with a severely injured right ankle and won; I had competed in the British Empire Games with a severely injured right thigh and won; I had beaten the Hepburn curse — something that no other alcoholic Hepburn had been able to do; I had resurrected a destiny thought hopelessly dead by myself and everyone around me, and I was now steaming towards fulfilling it. Of far more importance to me than any of the aforementioned, I had realized that what I was destined to accomplish was meant to be more for others than myself.

I spent the rest of the afternoon pressing my barbell and with each repetition I became more confident and energized. I was a pressure pump being primed; a boiler being stoked. "Thank you!" I prayed through tears of joy and relief. "You have kept your end of the bargain and I swear that I will keep mine!"

While I was exercising, Dr. Holloway appeared at the door, then left and returned with Dr. Maclean. They watched until I stopped for a breather. "I like it," I said, smiling. "More, it likes me. It's a marriage made in heaven that no man may put asunder, not even myself!"

Whether they understood, I have no idea. It made little difference. They were happy that I was cured and I was happy that I was cured. If lifting kept me that way, then more power to it — no pun intended.

Once my spiritual self was back on track, my physical and emotional selves quickly followed. Colleen and I spent more time together and little Brianna, now a tall eight-year-old, couldn't have been happier. God had taken her injured robin, but He had given her back a friend.

Every weekend the three of us would meet at the hospital and go for a picnic in the park or a long walk on the beach. After every outing I would tell Brianna a story about Mighty Matt with Colleen and myself acting out all the parts. The stories the little girl liked best were those of Robbie the Robin, an angel, who teamed with Matt to help forest creatures in distress. We would all clap and cheer at the end of each tale and it was as though we were cheering for ourselves as well, for we had weathered the bad times and now things would be better. Clasping hands, we vowed it would be so.

As previously noted, my hospital job was to help transport and care for out-of-control patients bound for the "East Berlin" section of the Hollywood Hospital. At this point in their treatment, the patients were often overcome with pain, physical and emotional, and wanted only to die. Some fought for the sake of fighting but most just hung limply or babbled incoherently. We stripped them of everything harmful, including their clothes, locked them in padded cells and began the arduous task of drying them out. Three to five times a day, seven days a week, we washed them, force-fed them and injected them with medicines designed to clear their minds and ease their cravings. After about a week, most settled down. Some were able to hold rational conversations.

Every night after completing my regular duties, I would sit outside the cell doors and read poetry. Mostly, I chose Robert Frost's "Stopping by Woods on a Snowy Evening" and "The Tuft of Flowers" because the poems were about the beauty of nature rather than the problems of the world. I also spoke of the joys of being alive with those patients capable of holding a conversation. Always, my message was the same: don't give up, there's a way to get yourself going again, you just have to find it. I would then explain how I was able to expel my own demons and, to my great satisfaction, found most patients receptive. They applauded my courage, vowed to show equal courage during their LSD confrontations and sincerely thanked me for caring.

Their resolve was usually short-lived, however. And what haunted me most about the severely addicted was how quickly they lost faith, pride and determination once they gave in to their cravings. It was as if the addiction had a mind and purpose of its own and monitored its effectiveness by how quickly and completely it could strip the addicts of their desire to carry on. It made no difference what the addicts wanted. The addiction was calling the shots and the addicts would say or do whatever it took to ease the pain.

Looking back on my "lost" time at Peden's cabin, I understood: count too much on something happening and you will emotionally shatter if it fails to occur. But as I studied the patients throughout the hospital, I realized that their addictions stemmed from a variety of sources.

Some, like myself, had never quite reached the success and fulfilment that they had spent their lives striving towards and had simply grown tired of trying. They had turned to alcohol to ease their frustration and had lacked the internal strength and drive to break free.

Others, however, had achieved staggering success, but had been unable to keep themselves going at what they had been so lucky to achieve. Strangely, the patients who had succeeded the earliest and with the least effort, seemed the most lost and miserable. When these "lucky people" became unable to keep sacrificing for something that no longer interested them, the alcohol allowed them to escape from the otherwise inescapable. The pain and humiliation of the addiction became more desirable than the frustration of their daily tasks and obligations.

As I watched the personal struggle of each patient on my ward I couldn't help feeling that I was being given a personal warning: Before continuing towards your final goal, be certain that you truly desire it. Success increases the need for sacrifice, especially when it affects the welfare of other people. Did I truly want to become the strongest man in history or would I find more personal satisfaction and fulfilment by remaining at the hospital? Since I had no answer, my only option was to remain at the facility until I did.

The "drying-out" process always left the patients extremely erratic. As I watched them roller-coasting along their emotional side roads, I was struck by how accurately my father had defined an alcoholic as "someone unable to get back to where he had first deviated from what was good and right in his life." One day the patients would be quiet and lucid; the next they would be ranting and paranoid. Regardless of how improved they appeared, there could be danger in their most innocent requests. Their good days required the most suspicion because they used their lucid moments to prepare for the "bad time" that they knew was coming. It was as if the demon of drink, John Barley-Corn, was forever taunting me with his unholy presence: "Ye may have escaped temporarily, Big'un, but see how many won't! Falter and I'll have ye back as well!"

One such example of patient untrustworthiness was a wealthy stockbroker who was forcibly admitted into "East Berlin" after he had smashed everything of value in his home, an estimated damage of over $200,000. As per hospital procedure, he was stripped, strapped in a canvas straight-jacket and locked in a suicide-proof cell. While he ranted, cried and threatened all who went near him, I patiently sat outside his cell door and repeated my message of hope. One quiet afternoon, he responded. "Doug Hepburn of Stockholm?" he asked weakly, his skin so pale and his eyes so sunken that he resembled a walking corpse.

When I assured him that I was and proved it with photographs and newspaper articles, his state of mind grew more lucid and our relationship became friendly. We discussed life in general, particularly those aspects which make living worthwhile as opposed to those aspect which make it unbearable and, after a few weeks, he politely requested to have a few of my newspaper clippings inside his cell plus a small lamp to study them by. His physical pain was intense and he needed something to occupy his mind. Dr. Maclean was cautious. "Not until we have ascertained his true intentions. Desire and ability are not always synonymous."

The man continued his requests, vowing to God that he would neither harm the clippings nor himself, and Dr. Maclean finally relented. "The articles, but not the lamp," he said. "Lamps have glass, cords and sharp edges, and have already claimed lives here."

As I placed the clippings in the man's thin, shaking hands, some of them full-page articles, I was rewarded with a look of true joy and relief. "Thank you," he said, clinging to my shoulder as though I had just released him from purgatory. "May God bless and keep you always!"

The next morning we found the man dead in his cell. He had asphyxiated himself by forcing crumpled newspaper down his throat.

Not all of my hospital experience was gloomy, however, and two rather unusual events deserve mention. The first concerned a particularly sizable logger named Joe who died in his cell late one night of acute liver and kidney failure. After Dr. Holloway made the pronouncement, Balfie Bowden, a thin, nervous orderly, and I were summoned to transport the body to the basement morgue. The dimly lit staircase was extremely steep with no room to manoeuvre a casket so we were forced to carry the body between us. Balfie went first, holding Joe's feet, and I followed with the rest of him. It was so awkward and weird with the steps creaking and our bodies casting grotesque shadows on the musty brick walls that we couldn't help giggling. Halfway down, Balfie slipped, causing me to lose my footing, and we all tumbled to the bottom. Joe suffered the most damage, having ended up beneath us, and Balfie eyed him and sniffed, "Lucky he's already dead!" This really started us off and we laughed until we cried.

The second incident concerned a sixtyish, male patient who we nicknamed "The Howler," after his strange habit of bursting into unprovoked fits of glass-shattering shrieks. A pair of orderlies were sponge-bathing him one afternoon when he suddenly broke free and bolted naked down the hall shouting, "I can fly! I can fly!" It took myself and the orderlies a good fifteen minutes to get him back in his cell. Again Balfie expressed it succinctly: "Good thing no windows was open!"

About this time friends and fellow athletes began visiting me at the hospital grounds, including talented lifters such as Paul Bjarnason, a heavy-set middle-heavyweight with a boyish face and an iron determination; Bill Gladstone, a "heart-of-gold" middle-heavyweight lifter with huge upper leg development, who owned two Vancouver rooming houses; George Dean, a middle-heavyweight/heavyweight lifter who became the first British Columbia lifter after me to win the Canadian Heavyweight Championship; Gerry McGourlick, a wiry light-heavyweight; and heavyweight wrestler and weightlifter Ernie Fulton — to name only a few. As we sat discussing the meets that they had attended and the training problems they were having, I sensed that it was time for the old "Hepburnius Rex," as Gladstone called me, to leave the hospital. I could do precious little to help the patients — they had to do that themselves — but I could, perhaps, do a lot to help promising lifters.

Packing my belongings into my trademark duffel, I thanked Dr. Maclean and Dr. Holloway for their help and support and strode purposefully to the front gate. As orderlies and patients watched from the hospital, I waved farewell, gripped the gate and, to my horror, was unable to step through. A familiar surge of energy-draining heat flooded my body and I had to sit on my duffel to keep from falling. Since I had left the grounds many times before with Colleen and Brianna, my weakness completely mystified me.

"Your previous departures were temporary so you knew that you would be returning to the things that made you feel safe," Dr. Maclean explained in his soft, matter-of-fact voice. "Your room, your doctors, your way of life. You felt no risk. Now you feel nothing *but* risk. What if you are unable to keep your life back on track and fall back into the old habits that you promised God you would steer clear of? Failing yourself or another mortal is one thing — failing God is another. You will be tied to this hospital until you are willing to risk living without it."

That night I prayed for strength and guidance but received no response: no dreams, falling stars or even an inkling that I had been heard. I wasn't surprised. Since I had created the problem, it was up to me to solve it.

Too ashamed to face the patients after being unable to follow through on all my big talk about the power of faith and determination, I exchanged my position as Athletic Director for that of "East Berlin" janitor in hopes that my time scrubbing cells, halls and toilet stalls would trigger whatever needed to be triggered to get myself going again.

Surprisingly, it happened a few days later, when Dr. Maclean approached my toilet-scrubbing with a smallish, sour-faced gentleman holding a long notepad, whom he introduced as the public health inspector for the area.

"That man," the good doctor said, pointing down at me, "was once the strongest in the world."

"What happened to him?" the health inspector sniffed.

They left without further comment, but the question remained.

I spent the remainder of the day attempting to avoid the inescapable answer that *I* had happened, me and no one else, then stood and dropped my scrub brush to the floor. "Just resting," I said aloud. "But the rest is now over!"

Having made my decision, I packed my duffel and again stood before the main gate with all eyes upon me. Sucking in a determined breath, I gripped the iron latch, but was again unable to open the gate. I thought briefly of returning to the hospital, then forced it from my mind. I had talked the talk, now it was time to walk the walk. Clutching the iron gate with both hands, I yanked it open as though I were cleaning a 400-pound barbell and stepped through. As everyone clapped and cheered, it was Stockholm, the British Empire Games and every other victory I had experienced — only better. I had overcome yet another obstacle and was now free to pursue my life in any manner that I chose. As I strode purposefully towards a waiting streetcar, I thanked God for leading me both to and from the hospital. "You're doing your part and I swear that I will do mine!"

I spent a few blissful days touring Stanley Park and its many beaches, then returned to Cloverdale. Two of my demons still resided there, and I knew that I could never be truly free until I conquered them as well.

Unable to afford the big house that I had shared with Roger Williams and his family, I again stored my weights in Brett Pine's shed and took a room at the Clova Hotel. Each morning, for fourteen consecutive days, I entered the bar, chatted with whoever was willing, sang along with the band or jukebox when asked (Frank Sinatra, Perry Como and Buddy Clark tunes, mostly) and had no urge to drink.

So much for demon number one: alcohol.

Each afternoon I strolled in the fresh air, feeling as contented as the birds and squirrels that were all around me, and every night I wrote strength courses, which I sold by mail-order: (*Strength and Bulk, Super Strength, The Bench Press, The Deadlift, The Two-handed Curl* and *The Two-handed Press*).

So much for demon number two: lack of desire.

One evening, as I happened by a smiling mother and father pushing their giggling daughter on a swing, I was reminded of Colleen, whom I hadn't contacted since leaving the hospital, and little Brianna, who had prayed for a sick robin to fly high in the sky again. At that moment, I truly wanted to sweep them into my arms and form a family.

Hurrying to the Cloverdale butcher shop, I once again found Colleen wrapping meat.

"You're out," she said.

"Yes," I replied.

"For good?"

"Yes."

"Where does that leave us? I won't be hurt again and I will not allow my daughter to be hurt again either."

Determined not to repeat past mistakes, we decided to take things slowly. I would remain at the Clova, Brianna and Colleen would remain at their Cloverdale apartment, and we would see what transpired. I would continue to train, she would continue to work and there would be no more drinking or stumbling. Brianna accepted the situation readily and as she, Colleen and I spent more happy times together, it seemed the logical time to start spending more time with my parents.

Since my mother and father kept completely clear of each other — her decision, not his — we were forced to meet with them separately. We visited my mother first at her West Twelfth Avenue home. To my surprise, she, Colleen and Brianna hit it off even better than before. They laughed and joked about my formative years and how I really needed to settle down, and, as my mother stroked Brianna's hair — an intimacy that she had never shared with me — I couldn't help wondering what had caused such a mellowing of her personality. Did she no longer feel the need to be strong and unyielding now that Bill and I were gone? Or was it the result of old age?

As we stood to leave, she held my hand and congratulated me for breaking my alcohol addiction. Although she tried to sound sincere, I knew she wasn't. Given all the times that she had heard my father promise her that he had quit for good, I could hardly blame her, but it hurt me all the same. After everything that I had accomplished in my life and everything that I was struggling to accomplish, my mother still didn't take me seriously.

Ivan, although extremely polite and kind to both Colleen and

Brianna, and perhaps even pleased that I was finally contemplating a serious relationship, was adamant in his belief that I had *not* quit drinking for good. "Once a Hepburn starts drinking," he confided to me as we sat together in the Waldorf Hotel bar, him slugging back beer and me sipping pop, "he will drink until he dies, so he must never marry. Remain friends if you can, even lovers. But under no circumstances marry. The pain of watching it crumble around you is too much to bear!" Although I knew that he was serious, I couldn't help wondering how much of his warning was a subconscious or even a conscious hope that I would not be able to stay alcohol-free because he had never been able to. It wasn't something that I wanted to believe about my father, but given what I had learned about the addicted mind and its need to concoct excuses, it was a possibility that I could not ignore.

Finally, it was time to retrieve loyal Buck from Peden's Serpentine River shack and I trembled with fear as well as anticipation. It was as if I were being lured back to hell and all its temptations, with a satanic Peden dancing on an altar.

As I neared the cabin, old memories choked me like a thick, sulphur smoke and I was forced to stop and catch my breath. My dread turned to elation as Buck, huge and healthy, rounded the corner, spotted me and stared. I dropped to one knee and called to him, praying that my nine-month absence (most of it due to my hospital stay) had not erased me from his memory.

It hadn't. Yelping, he charged into me like a four-legged steamroller and we fell into a tumbling, wrestling knot in the tall grass.

Peden was nowhere to be found. There were more shotgun holes in the framework and fresh animal pelts and carcasses hanging about — but no Peden. I scratched a charcoal thank-you note on the wall, left fifteen dollars pinned to a rusty nail beneath it and started back to Cloverdale with Buck. Eager to put that hell-cabin behind us, we were soon running as fast as we could. "Thank you for giving us our lives back!" I shouted to the clear heavens. "We promise to make the very best of it!"

Back at Cloverdale, things took a gargantuan hurtle for the better and it was as if we were back in the happy, productive days before my addiction. I printed and sold mail-order strength courses — enough to pay our expenses plus a little extra — lifted weights on a regular basis and read many poetry and philosophy books. In particular, I studied Plato's *The Republic,* where Greek philosophers Socrates and Thrasymachus argued whether the attainment of human excellence is a worthwhile endeavour. I sang in local bars and coffee houses, enjoyed treks to the park and beach with Colleen and Brianna — Colleen still attractive with her haunting smile and her long, auburn hair; happy Brianna, always humming and exploring — and was once again faced with a familiar dilemma: should I marry Colleen and adopt Brianna or heed my father's warning?

Each time I considered popping the question, reality made me mute. How could I properly care for a wife and daughter when I could barely provide for Buck and myself?

Colleen seemed to understand, at least more than she had before, and, mercifully, did not push the issue. This made things more relaxed between us and, as a consequence, enabled me to hoist heavier weight. The more I lifted, the more confident I became and the more confident I became, the more I lifted. To my surprise, at the post-prime age of thirty-six, I was soon nearing world record capability for the one-armed press and the one-armed dumbbell hold-out to the side, and was still able to perform the following drug-free, unassisted feats: a full squat with 720 pounds; a push press off the rack with 440 pounds; a one-armed dumbbell hold-out to the side with 113 pounds; a strict deadlift with 780 pounds; a strict two-handed curl with 240 pounds; and a right-handed military dumbbell press with 192 pounds.

Then the obvious question for a world-class strongman looking to get back into the public eye: why was I hiding these endeavours in the confinement of Brett Pine's shed? The more I thought about this question, the more I couldn't get it out of my mind. Did I really want to go public again, or was my desire just a half-hearted dream that I was using to keep myself going — or, perhaps, to keep myself from marrying?

Needing to find out, I packed my lifting apparel into a brown paper bag one quiet Saturday evening and headed down the street to a small but well-equipped Cloverdale gym. As I neared the front door, I felt the exhilaration that I had always felt when going to a public demonstration or competition. As my hand gripped the handle, however, I was slammed by the same searing, energy-sapping dread that had taken hold of me in Brett Pine's shed and at the Hollywood Hospital gate. During those times I had been afraid to proceed because I hadn't been willing to risk the pain. Did I fear entering this small gym for the same reason?

Certain that I had to be light years ahead of any lifter inside in both size and ability, I shoved my caution aside, entered and froze as everyone stopped and stared. I eyed the small change room at the far end of the gym but couldn't make my legs work. I searched for something witty to say but drew a blank. From somewhere, I heard a faint voice mumble, "Looking for a miracle, Hepburn?" But to this day I don't know whether it was my voice or someone else's.

Leaving as abruptly as I had entered, I hurried back to the confinement of my lonely Cloverdale room and cursed myself for being so undecided. Was this how I would always be: resolved for spurts of time, then an emotional and spiritual "wash-out" the moment I encountered the slightest obstacle?

I knew by my shaking and shortness of breath that I should return to the Hollywood Hospital for more therapy, but I couldn't force myself to do it. Letting myself down was one thing — I'd been doing that my entire life. Letting down patients who might have been inspired by my ability to take charge of my life and leave the hospital was unthinkable. I considered confiding my problems to Colleen and Brianna, hoping that their love and support would take the place of hospital therapy, but I couldn't bear to have them think that I was no longer a man of my word.

As if sensing my indecision, loyal Buck placed his head on my knee, and I forced myself to say, "Walk? Go for a walk?" Excited, as he always became at those words, he bolted for the door. Halfway there, however, his hind legs gave out and he went down with a yelp. The professional diagnosis was advanced arthritis complicated by severe vertebral degeneration. There was no cure.

Within a very short time, the brave husky that had always been so strong and robust had become almost completely incapacitated and I knew that the only humane thing to do was "put him down" as quickly and painlessly as possible. I also knew that I didn't have the heart to do it myself so I wrapped him in a blanket and carried him to the Cloverdale pound.

As I walked, I talked to him, reassuring him that he would soon be in a happier place romping with Chinook and Bernard. Fighting back tears, I remembered those that I had loved and carried — my mother, Chinook, Bernard, the little robin that Brianna had begged to "fly high in the sky again" — and couldn't hold back the pangs of self-blame. I had wanted only to help them and had been unable to, and now I was unable to help Buck.

At the pound, the emotionless, male attendant completely ignored my grief, acting as though Buck were already dead and only the paperwork remained. Leading me to the rear of the compound, he jabbed a thumb at what appeared to be an oversized, steel-plated oven attached to a thick, electrical cable and said, "Pop him in there and he'll never feel pain again."

If the comment was meant to comfort me, it did the opposite. I considered carrying Buck back home, but knew by his yelps of pain at even the slightest movement that home was no longer an option. Placing him inside the steel box, I hugged his thick, shivering neck as he weakly licked my face.

"Want the carcass?" the attendant asked, latching the door with a clang. "Or should I dump it?"

"I'll be back," I said, wiping tears from my eyes. "You don't dump a friend." I was thinking of better days and places, and a pair of husky pups with "bum-holes no bigger than shirt buttons." Soon they would be united again.

I took a long walk so that I wouldn't see the handle pulled or smell the fur and flesh searing. When I returned, I found Buck's still-warm body haphazardly wrapped in a pair of burlap sacks. Lifting him into my arms, I left the pound without a word and carried him towards the fast-moving Serpentine.

On the bridge where I had committed Chinook to her Viking burial, I held Buck over the edge and proclaimed softly: "May you both have tireless legs in a field that never ends." As I dropped Buck into the rushing water, weakness overcame me and I had to grip the wooden railing to keep from falling in. For a second, I considered throwing myself into the water after him, then stumbled back to my Cloverdale room. Flopping onto my bed, I vowed to cure myself, but the longer I remained motionless, the weaker I became. It wasn't depression as much as an extreme frustration of not knowing how to bring my cure about. Sick to death of always having to seek help from hospitals or psychologists or even God to get myself up and going again, I made up my mind to remain in bed until I had reasoned out the answer. When Colleen saw what was happening, she mistakenly diagnosed my condition as depression, begged me to return to the hospital, and became infuriated when I refused. "You promised Brianna and you promised me! Sickness is one thing, but this is quitting!" She stomped out before I had a chance to explain and I suddenly felt suffocated as if by sulphur smoke.

But I didn't give up. I considered phoning my mother, a person who had always shown extreme emotional balance in the face of adversity, but I was too ashamed. Here I was, the great strongman with all the answers and insights, but she was still the stronger in what really mattered: the ability to keep going. I thought about phoning friends, but was again too ashamed to pick up the receiver.

To make matters worse, my father, wearing his usual suit, tie and alcohol-induced sneer, suddenly appeared at the foot of my bed and stood there studying me as though I were something he'd found on the bottom of his shoe. As I waited for him to denounce me as a coward and a quitter, he did far worse. He told me that he wasn't surprised, and that the worst was yet to come: my return to alcohol. Although my father's expression remained stern, I could almost see him smirking behind it. "See how easily it happens?" I could almost hear him say. "Who's the weak-willed loser now?"

I wanted to respond, but my mouth was too dry. I wanted to jump up and tell him that he wasn't as smart as he thought he was because I was fighting, not quitting, but I couldn't find the strength. When his staring ceased to disturb me, he paced on the wooden floor and taunted me. "Why don't you get up and do something with your life?"

"Why don't you," I shot back. "You want me to fail!" I shouted, forcing myself up onto one elbow. "Where were you when Mother and I needed you? I'd rather be a hopeless drunk than a lying hypocrite!" I was immediately sorry for what I said, but he left before I could apologize.

A few minutes later I heard him sobbing outside. At first I wasn't sure what I was hearing and had to hold my breath to hear it clearly. I was so shocked that I cried myself. He hadn't been gloating after all. He had been trying to help me and I had been hitting back.

I had to do something, and quickly. Forcing myself across the floor to my dusty barbell, I pressed it above my head and, for that split second, my depression went away. I pressed it a second time and experienced the same sense of relief. Feeling as though I had finally found the means to fight back, I placed my barbell on the floor, went outside and hugged my father as hard as I could. He hugged back and when we stepped apart, neither of us wanted to lose the moment.

"I guess I just needed the right incentive," I said.

"Maybe we both did," he replied.

As I returned to my barbell, I felt myself filled with hope for the future. My weights were the key and as long as I kept to them I would be okay. And there was something else: if my father and I could make such a connection, perhaps my mother and I could. It was a satisfying thought that made me train harder.

CHAPTER 8

STARTING
BACK UP

*As people age, their desire is
the first thing to go.*
— DOUG HEPBURN
(Author interview, March 1998)

When I had diagnosed myself as "recovered enough to travel," I gave up my Cloverdale room, thanked Brett Pine for all his help and support and in the early part of 1963, at the "over-the-sticking-point" age of thirty-six, hopped a bus to Vancouver to reconnect with everything that my illness had caused me to lose track of. I spent the remainder of the day relaxing at Kitsilano Beach and watching the animals at Stanley Park's Lost Lagoon, then found myself in front of the same East Hastings Street rooming house that I had frequented after my return from Stockholm and White Plains.

At first, I wondered if this were an unconscious attempt to expel yet another demon. But the moment I descended from the bus I knew that I was searching for familiarity. In this ramshackle part of the city, I would not need to impress anyone and no one would try to impress me. For a mere four dollars a night or forty dollars a month, I could retreat into my one-room sanctuary, bolt the door from the inside and know that the world and all its troubles could not get at me — at least for a little while. And a little while was all I needed.

Since the rooms were cramped and equipped with only the barest of essentials — a doorless closet, a saggy cot, a single-element hotplate and a heavily chipped sink with shrieking taps — I had packed only what I needed: a few clothes, my Gestetner mimeograph machine for cranking out strength courses, a 100-pound dumbbell for light exercise and a couple of John Gunn's poetry books. The room contained no kitchen and the only toilet was at the far end of a long, dim hall, but I was content. I was back to my roots, free of the "mental flyshit" (as my father used to say) that had been impairing my thinking, and I was slowly becoming aware of how satisfying life in the present could be.

The next morning I rose with the birds, gulped down a mixing bowl of milk, honey, protein powder and raw eggs ("stirred, not shaken," as I liked to quip in response to the James Bond martini phrase of "shaken, not stirred") and packed my training gear into a brown paper bag. I then started on foot for the Western Sports Centre, located at 135 East Hastings Street. Although it was less than two blocks away, the morning was so crisp and tranquil that I purchased a large cup of coffee from a sagging corner store that catered to the morning "caffeine junkies" and relaxed on a bus bench.

As I watched local street people stumbling about, scrounging for cigarette butts, hustling change and scrubbing the night's redness from their eyes, a rather bedraggled man of about my own age wandered my way and picked through the cigarette butts near my bench.

"Nice morning," I remarked, remembering my own dark times.

"Better than the night," he mumbled. He finished picking, arranged his treasure in a wrinkled plastic bag according to length and thickness and eyed my cup. "Any more of that?"

"No," I replied, bemused by his directness. "Let me buy you one."

Accepting my change as though it were the deed to a gushing oil well, he quickly exchanged it for a large cup of steaming beverage that he sipped slowly. "Bet you eat a lot for breakfast," he said, eyeing me up and down.

I chuckled in a way that told him that I couldn't afford to buy him anything more and he shrugged and left without a word. As I watched him depart, alternately sipping and scanning the streets for more kind-hearted "marks," I wondered how much wasted potential I was watching. What might this man have become under other circumstances — what might he still, if afforded the opportunity? I knew that such a break would have to come from someone other than myself, so I drained my cup, jammed it into a stinking, overflowing trash barrel and headed for my workout.

At the gym, I paid the daily workout fee to a young attendant who seemed surprised to see me there, changed into loose-fitting sweats and regulation lifting shoes and weighed myself on an ancient but accurate bar-and-balance scale: 276¼ pounds — not too shabby for a thirty-seven-year-old lifter who had been counted out too many times to count. As I studied my 22-inch arms and my 51½-inch chest in the mirror I wondered: what is *this* man capable of if he chooses to give it one last try?

On a whim, I flipped up into a handstand and hand-walked out onto the training floor — straight into a smiling Bill Copeland, who was also in for a workout. He was still working in the fire department, with thoughts of running for union office, and he offered a familiar solution to my equally familiar dilemma of not knowing what to do with my life.

"Start a gym!" he said with a wide, infectious grin. "You're a famous strongman and that's what famous strongmen do in their later years. How else can they pass on their experience and expertise to posterity?"

Since I had already founded and lost three gyms, I was less than enthusiastic. Bill, however, would not be dissuaded. "This time will be different," he said, acting as my weight-spotter as I performed a short set of 450-pound bench presses. "We'll rent space farther out of town where it's cheaper and really save by constructing the equipment ourselves. With such a low overhead and your famous puss, how can we lose?"

The question seemed the epitome of famous last words, but since I had no plans and really owed Bill for his help with my dog breeding business, I agreed as long as he was willing to "front" the first load of steel and the first month's rent, which I certainly didn't have.

Bill agreed without hesitation and, as we sealed our arrangement with a handshake, I was struck by how truly special this man was, both as a friend and a person. Although he had a family to raise and bills of his own, he was always willing to extend a helping hand even if it meant digging into his own pocket.

After my workout, I met with Colleen and Brianna at the Stanley Park Zoo. We fed popcorn to the monkeys and ducks and enjoyed a picnic of sandwiches and juice at a quiet area overlooking Burrard Inlet. Everything felt so relaxed and right that I again considered marriage. I could tell by the way Colleen held my hand and leaned her head on my shoulder that she, too, was considering the idea, and I wasn't sure whether to laugh or cry. Since we were both in our late thirties, I knew that a decision would have to be made soon — "play her or trade her," as the saying goes — and I was never much good at games.

Lack of money to raise a child properly had always been my excuse for waiting, but that problem was quickly solving itself. Brianna was growing up, with a life of her own to follow, and I would soon be out of excuses — if excuses were what it was about.

After our meal, we dropped in to see my mother. After the usual snacks and small talk, she hauled out her sprawling record collection and invited us to make a selection. I had always been partial to "crooning" songs, so she put on one of my all-time Buddy Clark favourites: "Impossible." I sang along, adding to the moment by standing and singing to each of the three women in the room, and received a standing ovation.

"Singing Samson," Brianna quipped. Everyone laughed.

Then my mother played one of her favourites — Mrs. Oakley Fox's rendition of "Redwing" — and we all sang along as Colleen, Brianna and I danced. On impulse, I played the song a second time and asked my mother to dance. To my surprise and delight she accepted and we "Hepburn-hopped" around the room until we were all shrieking with laughter.

Colleen and Brianna clapped when we finished and, as my mother offered a quick bow, she happily allowed me a peck on the cheek. She smiled and squeezed my hand and I can't put into words how that made me feel. Throughout our lives my mother and I had been able to express only the barest of emotions to each other, but now, because I had mustered the courage to side-step the pain of the past, we sensed a new closeness growing between us.

I patted Brianna's hand for the courage that she had shown in taking that same first step with me the sad morning that her robin died. By the way she smiled at me, I was certain that she was remembering as well.

That night, as I sat on my lumpy cot, listening to the traffic outside my room, I wondered if I would continue as a strongman or put it all aside and spend the rest of my days as a contented family man. I gripped my 100-pound dumbbell with my right hand and easily military-pressed it. I did another three repetitions and placed it on the floor. How many men my age — even on steroids — could match that?

Crawling into bed, I dreamed that I was helping Robbie the Robin construct a giant nest overlooking Trout Lake. As I military-pressed log-sized lengths of string to Robbie, he took them in his beak and wove them into an intricate design.

Early the next morning I met with Bill Copeland to work out the details of our arrangement. More enthusiastic than ever, he told me that he had everything planned. He would order the steel that very morning from work and we would begin construction in the basement of his Burnaby home as soon as it was delivered.

When I spoke to Colleen, Brianna and my parents about my

plans, they were all for it despite my certainty that they wouldn't be. My father, a gifted salesman when free of John Barely-Corn's influence, offered to help with the daily running of the enterprise, the women offered to help with signs, leaflets and other forms of advertising, and I began to suspect that perhaps this gym had been fated all along.

True to his word, Bill had a load of steel pipe and tubing stacked in his carport along with tools, blueprints and coffee when I arrived that evening. He would do the cutting and measuring, I would do the welding and bolting (I had learned welding basics during my earlier stint as a cowling fabricator) and we would both do the painting and upholstering.

For the most part, this system worked quite well. One time, we were using a thick, black grease to lubricate equipment parts and as Bill took a break to use the bathroom, I squeezed a glob inside each finger of his rubber glove. Struggling to keep a straight face, I donned my welding helmet and waited for his reaction. To my disappointment, he showed little. "Must have a hole in it," was all that he said. He changed gloves and no more was mentioned about the incident but it had not been forgotten. About a week later, as I knelt welding a pair of steel support brackets, my viewing glass suddenly turned completely black, causing me to leap to my feet, slap my welding helmet from my head and hop around searching for the cause. As it turned out, someone had coated the inside of my helmet with a thick layer of the same black grease that I had dropped inside Bill's glove, and the heat had caused it to blacken everything inside, including my forehead, face, hair and teeth.

Within a few short weeks, we had produced power racks, bench press machines, free weight racks, a leg press machine and a set of parallel bars. We decided to keep up production. We could sell what we didn't need, along with a line of accessories that we could order from wholesalers, and the equipment would be a financial supplement to the gym memberships. When my father agreed with our plan, offering to act as liaison between ourselves and the wholesalers, Bill and I set out to find a suitable location for our gym.

The stars smiled on us and within a few days we had secured an ideal location at 4605 East Hastings Street in North Burnaby. A mere fifteen-minute bus ride from my rooming house, it was situated beneath a large, popular pool hall and was owned by an older Chinese gentleman and former student of mine, Simon Kwok, who agreed to give us reduced rent in exchange for free strength lessons and unlimited use of the equipment.

We signed a six-month lease, spread the word that "The Strongest Man in History" was back in business and within a blink had enough members to pay the monthly expenses with a bit left over for our time and effort. Old students returned, as did experienced lifters such as Paul Bjarnason, Bill Gladstone, George Dean and my cousin John Fraser, a large, blondish youth who, although quite a few years younger than me, could bench press well over four hundred pounds. Everyone went overboard to make the gym successful.

By June of 1963, we were the gym of choice for serious lifters and I was the happiest I'd been in years. I exchanged my East Hastings room for a tiny, forty-dollar-a-month house that was located on Hastings Street, a couple of blocks west of the gym, purchased a large griddle and pressure cooker for making wheat cakes and yogurt, and traded a bench press machine for an old but fairly reliable Ford Ranchero that had good tires, artificial wood-grain doors and no muffler. Surrounded by friends and family, I had little stress or worry; I was able to train as hard and as long as I wanted — even to the point of vying for a second world title, if I so desired.

One day, a new student who hadn't been with me long enough to understand who I was or what I stood for in the field of weightlifting strength, asked, "Why don't you take steroids like some of the other world class lifters? Not forever — just long enough to regain the title?"

"Is there a difference," I asked him, "between one time and one thousand times? In anything we do in this life? Don't you see that for me to even *think* seriously about doing it one time would make everything that I have accomplished in my life meaningless."

Anabolic-androgenic steroids first appeared on the weightlifting scene in late 1952 in York, Pennsylvania and immediately had an impact on the sport. The athletes swallowed or "hyped" these drugs into their bodies and, within a short training time, were able to lift as much as 30 to 35 percent more, according to experts.

The dangerous effects of these drugs, however, were staggering: violent mood swings ("steroid rages") which destroy the lifter's emotional well-being; liver and kidney problems, which lead to premature death; shrunken testicles; premature baldness; acne; breast enlargement ("steroid tits") — to name only a few. As the problem increased, I became more passionate about warning potential victims. "You do not need them!" I would calmly but emphatically state. "They will give you quicker results for a short time, but in the long run they will do far more damage than good. What use is a competition where the goal of most athletes, coaches and sponsors is to see who can cheat the best? Why not a hydraulic crane-lifting contest with each contestant at the controls of a mechanical device?"

Nevertheless, the issue of steroids persisted among other members of the lifting community who had succumbed to the lure and who would have loved to have seen me fall to their level. "If you can lift so much without drugs," they would ask, "how much could you lift *with* them?" One such person even did the math by increasing my best *recorded* lifts by the 30 percent advantage that steroids would have afforded me. I refused to look at them. "The importance lies not in how much more I could lift by cheating," I said, "but in how much less cheaters could lift by doing it honestly. Do the math that way and draw your own conclusions."

As gym attendance increased, so did the demand for our customized equipment. Bill, my father and I found ourselves working long hours. Bill took over manufacturing, my father took over the

day-to-day operations and I spent eight to nine hours a day instructing our members. As a result of our efforts, our reputation
grew and we attracted many well-known personalities to our gym.
The two most famous were Vancouver lawyer and alderman, Harry
Rankin and concert piano accordionist, Leo Aquino. From other
fields of athletics, there was champion bodybuilder, Jimmy Pratt,
title holder of Mr. B.C. and Mr. Pacific Northwest, who could deadlift well over 600 pounds; Dave Steen, a six-foot-six Canadian and
British Commonwealth Games champion shotputter who could
power-clean over 350 pounds; Bill Lasseter, a 220-pound B.C. Lions
running back turned linebacker who could snatch his own body-
weight; "built-like-a-tank" Tony Toljanich, who played junior football with the Vancouver Meralomas; and B.C. amateur heavyweight
wrestling champion Ernie Fulton who could squat well over 450
pounds. In the field of weightlifting, there was Stan Gibson, the
Canadian lightweight champion, who was also voted "most outstanding lifter in the Pacific Northwest" (1952, 1953 and 1954).
He participated with me in the 1954 British Empire Games. Also
included was Gerry McGourlick, who became both a B.C. middleweight and light-heavyweight champion.

From 1963 to 1964, our facility was the only gym in Canada with
five members capable of military-pressing over 300 pounds. Those
members included myself, at a body weight of 270 pounds; Paul
Bjarnason, at a body weight of 200 pounds; John Fraser, at a body
weight of 250 pounds; George Dean, at a body weight of 210
pounds; and Tony Toljanich, at a body weight of 220 pounds.

Employing the same heavy weight and low repetition principles
that I had originated so many years ago, and that had won Canada
two gold medals in international competition (refer to Appen-
dices 1 and 10 for a detailed explanation), I was able to keep everyone making steady and predictable gains without the use of drugs
or tricks. Within a short time, some of the more dedicated lifters
were approaching world class lifts. Two such athletes were heavyweight lifter, Tony Toljanich, and middle-heavyweight lifter, Paul
Bjarnason. Both lifters were pressing about 240 pounds when they

began my heavy singles program and within six months both had progressed to over 300 pounds.

Another lifter, George Dean, won gold in the heavyweight division at the 1964 Canadian Weightlifting Championships, held in Ottawa. Paul went on to become the first B.C. lifter to compete internationally for Canada since my BEG win in 1954. Paul also won gold in the 1966 Canadian Championships, won silver in the 1967 Pan Am Games, competed in the 1968 Olympic Games and won gold in the 1970 Canadian Championships. During his last competitive appearance in 1973, he set three Canadian records: a 305-pound snatch, a 390-pound clean-and-jerk and a 695-pound total.

One June afternoon in 1963, while I was watching Paul and Bill Gladstone go through their workouts, I placed a 400-pound barbell on the power rack and military-pressed it. Feeling spry for my over-the-lifting-hill age of thirty-seven, I increased the weight to 415 pounds and pressed that as well. Both Bill and Paul became quite excited.

"You're number one again!" Bill shouted. "World Champion Yuri Vlasov of the USSR holds the world military-press record with 413 pounds and you just beat it!"

"With ridiculous ease!" Paul quipped.

Eager to have me show the world, and perhaps initiate a "comeback" as a professional strongman, they encouraged me to accompany them to the Pacific Coast Weightlifting Championships, which were scheduled for Portland, Oregon on July 17, 1963. They would make the arrangements, I would duplicate the press and we would see what transpired.

I drove with Paul, Bill Gladstone and Bill Copeland to Portland and, before a packed house of curious and excited spectators and lifting officials, military-pressed 420 pounds — breaking Vlasov's world record by seven pounds. It was unofficial because I had shouldered the weight from the rack instead of cleaning it from the floor, but it was a world record just the same and everyone gave me a standing ovation.

Vancouver papers made little mention of it, however, and I

took it as a clear message that my draw as a competitive lifter — in Canada, at least — was definitely over. Satisfied that I still possessed world championship capabilities, I returned to Vancouver, where I was determined to get back to the more important business of enjoying my life and spending more time with my friends and family.

My increasing gym obligations made that more difficult each day, however, and I soon found myself searching for ways to reduce my workload.

CHAPTER 9

CROONING AND
CREATING

*Music is like a love affair that
has never been consummated. Top singers like
Sinatra have learned to woo the woman.*

— DOUG HEPBURN
(Scott Macrae, "He's Dreaming of a Hit Christmas,"
Vancouver Sun, December 12, 1975)

Since singing had always been one of my passions, I began
doing it to relax after the rigors of my job and workout. At
first, I sang along with my radio or record player but as people
took an interest in my ability, I found myself performing in the
Fraser Arms Hotel in Vancouver, as well as Nield Longton's
Espresso Cafe and the Cave Supper Club in downtown Vancouver.
I enjoyed the applause and respect from my musical sideline and
one night Colleen voiced what had been rattling around in my
own thoughts: "Why not singing as a career?"

The more I hashed over the idea, the more determined I
became to make it happen. The financial reward was minimal,
when it existed at all, but it was something that I enjoyed — and

enjoying the present was what counted most for me at that time. More, it was something that I could do with both friends and family — a bond rather than a wedge — and I flew at it with little regard for anything else.

Some of my most memorable experiences occurred during this time. When my singing idol, Frank Sinatra, was booked to perform at the Pacific National Exhibition Forum, located at the corner of Hastings Street and Renfrew, I was hired to act as head of security in case things got out of control. He always travelled with his own security team, of course, but I guess the PNE was looking to do a little bragging of its own, so it called in "The Biggest Arms in Canada" for the occasion.

Certain that I would at least get a chance to shake Frank's hand, I rehearsed what I wanted to say to him until I could recite it gargling. When the big night came, however, the Forum was packed and boisterous, both inside and out, and Frank was whisked past me before I had a chance to utter a word.

I watched his performance and when he finished, amid a thunder of applause, I handed the following handwritten note to his head of security:

Dear Mr. Sinatra,
My name is Doug Hepburn and I was once crowned World's Strongest Man. I enjoy your singing very much and would be honoured to meet you.

About fifteen minutes later, his head of security returned and whispered, "Mister Sinatra regrets that he will be unable to meet with you. He's heard of you, though, and thanks you for your compliment." Although I was extremely disappointed, I made myself satisfied with the fact that Frank Sinatra had heard of me and thanked the security head for acting as liaison.

When gorgeous singing and dancing star, Jane Mansfield, was scheduled for a week's appearance at the Cave Supper Club, I was again called in to help keep order. I was also asked to sing on the undercard, which I accepted as a huge compliment. Although her handsome husband and manager, Mickey Hargitay (Mr. Universe 1955) kept a watchful eye on her, I eventually managed to introduce myself and found her to be extremely friendly and down to earth. She also gave me complimentary tickets to hand out to my friends.

One night after one of Jane's shows, my father and I stopped off at my gym to pick up some paperwork. Entering through the back door, we grabbed what we needed and were about to leave, when we were intercepted by a pair of RCMP constables holding drawn pistols. They had found the door unlocked and had slipped in, hoping to find a B&E in progress. Although neither of them recognized me at first (much to my father's disgruntlement) my driver's licence finally convinced them of who I was and I gave them two front row tickets to Jane's performance to show that there were no hard feelings.

When they arrived at the Cave the following night, my father treated them like two long-lost brothers and made a point of plying them with drinks until all three of them were well-lubricated. When I asked him why, since he hadn't seemed too pleased with them the night before, he produced a camera and whispered, "Everyone should have their own 'get out of jail free' card."

Another fond memory of this time concerned Vancouver big band legend, Dal Richards. When Dal and his orchestra agreed to play a charity benefit at the old Georgia Auditorium near the corner of Georgia Street and Denman Street, I was also asked to participate — as a singer, not a bouncer. Happily agreeing, I sang two songs with Dal and his band and we all received a standing ovation. Although I can't remember what I sang, I *can* remember thinking: wouldn't it be something if Frank Sinatra were singing on stage with me. "Old Blue Eyes" and "Young Big Arms" — wouldn't that be one for the record books.

Although I kept up my training because I knew that my weights were what kept me strong, the remainder of my time was spent singing or analyzing songs and singing styles. In the privacy of my small Hastings Street house, I would spend hours playing a particular record as I attempted to pinpoint the phrasings, inflections and other quirks of delivery that made it appealing. When I felt that I "had it down," I would replay the record and sing along, trying my best to imitate what I had learned.

In the beginning, I found it quite difficult to stay in sync with my accompaniment and still maintain the "crooning" style that I was striving to master. Although I always took it in stride, a lot of my accompanists didn't, as I pointed out in a newspaper interview a few years later:

> When I first started singing, I had the piano player breaking out in shingles because he's only got so many beats to the bar and I don't realize it. It doesn't matter how strong you are, you can't beat that guy on the piano.
>
> Doug Hepburn (Scott Macrae,
> *Vancouver Sun,* December 12, 1975)

All the fun and late nights adversely affected my efficiency at my gym, however, and it wasn't long before both Bill and Ivan were nailing it out to me in spades. Bill was working two jobs, my father was working two jobs, and I was working half a job, when I managed to show up at all. Members were quitting because they weren't receiving the necessary personalized instruction that they had been promised. I was also selling our gym equipment so cheaply that we were always scrambling for money to construct more and some of our T-shirts and food supplements were actually losing money.

My excuse was that our low prices gave the members less reason to go elsewhere, but I knew that it was my way of ignoring the situation. I had vowed to avoid any form of stress, and, with my new singing career about to kick in at any moment, what did a few lost dollars matter?

As I look back, I'm amazed that I couldn't see how selfish I had become. My father was sacrificing time and energy that would have better served him in the insurance arena, and I acted as though he were obligated to help me. Although he constantly came up with training schedules and cost breakdowns that would have vast-ly improved our efficiency, I went out of my way to ignore them. Perhaps, deep down, I resented the fact he could do something that I couldn't, and I was trying to get back at him in some irra-tional manner: the way I had tried to get back at the world by pun-ishing myself with alcohol.

If this was true for my father, I have no idea why I ignored Bill. Here was a loyal friend and equal partner, whom I was treating like neither. Even when he and my father expressed thoughts of quitting, I barely gave it a second thought. Dissension and thoughts of quitting were the stuff that stress was made of.

As things turned out, this was both the right and the wrong atti-tude for me to adopt. It was right for my physical, emotional and spiritual well-being. But it had a devastating effect on my financial situation. Ivan, exasperated with my refusal to make the changes that were needed to keep the business going, finally quit and returned to selling life insurance full-time. As he explained, "You can lead a horse to water but you can't keep him from crapping in it — especially if he's got the runs!"

Bill also quit. He was voted in as business agent for the Vancou-ver Firefighters' Union and it was an opportunity that he couldn't pass up. As he put it, "Why should I care if you don't?"

Actually, I did care. Pride and stubbornness kept me mute, however, and within a few short weeks, I discovered just how rot-ten a businessman I was. Equipment production stopped because I had neither the time nor the expertise nor the money to keep it going, and so did the enrolment of new members. Instead of launching a last-ditch effort to salvage whatever was salvageable, I withdrew into myself until I was once again facing bankruptcy.

Enter long-time friend, and the man who had introduced me to weightlifting so many years ago, Mike Poppel. Still strong and muscular, and already a rising force in the field of finance, he strode into my gym one afternoon and proclaimed, "Time to get you back on your feet again. Re-establish you as a functioning member of society!" He placed a large bag of protein powder on my desk and explained that he had arranged for a manufacturer of food supplements, located on Dundas Street in Vancouver, to provide me with a special blend of protein that contained 92 percent of the complete amino acids necessary for muscle growth and development. Taken in conjunction with heavy weightlifting, the supplement allowed lifters and bodybuilders to increase in both size and strength while drastically reducing the time that they needed to fully recuperate from strenuous workouts.

True to Mike's word, the manufacturing company produced the bulk protein in both powder and tablet form, and delivered it to my gym at no added cost. I packaged it, affixed my own *Protein 92* labels (which I produced from stencils and photographs) and sold it via phone solicitation, media ads and in conjunction with my six strength courses. The protein sold well and I soon had a large and regular clientele of gyms, schools, reform facilities and construction camps.

For the next few weeks, I basked in the elation and security of my new-found success. Then, unable to ward off my ever-increasing desire to return to singing and performing, I hired a female gym member to manage the business in my absence. Sales immediately dropped, and by the time I realized that it was my name and telephone presence as much as the quality of my product that had kept the orders coming, my protein business had dwindled to a point where it was no longer worth pursuing — or, at least, that was what I told myself. My bills again overtook me and I was soon forced to close down all operations including my gym.

Selling some of my gym equipment to settle outstanding bills, I stored the remainder at the home of another of my students, a physical education instructor who owned a large shed near the outskirts of the city. He afforded me free storage in exchange for his unrestricted use of the stored items until I returned for them — if ever — so the arrangement suited us both.

Before I went to bed that night, I listened to a recording of Frank Sinatra belting out his incomparable rendition of "My Way" and wondered what might have happened if I had been lucky enough to meet him. As I drifted off to sleep I thought about asking Jane Mansfield to arrange it but decided against it. Frank was a busy man, New York was a long way off and I really hadn't a thing to wear.

The next morning, free of all financial obligations, I concentrated on what I really wanted to do: develop a professional singing career. This seemed to satisfy Colleen, who saw it as more viable (more fun, at least) than a career in strength instruction, and we began spending every night together — me crooning along with the piano and she, in the audience, leading the applause.

To my surprise, I was soon back in the news. A middle-aged athlete breaking world lifting records was no longer of any interest to the reading public, it seemed, but a middle-aged athlete "breaking the sound barrier" (as I loved to quip) apparently was. After catching my June 15, 1965 rendition of "Prisoner of Love" at Nield Longton's Espresso Cafe, a newspaper columnist penned the following:

> Never reluctant to try something new, Doug has taken up singing because he likes to sing, and he's good at it. Sounds like Vic Damone. That's the professional opinion of one of our entertainment buffs, Jack Moore, who has been known to carry a tune himself without the aid of a bucket.
>
> (Clancy Loranger, Vancouver *Province,* June 16, 1965)

One evening, after giving a well-received rendition of "Strangers in the Night" at the Fraser Arms Hotel, I returned to my table to find Colleen conversing with a smiling, flashily dressed, middle-aged musician by the name of Wilf Wylie. He had been following my progress and wished me to become the lead vocalist for his band, the Wilf Wylie Trio. He could guarantee regular, paid gigs (not great money, but money all the same) and I would receive an equal share — more, if it turned out that my reputation as a world champion weightlifter and strongman was adding to the draw. Since this was more appealing than my always having to scramble for accompaniment, I agreed.

True to his word, Wilf kept us performing at most of the entertainment pubs and coffee houses around town and we soon began
drawing a reasonable crowd. As he had cautioned, it wasn't great
money, but it was enough for Colleen to bring up again the question of marriage. I still wasn't prepared to make a commitment
without more financial security than a "maybe" vocal career, and
we again elected to wait. I could see that her patience was erod-
ing, however, so I searched for a way to supplement my income in
case my singing career was slow to take off.

Comparing what I enjoyed doing with what I was able to do
(the last thing I needed was another source of frustration), I drew
a blank. I returned to mail-ordering my six strength courses and
protein powder to make ends meet. To help boost sales, I purchased a few cases of a popular "weight gain" formula that was
manufactured by the Weider company. Unfortunately, I didn't
discover until afterwards that the formula contained a high percentage of alcohol. When my father found out, he slipped into
the gym one night and drank the entire stock — without gaining a
pound.

In 1966, I was inducted into the British Columbia Sports Hall
of Fame (now located at 777 Pacific Boulevard South, in Vancouver) where short film clips of my British Empire Games gold medal
lift and the Landy and Bannister gold medal race soon became
the two most popular displays. The following year, I was the subject of a CBC Times documentary entitled *The Strength of Giants,*
which was also well received, but did little to threaten my unofficial title of the "poorest, best-known man in Canada." As my
father gloomily prophesied, "You're doomed to the cold, gray
world of purgatory until your luck changes."

Determined to remain upbeat, I headed down to the Western
Sports Centre for a late afternoon workout. As I entered, I noticed a couple of bulky lifters doing heavy squats in the powerlifting section of the gym and wandered over to watch. I could tell by
the way they suddenly stiffened and became sombre that they had
recognized me.

Halfway through a heavy clean-and-jerk, one of the lifters stumbled and fell backwards. He managed to avoid the falling barbell, thereby preventing a perhaps fatal injury, but he was shaken all the same.

"What we need," he mumbled as we helped him to his feet, "is light weight! Heavy when you need it, but light if you fall, so it don't kill you!"

We all laughed because we knew that what he was describing was impossible. And by the time the two lifters had departed, I had pushed the words from my mind. The conversation returned that night, however, and played havoc with my dreams. "Light weight: heavy when you need it, but won't kill you when you fall."

Fish-flopping until daybreak, I rolled out of bed more exhausted than when I had rolled in. I donned my pants, yanked my belt tight and froze. The harder I pulled the belt, the more difficult it became because my body compressed and created a resistance that, in effect, pulled back.

A form of light weight?

For the next two days I hashed over the problem, trying to figure out what I had, exactly, and what "canned weight" would be worth on the open market. I could envision it already: flick a switch or turn a dial and there it was.

Turn a dial and create friction.

To create a working prototype, I purchased a broom handle and a pair of four-foot lengths of rope. I attached one end of each rope to each end of the handle and held the handle horizontally with both hands (the two free rope ends hanging down) as though I were preparing to curl it. Standing on the two free rope ends to create a resistance, I allowed the ropes to slide through my toes as I curled the handle. The harder I stood down on the rope ends, the more resistance I created — and the more my muscles strained to perform the curling movement.

I had it — light weight!

Sort of. I had the basic idea but I still had to develop a compact device that was easily adjustable and able to exert resistance from zero to at least a few hundred pounds. To make a long, problem-riddled saga short, the solution was a clutch system composed of alternating plates of steel and leather that could be squeezed together and held at a desired resistance by a dial. The clutch system was housed inside a hollow platform that the lifter stood on, and a spring and pulley system (also inside the platform) was attached to the clutch system to keep the two resistance cables tightly wound, and the lifting bar snug against the platform. The dial kept the cables unwrapping at a constant resistance during any exercise movement and the spring automatically rewrapped them at the end. Once the cables stopped, so did the resistance, with the result that the athlete was never in danger if he slipped. He simply stepped away from the bar, allowed the cables to re-wrap and began again.

My next step was to test the device. To my great delight, I found that it worked smoothly and had several advantages over conventional weights and barbells: it was light and easily portable; it was a lot cheaper than conventional free weights; and it produced a much more efficient workout because the pre-set clutch resistance remained constant throughout the full range of every exercise movement whereas the gravity-based resistance employed by barbells and dumbbells did not.

At first, because these advantages were not readily apparent to the athlete, the idea of promoting it as "a new and more efficient form of strength development" was received with reserve (if not with down-right scepticism) by the lifting community.

Once people experienced its solid results and ease of operation, however, the mood quickly changed and everyone wanted to become involved. I borrowed enough money to start building the devices in the hall and living room of my small house and within a very short time, had people contracted to sell them in a variety of ways: including phone solicitation, mail order and door-to-door sales. My percentage of the proceeds kept me happy.

Once the device began selling well, a pair of brothers who worked for the C.M. Oliver investment firm in downtown Vancouver (and whom I will refer to only as Don and John) approached me with a plan that they assured me would make us all millionaires. They would raise money on the Vancouver stock exchange and heavily promote the Hepburn Exerciser (as it was quickly dubbed) via a chain of bar/gyms, where they could, as Don loved to quip, "break them down on one side and build them back up again on the other!" In exchange for my exclusive rights and endorsement, I would receive a contract and a generous royalty for each unit sold — one to two dollars a unit, depending on gross monthly sales. Creative marketing would do the rest.

Since I had neither the time, floor space nor desire to keep manufacturing the Exerciser at home, it was an offer that I could not refuse. I obtained a legal evaluation of both the contract and the deal, signed on the dotted line and waited for the promised "good life" to kick in.

No one else shared Don and John's vision, however, and the idea never got past the planning stage. The required funding was never realized, full rights reverted to me and I was left with my original problem of trying to launch an invention that I had neither the funds nor the expertise to mass-produce effectively on my own. As I commented about the situation years later in a newspaper interview:

> My Exerciser, my Horatio Alger thing? Nothing but trouble and static and I'm ready to write the whole thing off. As my lawyer told me, it's a messy business.
>
> Doug Hepburn (Scott Macrae,
> *Vancouver Sun,* December 12, 1975)

When other groups and individuals were also unable to keep the Exerciser selling regularly, I was forced to conclude that the problem might be due (in part, at least) to the device's lack of versatility. Since the user had to stand on its platform and grip its handle with both hands to make it work, there were only so many types of exercises that could be performed. To the average strength enthusiast who was used to the versatility of a fully equipped gym, these limited exercises might have appeared incapable of providing a *complete* body workout.

Since understanding the problem did little to provide a solution, however, I elected to "throw it all in the corner" for a time and sweat away my frustration at the Western Gym. There, halfway through a set of heavy, two-handed curls, I was struck with an idea. Why not a smaller, more versatile version of my original friction device that could be held and operated with one hand as well as two: a dial, clutch and spring mechanism no bigger than a soup bowl with a hand-hold on one end and a foot-hold on the other? In effect, a friction-powered dumbbell.

The more I considered this concept, the more I wondered if I was the dumbbell. Hadn't I just wasted months, going on years, trying to launch my last "brain storm"? No, I concluded. Others had created the waste because I had allowed them too much control. This time would be different. I would always retain at least a 50 percent interest in the device, thereby retaining an equal say in all business decisions. Potential partners could either accept such a condition or leave it as they saw fit.

Rushing back home, I spent the remainder of the day and night sketching a viable design, then rose with the robins to ferret out a capable manufacturer willing to build the device on credit. I had little luck. Since the demise of the Exerciser was still vividly remembered by most Vancouver businessmen, none of them wished to waste either time or money flogging a horse that, in their minds, had already proven itself commercially dead.

On impulse, I stopped in at an engineering company at 3121 West Sixth Avenue and spoke to a master machinist by the name of Josef Bingisser. Showing him sketches of my idea, I offered him a 50 percent partnership in exchange for a working prototype and the means to mass produce it. He agreed, on the condition that the patent be filed in his name alone until I was able to come up with my share of the expenses. I agreed and we filed for a United States patent through the Vancouver law firm of Carver & Company (application number 515,129). Josef immediately set about hand-crafting a working model that was sleek and efficient beyond my wildest expectations. He also constructed a set of jigs and ejection moulds that enabled us to produce every part of the machine, right down to the dials, spring assemblies and jet black plastic handles and housings. Dubbing it the Dynatron, I drew up an elaborate advertising campaign that included glossy brochures and detailed instruction manuals and got set for the success I was certain would come.

Taking the first step towards that success, Josef and I assembled a few hundred units and embarked on a serious quest to secure a contract with a company that had international distribution capabilities. It never happened. While most of the interested companies lacked the expertise, the rest were either too greedy — "You supply everything and we take most of the profits" — or too preoccupied with other projects. Josef and I tried selling it by mail order and door-to-door for a while, but lacked the funds to get it off the ground. Josef ended up walking away, and I was reduced to flogging whatever I could out of my back door like some sidewalk hustler.

In the summer of 1968, friend and fellow British Empire Games weightlifting team member Stan Gibson journeyed to Mexico City to watch the Olympic Games. As a favour, he took along a Dynatron and soon found a large sporting goods company that was willing to pay $35,000 cash plus a generous royalty for the exclusive distribution rights to both the Hepburn Exerciser and the Dynatron. Although the company was only interested in the more versatile Dynatron, the rights to the Exerciser were also part of the package because both inventions shared a common design.

Within days of the Mexican offer, I received an identical offer from a North Vancouver lawyer, whom I will refer to only as Harold. Since North Vancouver was closer than Mexico City, I elected to go with Harold. A contract was signed, the required funds changed hands and the stock-piled Dynatrons were forwarded to Harold for sale. Results were immediately positive: I began receiving regular royalties and it wasn't long before

Colleen and I felt that it was time to start enjoying my new-found affluence. We purchased a spanking new, fully-loaded, black Lincoln Continental. Perhaps I bought such an elaborate vehicle to make up for the Cadillac that I had been forced to sell after my wrestling fiasco, or perhaps it was my way of honouring Yukon Eric, whose pride and joy had been his trademark Pontiac convertible. Whatever the reason, the black Lincoln soon became my trademark around town.

A new house in Tsawwassen with a sprawling backyard quickly followed and Colleen was ecstatic. "It'll take dynamite to get me out of here," she cooed a couple of days after we moved in. "Whoever says money can't buy happiness isn't trying!" As expected, the subject of marriage soon resurfaced and although there seemed no reason to postpone, a tingling in the back of my mind kept me cautious.

It was the right decision. Within a few months, the supply of assembled machines was exhausted, my royalties stopped and a major stumbling block appeared between Harold and me. The good lawyer, in his zeal to secure a contract, had failed to realize that he had purchased only the distribution rights and that I still held the manufacturing rights. When I offered either to sell him the manufacturing rights for another $35,000 or provide him with more assembled machines for a yet-to-be-negotiated price per unit, he hit the roof. As far as Harold was concerned, we had formed a deal, I had reneged and he would fight me to the last ditch until I fulfilled my legal obligation. If he couldn't manufacture the Dynatron without me, then he would make damn sure that I couldn't distribute it without him, and that was where we would both sit until common sense prevailed or the patent expired in approximately twenty years.

Since I considered Harold more responsible for his problem than me, I also dug in my heels and our differences quickly became irreconcilable. I lost the house, the car and, eventually, Colleen. According to her, I was destined to remain poor and alone — perhaps I even craved it — and she had no more time to invest. We embraced one rainy afternoon outside the Fraser Arms Hotel and never saw each other again. Stuck for options, I returned to the East Hastings rooming house that had given me solace so many times before and sat back to see what the future would bring.

In early May of 1972, as if to add insult to my emotional injury, the International Olympic Committee dropped the Olympic clean-and-press — the lift that had allowed me to become the strongest man in the world — from all weightlifting competition. The official reason was that it had become too difficult to distinguish from the clean-and-jerk, but, to me, in my rather "out of it" state of mind, it was but another instance of the world going out of its way to kick me when I was down. "See, Hepburn? You think what you're trying to do is important, but it's only important if we say it is — and we don't!"

I immediately responded by deciding to set yet another world strength record. Since the one-armed military press was what I did better than anyone else on the planet at that time, I went after the current world record holder: Dennis Hillman of Great Britain. He had set the record in 1964 by hoisting a respectable 147⁷⁄₁₀ pounds, and on November 18, 1973, at the over-the-lifting-hill age of forty-seven, I easily shattered it with 170 pounds. Although the feat was officially recognized and celebrated throughout the world, it did little to improve my financial situation. I was still a failed businessman at the mercy of an uncaring world, the rights to the Dynatron and the Hepburn Exerciser were still trapped in legal limbo, and I still had no idea how to proceed.

A couple of weeks later, to keep my comeback as a world-class strongman rolling, I began training at the Broadway Gym, located at the corner of Broadway and Kingsway. It had a regular clientele of serious lifters and was owned by my ex-partner, Ray Beck, who welcomed me with open arms and invited me to train free of charge for as long as I liked. Other ex-Hastings Street gym members such as long-time friend Gerry McGourlick also began dropping by and we all spent many happy times discussing politics and religion after hours at the Green Door and Mai Woo restaurants. Within a short time I was able to focus myself back to hard and regular training.

My enthusiasm was short-lived, however. Since it was obvious that many of the members were using steroids in place of my established training procedures, I couldn't help feeling that I was wasting my time as an honest trainer and role model. The last straw came one afternoon when I was approached by a group of young lifters who showed me a recent muscle magazine article about a well-known American strongman who had broken many world strength records.

"Is he using steroids, growth hormones or some other strength-enhancing drug?" I asked, trying to remain patient.

"Possibly," they acknowledged. "Pretty hard to compete without them when everyone else is using them."

"Then let's subtract 30 percent from his maximum lifting ability to compensate," I said. "Does he wear one of those heavy lifting suits for added muscle support?"

"Yes," they acknowledged, since the photograph clearly showed that he did.

"Knock off another 10 to 15 percent. How about one of those extra-springy lifting bars to help offset gravity?"

Since the photo clearly showed that this was also the case, the young lifters scowled. "Making the lift is making the lift! What difference does it make how you do it?"

When I saw a lot of the other lifters nodding in agreement, I knew that I was wasting my time. I could no longer remain in such a negative, dead-end environment. Saying goodbye to Ray Beck, I made it known that I would privately guide and instruct any athlete who was willing to do it honestly, and left it at that.

When no one took up my offer, I accepted it as the will of fate and made one last-ditch attempt to revitalize my singing career. Since I had broken with Wilf Wylie when my invention royalties had kicked in, it was back to singing whenever and however I could. I was received with only moderate enthusiasm. Since I knew that I was improving in both tone and delivery, I found myself wondering how much of my problem was due to my size and reputation as a strongman. No matter where I sang or how much emotion I delivered, I sensed that the audience was there to see me bend a railroad spike or perform some other feat of strength, and that my singing was but "filler-stuff" until the big moment arrived. It made little sense, since no strength feats were ever advertised, but my insecurity remained.

Late one evening while strolling home from the Espresso Cafe, I decided to reduce to the size of an ordinary man and find out. I constructed an exercise program that was designed to shed pounds rather than gain them, purchased an old bicycle that I pedalled at least ten miles a day, and limited my daily diet to three slices of plain Roman meal bread, two slices of cheddar cheese, honey, one small tin of salmon and two cups of weak tea.

In less than two years I lost over 105 pounds and felt as though the "other Hepburn," the larger-than-life athlete whose shadow had hindered my singing progress no longer existed. I remained powerful by concentrating on "tendon and ligament strength" rather than "muscle strength" (refer to Appendix 1 for a detailed explanation), but, in the singing spotlight, looked nothing more than your average 185-pound man.

It made little difference to the audience. They reacted as unenthusiastically to my singing as ever. The only thing that changed was that they no longer waited for me to perform strength feats — probably because they assumed that I was no longer capable — and I quickly became less popular, both as a singer and as a celebrity, than I had been. I felt as though I had completely wasted the last few years of my life and couldn't blame a newspaper columnist for more or less stating that:

> You remember Hepburn. The local boy who made good with the barbells over in Stockholm. The underprivileged 285 pound Gulliver out of Vancouver's East End whose travels since scaling the peak have gone backwards, sideways and off in strange, meandering circles.
>
> (Eric Whitehead, Vancouver *Province*, December 2, 1975)

My reaction was quick. As suddenly as I had worked my body weight away, I worked it back again. I initiated a concentrated weight-gain diet and exercise program and within a year was back to straining the scales at 260 pounds, lifting heavy and feeling strong on all three levels of my existence. Once again, my barbells had brought me back to who I was and who I would always be. I was a good singer, but not a great singer. And since good is rarely able to compete with great, I elected to keep my music as a hobby and get back to what I had proven myself to be great at.

How? was another matter.

While I awaited inspiration, I rented a small, commercial area at 250 Kingsway, which I dubbed International Exercisers Limited and which allowed me to live in the back and build gym equipment in the front. I kept up with my singing, but traded public appearances for a sound system that allowed me to produce my own singing tapes and sell them in conjunction with my gym equipment, protein and strength courses. I also set up a private gym that allowed me the convenience of heavy training at home and — all in all — things went along well. I wasn't making a lot of money but I was getting by and, as Colleen had pointed out at her departure, perhaps I had never really wanted to be rich in the first place.

With more time to relax and contemplate the world and my place in it, my thoughts turned to writing and I found myself submitting articles to muscle magazines such as *Milo, Muscle Builder* and *Strength & Health*. In my more reflective moments, I composed poetry and songs. One such musical composition, "It's Christmas Time," struck such a cord with listeners that I decided to put out a record. Unable to interest an established record company, I scrounged every cent that I could and paid $90 an hour to have the song produced in a 45-rpm format. A local group, the Charles B. Curtis Trio, accompanied me as I sang. The trio also did the flip-side, "I Love You Charlie Brown," and the record went out on the Shelly International label, selling for $1.98 at all Jack Cullen record shops. A newspaper columnist reviewed it:

A laffer? Forget it. "It's Christmas Time" is very good. Both the song and the way Hepburn sings it. Light, lilting, infectious, a delicious thing. Maybe no immediate threat to Bing Crosby's "White Christmas," but several cuts above the pretentious pot-boilers that always surface this time of year. You have to admire a "tryer," especially when he comes up with a good one. And this is.

(Eric Whitehead, Vancouver *Province*, December 2, 1975)

"I know it's not Tony Bennet," I confided to Mr. Whitehead, during the post-performance interview, "but I'd like to realize enough from it to put out an album."

The record sold only moderately, however, and I resigned myself to spending the remainder of my days in the solitude of my Kingsway walls, content to be a "tryer" rather than the "settler" my mother had warned about so many years ago. If success was being relatively happy with your lot in life, then I was successful. If there was more that I had to learn on the subject, then I would await it in peace — building, reading, writing and singing.

At the age of forty-nine, when most lifters and strongmen had long since hung up their lifting shoes, what else was there?

CHAPTER 10

LOOK EAST, YOUNG MAN

The more complicated a man
becomes on the inside, the more simply
he can live on the outside.

— DOUG HEPBURN
(Archie McDonald, "Hepburn's Legend Lives On,"
Vancouver Sun, December 7, 1994)

Life at my Kingsway abode quickly settled into routine and although I had no complaints about the way I was living, I sensed that something was missing: there was an emptiness inside me that I couldn't identify. Given the time I spent with my mother, father, friends and customers, it couldn't be loneliness. Nor was it a yearning to be in the spotlight again. Still, I couldn't shake the feeling that I was allowing something important to pass me by.

I threw myself into my weightbuilding, singing, exercising and reading, but the feeling remained. Upon discussing it with friends, customers and a couple of well-meaning doctors, I received a common response: "Life is what you make it; get out and do things, if you're feeling left out; become more involved."

For a while I tried — regularly attending gyms, movies, restaurants, parks, beaches and other public places. Nothing helped. It was as if I were trapped aboard a runaway train with no way to prevent the inevitable pile-up. As one acquaintance aptly described my apprehension at that time, "They're walling us in and when they do, there ain't gonna be no air!"

In an attempt to find peace, I turned to the books that friend John Gunn had given me many years ago while I was staying at his Langley poultry farm and chanced upon a text entitled *Philosophy of the Masters,* written by Huzur Maharaj Sawan Singh. More spiritual than religious, it was an instruction guide for the practice of Sant Mat (also called Surat Shabd Yog), the yoga of uniting the soul with the Sound Current. The author claimed that this current (also referred to in the text as the Shabd or the Holy Spirit), is the manifestation of God that resides in all human beings, and states, "It [Sant Mat] is the inner experience of connecting the soul with the Lord" (p. 4). In short, the book outlined the way by which the soul could return to the Sound Current and free itself from the cycle of life and death. According to the author, this path could only be shown by a living Master (also referred to in the book as a guru or spiritual advisor) and that any attempt by a student (referred to in the book as a disciple) to follow the path alone was dangerous because there were obstacles that only the Master could remove.

Sant Mat is easy to practise. The student merely relaxes in a secluded spot away from noise, closes his eyes and focuses all of his concentration on his "third eye" or "eye centre," which is located behind the eyes and between the two eyebrows. He performs this meditation at fixed times, once in the morning and once in the evening, and, in the beginning, the goal is to try to visualize clearly the astral figure of his Master. The student does this by systematically closing his nine "doors" to the outside world (two eyes, two ears, two nostrils, mouth and two lower apertures) as he listens for the Sound Current. Once all worldly distractions are blocked, he will hear it clearly and it will it attract his soul like a magnet, allowing him complete single-point concentration. According to Singh, "When a person listens attentively to the heavenly sound, he begins to be enraptured by the bliss and automatically turns his back on the world" (p. 57). At this point, the student will clearly see the bright astral form of his Master, who will then begin the arduous and often dangerous task of guiding him back to the Sound Current:

> The first region to be entered is the thousand-petalled lotus, which is the centre of the astral region and very brilliant. Here, the "Negative Power" places certain obstacles in the disciple's way, but the Master removes them and takes the soul across. After passing through many other spiritual regions, the Master leads the soul to "Sach Khand," the true region, where it obtains release from the mind and the illusion, pain and pleasure, duality and birth and death.
>
> (*Philosophy of the Masters,* p. 59)

Once released, the soul can become a living Master.

Although eager to try Sant Mat, I had no living Master to guide me and had no idea where to find one, short of writing to the author in India. Studying the text, I found the following passage: "It is immaterial whether the disciple is near to, or far away from the Master. He [the Master] has a long reach, for his hand is the hand of God. His hands wield the power of God." Since distance was not an obstacle, I decided to search for a Master through meditation. I locked my office door, closed all the blinds, took the phone receiver off the hook and relaxed in my most comfortable chair. One by one, I mentally closed my nine apertures and listened intently for the Sound Current as I attempted to visualize the astral form of a living Master at my eye centre. Although I meditated twice a day for a month, I saw no visions and heard nothing other than my own breathing. A couple of times I even dropped off to sleep.

I again considered writing to India, but as I searched for pen and paper, I realized that I *had* made progress in one very important area: the ability to concentrate without becoming distracted. What would happen, I wondered, if I used this single-point meditation in my lifting regimen?

I decided to find out. Retreating to my secluded chair, I closed my eyes and attempted to visualize a 300-pound barbell lying on a lifting platform. At first, the image was fuzzy, continually flashing in and out of my eye centre. Within a few weeks, however, I was able to keep it as clear and stable as if I were staring at a black and white snapshot. I was soon able to watch myself grip the bar and prepare to lift, and was surprised by how relaxed I became. Without Sant Mat, I had always wondered if I would be able to will the necessary amount of adrenaline into my body at the necessary time. Now the opposite was happening. As I willed the weight into the air, it was as if I were an exploding bomb with unlimited power and focus. At times, I even found myself sweating and shaking from the exhilaration.

Once I felt that my powers of concentration were strong enough, I again searched for a living Master through meditation. Although I tried as sincerely as I could for a month, I experienced no more success than I had the first time. I returned to my *Philosophy of the Masters* for guidance and eventually realized that becoming worthy of returning to the Sound Current meant adopting a new lifestyle. As well as regular meditation, I would need to help people while I was of this world, make my own way and be a burden to no one, remain pure in thought and deed, and adopt a vegetarian diet to keep the functioning of my body as pure as possible. I knew that re-adjusting my eating habits would be the hardest for me (I was a man who loved to eat meat) but I also wanted to master Sant Mat, so I vowed to follow its tenets to the letter. I became vegetarian and began frequenting vegetarian restaurants in my area, and one restaurant owner in particular, Paul Dhanoa, of Greens and Gourmet at 2681 West Broadway in Vancouver, went out of his way to explain all the available dishes to me. He even invited me to eat there for free any time I wished in exchange for the odd tip on strength development.

A few weeks later I visited Mount Pleasant Community Centre at 15th Avenue and Ontario Street. Although there was no perfect master present, I was invited to attend lectures whenever I chose and helped with meditation techniques. The more I studied my philosophy, the more it seemed to answer my questions and give direction to my life. I would continue making my gym equipment and proving to the world that super, enduring, drug-free strength was available to anyone who honestly desired it — thereby fulfilling my worldly obligation — but I would also devote equal effort to elevating my spiritual self. What would be in this physical existence would be, and I would entertain no more expectations or demands of it. My reward would come on another plane.

Filled with the elation of my conviction, I set out to share it with others, beginning with my mother. "That's nice, Douglas," she said, neither smiling nor looking up from the cutlery that she was polishing. "What does it say about your being able to support yourself in later years?"

I had no answer and knew that I would be bouncing it against deaf ears if I had, so I left her to mull it over in the privacy of her kitchen and set out to find my father. If ever a man on God's green grass needed a way to keep himself focused and free of his "stinking thinking," as he so aptly termed it, it was the irrepressible Ivan Clifford Hepburn.

He disagreed, however. "Why don't you go the whole donut and become a Hairy Critchna?" he asked, eyeing me as though my brains had just fallen out onto the floor. "Shave your head and bounce around like a gut-shot goat? At least they got the brains to ask for money!"

"The Krishnas or the goats?" I asked. "What if this is your last chance at this life and you're blowing it?"

"What if it ain't and you're doing the same?" he snapped. Shooting me a look of disgust, he danced away, chanting, "Boogala, boogala, boo — they're making an ass outta you!"

Desperate to steer at least one needy soul in the right direction, I explained my new-found philosophy to every friend and customer who entered my shop and received a variety of responses. Some went away nodding, some went away laughing and some just went away. The more I explained, the less response I received until I eventually realized that each of us has to find his or her own way. As with my work at the Hollywood Hospital, I could do little more than offer advice when asked and hope that it would be heeded. I let it be known that I was available to discuss spiritual issues at any time and left it at that. As my father was so fond of saying, "The line's in the water, let's see who's worm-hungry!"

Determined to remain true to the second tenet of my *Philosophy of the Masters* doctrine of always making my own way in the world, I concentrated my efforts on increasing my monthly sales by mail-ordering my protein, strength courses and singing tapes. The more I made, the more my landlord raised my rent, however, until I was forced to seek a cheaper establishment after only one and a half years.

With the help of my father and friends, I moved to a large, three-level warehouse at 38 East Fourth Avenue in Vancouver. The owner, Mount Pleasant Furniture Limited, which did well at leasing antiques to the movie industry, kept the upper level and allowed me the basement and main floor levels. I did my packaging and fabricating in the basement, my sales and weightlifting in the front portion of the main floor, and lived in the rear area of the main floor, which I equipped with a fridge, stove and small shower. I also built a small but efficient recording system that I used to produce cassettes of my songs — at least one cassette a day.

After working on my music, I retired to my office and meditated for two hours in the manner prescribed by my Sant Mat discipline. Leaning back in my easy chair, I systematically closed off my nine apertures, listened for the Sound Current and attempted to contact a living Master.

After my meditation, I moved to my weightlifting area and performed my workout — again employing as much Sant Mat technique as I could. Standing before my loaded barbell or dumbbell I would grip it with both hands, close my eyes and sever all contact with the outside world. When only my barbell or dumbbell was visible in my eye centre, I would visualize myself lifting it. Then I would open my eyes and perform the lift for real. I always experienced an extreme feeling of exhilaration, and, at times, I became so focused that I barely remembered making the movement. I soon experienced a soaring success rate and at the age of fifty-three, was again setting world strength records for my age group.

Eager to stun the world, I packed my training garb, donned my Donegal tweed cap and headed to the Spartacus gym which was located at 1522 Commercial Drive, a few blocks south of my two previous gym locations. Inside, I was met cordially by the many lifters who were clanging, grunting and sweating through their "daily grinds." When I explained that I intended to break a world record for my age group and prove once and for all that a lifter doesn't need drugs or tricks to attain super, enduring strength, I was all but ignored. "That's nice, Doug," a couple of them said, trying, at least, to be civil.

Seeing the tell-tale signs of steroid abuse — stiffness in the joints and a sponginess in the muscle tissue — in nearly all of the serious lifters present, I could well understand why they might feel threatened by someone coming to repudiate the idol for which they had traded their souls and countless hours of gru-elling training. Yet there were also a lot of beginners present who had not yet succumbed to the "false lure" of drugs, and I directed my point to them. Expounding on both the short-term and the long-term dangers of strength-enhancing drug use, I placed an Olympic bar on the power rack, loaded it to 420 pounds and mil-itary-pressed it.

To my surprise, no one said much. A couple nodded or shrugged, as if to say, "Yeah — not bad." But I could tell by their expressions that the sight of a middle-aged man lifting weight — even world record weight for his age — did little to inspire them. One by one they returned to their workouts or to watch the cheaters train. I left the gym perplexed.

What was the message? That they didn't respond because they weren't ready to respond? Or that I was spending too much time worrying about mundane physical matters that had little to do with elevating my spirit?

On a whim, I journeyed by bus to the B.C. Sports Hall of Fame at 777 Pacific Boulevard South and stared at a movie clip of myself winning gold at the 1954 British Empire Games. As I studied the look of complete confidence and concentration on my face — my gigantic, drug-free muscles moving in perfect harmony — I asked myself: "Who is this guy? How much of this guy do I want back? How much do I need?"

As if in response, a man who was touring the exhibit with his two sons eyed me and asked, "Aren't you Doug Hepburn?"

"I used to be," was the best that I could muster.

More confused than ever, I returned home and sought advice from my *Philosophy of the Masters* doctrine. Although it didn't address my question directly, it stated clearly that enlightenment cannot be hurried or forced. As long as I was trying my best to help as many people as I could during my life, I was fulfilling my worldly obligation. Since the help offered could be either physical or philosophical, I elected to remain with the less stressful philosophical.

Returning to the Spartacus, I made it clear that I would help and instruct anyone looking to adopt a drug-free strength regimen — lack of money was no object — and returned home to see who showed up.

As it turned out, no one did. And two incidents quickly proved to me that leading a selfless existence in a self-driven society did indeed have its price. First, a young homeless woman of about thirty entered my shop one late afternoon looking for a handout. She swore that she hadn't eaten for two days and that all she wanted was enough change to purchase a small loaf of bread, with perhaps a little jam or margarine to spread on it. Remembering my own dark times, I gave her what money I could afford, plus some fruit and hazel nuts that were to have been my supper. She accepted it tearfully, promised that she would never forget my generosity, and left. The next day I was visited by another homeless woman with much the same story, and two more homeless people the day after. As it turned out, someone had painted a large "X" on the front wall of my front shop — the panhandler's code for "a mark lives here" — which was why I was suddenly so popular. When I began dispensing spiritual advice in lieu of money and food, the visits quickly ended.

I laughed at the absurdity of it. Refusing to let this incident hamper my spiritual growth, I devoted more time to meditating and lifting and, by February of 1980, at the age of fifty-four, I found myself breaking records for my age group more easily and by a greater margin than the year before.

Once again feeling the need to "show the world," I decided to make a comeback as a powerlifter and strongman. At first I toyed with the idea of giving my demonstration at a public gym. I was received with such reserve from local gym owners, however — in some cases, with downright antagonism — that I decided to make my statement in such a way that the results could not be ignored or suppressed.

On the morning of July 1, 1980, I sent out a news release to gyms, newspapers and muscle magazines, outlining my intentions and inviting anyone who was interested to attend. Then, on the evening of July 7, 1980, before a running videotape at my Fourth Avenue shop and using calibrated weights so that there could be no doubt about the poundages, I easily broke four world records for my age group. A strength reporter confirmed the feat in a popular strength magazine written years later:

> And his strength is lasting. At the age of 54, Hepburn made a comeback. He proved his claim that natural strength nurtured by proper nutrition and coupled with the force of the mind is enduring. He squatted 600 lbs. for 8 reps, pressed 390 lbs. off a rack, curled 260 lbs. and performed a right hand military press of 170 lbs. . . . Hepburn wants to show the world that a true strongman is *always* a strongman. He wants those of us who aspire to strength and health to know that chemically produced muscle is, at best, temporary and at worst, injurious.
>
> (Eric J. Murray, "Doug Hepburn — The Fountain of Strength," *Milo* magazine, March 1997, vol. 4, no. 4)

Although the feat was spectacular and unique in the history of the sport, public reaction was mixed. While a few people travelled to my store to shake my hand and wish me luck, others accused me of rigging the results. When I offered to let the skeptics weigh and load the barbells themselves, no one took me up on it, so I suppose my point was made: I was the strongest natural lifter in the world for my age and there wasn't a thing anyone could do about it.

Actually, I was probably stronger than *any* lifter my age — whether they were on drugs or not. The more the lifter ages, the more steroids and other strength-enhancing drugs ravage various organs of the body, until the lifter finally ends up weaker than if he or she had remained drug-free. The drugs also take a huge psychological toll. Bobby Hindley, President of the B.C. Powerlifting Association and an avid lifter himself, once described the situation: "It takes a lot of mental determination and discipline to prepare for a powerlifting competition. If the competitor trains naturally without drugs, he will develop these attributes as a consequence of his training. If he derives them from illegal drug use, however, he will find himself unable to rise to the occasion once the drugs are taken away."

Although eager to initiate more demonstrations and prove my point more emphatically, I was forced to put it all on hold when, in early March of 1981, my father's many years of alcohol abuse caught up with him and stripped him of his ability to live and function on his own. He was diagnosed with severe stomach cancer, complicated by liver and kidney degeneration, and it soon become evident to everyone that his days were numbered.

At first, being Ivan, he stoutly refused to go to a hospital. "They'll gut me like a trout!" he screamed. "And you know what happens to gutted trout!"

"Trout or pickled herring?" I asked, trying to lighten the mood.

But eventually his extreme and constant pain overshadowed his fear of being filleted, and I managed to taxi him to the parking lot of the Shaughnessy Hospital on Vancouver's West Side. Always the clown (I think he was clowning), he immediately flopped to the ground and spread his arms. "Put me out of my misery right now and save us all a lot of trouble."

Inside the hospital, he remained remarkably upbeat, perhaps determined to make up for the other times in his life when he had lacked the strength. Once, during visiting hours, I found Ivan and another patient of about his age, Frank Stevcon, playing five card draw poker in the hospital lounge. Frank, a short, rotund man who was always noisily wiping his nose with the back of his hand, had recently lost his leg in a car accident so they were playing for body parts. If my father lost, Frank would get my father's leg. If Frank lost, my father would get his stomach. As I arrived, they had just dealt their final cards and my father hustled me aside and showed me his full house: jacks over threes. "Are liver and kidneys part of the stomach?" he asked. "I gotta get the most outta this I can!"

Another time, as my father and I played checkers in his room, the hospital chaplain happened by and asked my father if he would care to chat a bit. My father shook his head. When the chaplain had left, my father turned to me and smiled, "Wants to save me in fifteen minutes from what it took me a lifetime to do."

In the hours before his demise, he told me his last request. "Bury me under roses — I been a stinker all my life!"

After my father's death, I complied with his wishes by spreading his ashes among the roses in New Westminster's Queen's Park. "Ashes to ashes, dust to dust," I said solemnly. "You had a wild ride, but enough is enough." Feeling that he would have appreciated the humour, I returned to the solitude of my Fourth Avenue sanctuary, locked the door and leaned back in my chair to meditate on all the things that had made Ivan who he was.

I remembered how tall and muscular he was, and how out of place he looked trying to cut the grass while he was "half-in-the-bag." I remembered how glad I was when he jack-knifed the cast from my infected right leg and how scared I was when he and my mother had their last fight. Above all, I remembered his sardonic sense of humour.

How my mother felt about my father's death, I have no idea. I never asked and she never said. But sometimes when I caught her staring off into space, immersed in her thoughts, I wondered if it was Ivan she was thinking about. Or perhaps I was just hoping it was.

For the next seven years, my life was relatively clear of mishap. I spent more time lifting and meditating in the solace of my shop, and soon found that as other lifters my age lost their drive and ability to hoist heavy poundages, I did not. I could no longer match what I had lifted at my prime, but I could still easily set world records for almost every power and Olympic lift in my weight class.

On November 27, 1984, a U.S. patent (file number 4,484,741 in the name of Josef Bingisser) was finally granted for both the Hepburn Exerciser and the Dynatron, but since both devices remained in legal limbo, it made little difference to my financial situation or plans for the future. I would continue to lift my weights and elevate my spirit.

On March 13, 1988, as if in response to my refusal to toss in the weightlifting towel, weightlifting associations worldwide, including the International Olympic Committee, adopted a new body weight classification system. As a result, they discarded all lifting results to that date — including my many world records. I had little reaction. As far as I was concerned, the world could do as it pleased. I even reduced my hours of business so that I would be less distracted by its pain and greed-driven workings.

I did not stop enjoying my life, however. I merely concentrated on thoughts and activities that I was passionate about. At least once a week, I shared a vegetarian meal with my mother at her West End apartment, where we sang, talked and listened to records until the "wee hours." I gave her copies of my homemade singing tapes and, as she got older, I noticed that she played them more. During each of my visits, she asked if I had enough food and money and always offered me both. Although I always declined, assuring her that I was doing fine, I found it slightly hurtful. Throughout my life, I had wanted to support her in style, the way I had promised that sad, starry evening I had carried her along the beach. I had never been able to manage it. But I knew that she would always have enough income from her pension and savings to live as she desired, so I consoled myself with that.

Another great joy of my life was riding my bicycle through Stanley Park. I would first get myself into the mood by watching the many types of waterfowl at Lost Lagoon. Then I would suck in a couple of deep breaths to get my heart pumping and pedal around the park until exhaustion forced me to stop. Out in the real world I aged like everyone else, but astride my moving bike time stood still as though the turning of the bike wheels counteracted those of time. Of particular significance to me was the long hill near Lumberman's Arch. I knew that as long as I kept making it up that steep grade without stopping, I would remain young on all three levels of my existence. As I said once to a Vancouver newspaper reporter:

> When I hit that hill I'm 17 again. I pumped and got out of breath then, and I still do. I don't have any age when I go up that hill.
> (Archie McDonald, "Hepburn's Riches are Strictly Spiritual," *Vancouver Sun,* 1990)

Another of my passions, and one that most health authorities agree can add years to your life, is pet ownership. And I always made sure that I had at least one pet around me at all times. With the passing of Boris and Wizard, my dog and cat from my East Hastings era, came another black cat by the name of Ninja, probably the best mouser I have ever run across.

Another cat appeared one stifling June afternoon while I was packaging protein near my shop's open rear door. He poked his head inside to check the place out, saw me and froze. We stared at each other for a couple of seconds, and then he bolted. He returned the next two nights, however, and on the third night placed a freshly killed mouse on the floor inside my door. Unsure of how to respond, I mixed up a little milk and protein powder in a cereal bowl and nudged it towards him. When he took a couple of steps back, I did the same and waited. To put it simply, he lapped the milk, I garbage-canned the mouse and we became roommates. I christened him Cupcake.

What had always intrigued me about Cupcake was his apparent ability to read my mind. Whenever I felt sad or lonely, he would hop onto my desk and nuzzle my neck until I petted him. Sometimes, when he woke me up in bed too early, I simply stared at him and he departed to let me sleep.

During this peaceful era of my life, I continued to lift and meditate regularly and, all things considered, found my existence quite satisfying. I was venturing out into the world less, but friends, customers and fellow lifters were dropping by my shop more so it all balanced out.

Then on January 12, 1991, as though the universe was obligated to offset all happy times with an equal dose of sadness, I was notified by a fellow lifter that my friend and lifting coach, Charles A. Smith, had died in Austin, Texas, as the result of a cancerous growth located on the top of his skull. Long-afflicted with diabetes, he had been confined to a wheelchair by the loss of one of his legs and had taken to consuming copious amounts of beer to deaden his emotional pain. I was extremely saddened by the news and it took me a long time to come to terms with it.

But the worst was yet to come. In the early part of November 1993, my mother was diagnosed with terminal cancer and quickly degenerated so far that she needed a full-time careworker. Within weeks she was bed-ridden and only able to sit on a chair or toilet for fifteen-minute intervals. She had her magazines and record player for solace, but since she was too weak to read much, our visits tended more towards listening to music than chatting. We rarely thumbed through her photo albums. Whether it left her too sad or too tired, I have no idea. She would suddenly turn away and say, "I no longer feel like it."

As her condition deteriorated, she became crankier and would "tee-off" at me for the slightest provocation. Although it upset me greatly, the careworker would just smile and tell me that it was her way of protecting me. My mother berated me so that I wouldn't miss her as much when she was gone.

One of the reasons that I dreaded her passing was that in all the time we had spent together I had never been able to tell her how I really felt about her. In the privacy of my Fourth Avenue shop, I vowed to muster the courage while I was still able and the opportunity presented itself sooner than I could have imagined.

One evening, when I was meditating alone in my locked storefront, I felt an overwhelming need to go to my mother. Although it was pounding rain, I raced my bicycle to her West End apartment — almost sliding into a city bus in the process. I rang her doorbell and got no response. I yelled, pounded the door and was about to bolt in search of the landlord's pass-key when I heard a feeble voice from inside. Shouldering-in the door, I found my mother lying exhausted in the middle of the hall. She had dragged herself across the floor to answer the door but had lacked the strength to make it all the way. Scooping her into my arms, I carried her to her bedroom and tucked her under her covers.

"Like the night you carried me through the park," she said weakly.

I was suddenly so overcome with emotion that I held her hand and poured out everything that was inside me. With tears in my eyes, I told her how much I would miss her and how very much I appreciated all the times she had fed, protected and cared for me. I apologized for being unable to care for her in the same manner, and for failing to be the kind of son that she had wanted and deserved. I told her how much I wished that our relationship had been closer and how much stronger in spirit she had always been than either Ivan or myself. I told her how much I envied her unyielding courage and determination and that I understood why she had needed to be hard at times — to offset the frailties of others around her.

While I spoke, she stared at her covers and uttered not a sound. Whether she lacked the words or the strength, I have no idea. It

▲ Doug relaxing with his arms folded in the early 1950s.
(COURTESY RAY BECK)

▲ Doug and fellow lifters watching Roy Hilligenn clean 330 lbs. at the
Western Sports Centre on Hastings Street in the early 1950s.
(COURTESY STAN GIBSON)

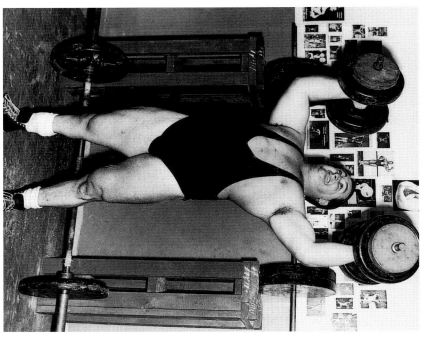

▶ Doug performing a press with dumbbells, a lift in which he had no peers. (COURTESY RAY BECK)

▶ Doug pressing 370 lbs. in the early 1950s, which was above the world record at this time. (COURTESY RAY BECK)

▲ Doug performing a bench press, one of his trademark lifts. Eventually he managed 580 lbs. in this lift. (COURTESY LEO AQUINO)

▲ Doug performing a heavy squat. He eventually reached 800 lbs. in this lift. (COURTESY RAY BECK)

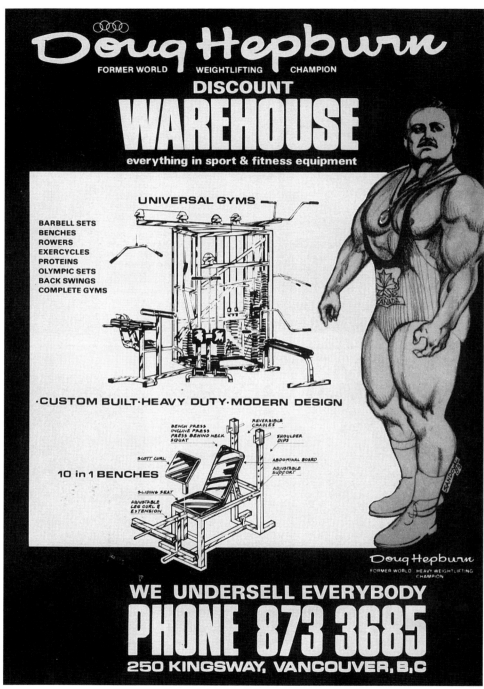

▲ Advertising in the magazine *Muscle Canada* for Doug's fitness equipment, which he himself constructed. (COURTESY DENNIS WONG)

▲ Doug's arm wrestling machine that he invented in the early 1990s. (COURTESY STAN GIBSON)

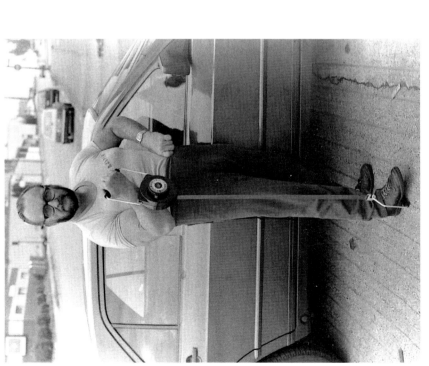

▲ A slim Doug Hepburn posing with his newly developed Dynatron in the mid 1980s. (COURTESY PAUL BJARNASON)

▲ Doug at age sixty-one with his trademark Donegal tweed cap.
He continued to work out with weights regularly.
(PHOTO: MARK VAN MANEN, *VANCOUVER SUN*)

▲ Doug at age seventy-one doing a world record curl for his age group
(170 pounds) at his World Challenge in 1997. (COURTESY SYD BRUNT)

▲ Doug in 1997 cooking a typical meal of beans on a hot plate in his one-room shop and living space on 4th Avenue in Vancouver. (COURTESY STAN GIBSON)

▲ Doug in his 4th Avenue shop with posters from his 1997 challenge.
(COURTESY STAN GIBSON)

▲ Doug's memorial service on December 9, 2000 at the Hamilton-
Harron funeral centre in Vancouver. (COURTESY STAN GIBSON)

didn't matter because I had finally bared both my heart and soul and I felt a thousand pounds lighter. Certain that her time was near, I leaned down and kissed her lips. It was one of the few times in my life that I was able to show that emotion.

Then the careworker appeared — she had popped down to a convenience store for a couple of things — and after she had examined my mother and made certain that she was resting comfortably, I repaired the lock on the front door and returned to my Fourth Avenue sanctuary to meditate on what had occurred. Later that night, on December 19, 1993, my mother left her physical existence without pain or regret. She had smiled up at her careworker and said, "I know Doug loves me, because he kissed me!"

She was cremated and laid to rest with her late husband, Bill Foster, and, after the service, I returned home and meditated on the aspects of her character that had made her special. I remembered her sitting at the kitchen table stubbornly pouring drink after drink for Ivan, who only wanted to leave. "If you are going to do it," she said, "you will do it here." I remembered her always moving — always trying to do better for herself and everyone under her care. I remembered her admonishing me for bringing stray animals into the house, then petting and feeding them when she thought no one was looking. Most of all, I remembered her weakly informing me that she wanted to be cremated so that I wouldn't embarrass her by showing up at her funeral with "the ass out of my pants."

The last image made me smile and I felt better because I had again been able to turn a negative into a positive. I was sad that she was gone, but I was happy that she would never be gone from my thoughts. Closing my eyes, I imagined her frolicking in an expansive field of flowers with Buck, Chinook and Bernard, and prayed that I could one day join them.

With her passing, I wondered if my need to keep proving myself would also pass. To my surprise, the answer was no. Although I loved my mother dearly, I knew that what I was destined to prove in my physical life transcended mortal ties. My job on this planet was not just to show that super strength was possible without the use of dangerous drugs, but to prove that naturally developed strength far outlasted drug-assisted strength, without dangerous side-effects. This truth could not have been presented earlier because I was the proof. It took my lifetime of honest training and living to provide the required example. They could toss out the Olympic clean-and-press (the lift that had made me a "world strength institution"), they could strike from the official record books the twenty-five world strength records that I had set in as many different lifts and they could accept increasing drug abuse in weightlifting as a natural evolution of the sport. But they could *not* erase my ability to keep breaking world strength records long after drug-assisted athletes my age had either quit or died.

To this end, I immediately made plans for another demonstration: something that would really make the world sit up and take notice. Not only would I break a series of world records, I would do it within a specified time limit, thereby setting the record for setting records. Compiling all the most recent competition results — both in the Open category (where all ages competed) and the Masters category (where competitors were restricted to their age groups) — I retired to my private gym to see how I fared in both divisions.

To my satisfaction, I found that not only was I able to break the majority of the world Masters records in my sixty-five to seventy-year-old age group plus at least one record in the Open division, I was able to break these records by a far greater margin than in the previous year. I credited this increase to the incorporation of my Sant Mat meditative techniques and tentatively scheduled my "Demonstration to the World" for the middle of September 1994.

On August 15, 1994, my training was interrupted by more sad and shocking news: friend and Olympic Weightlifting gold medallist, Paul Anderson of Toccoa, Georgia, was dead from kidney and liver complications at the early age of sixty-two. Taking it as a sign that what I was doing was indeed important and had the potential to help a lot of people (here was a younger lifter who was dead while I was still alive and about to set more world records), I decided to proceed with my demonstration as quickly as possible. Settling on an exact time and place, I had friend and freelance writer, Barry Whittaker of Vancouver, send out the following press release:

Attention: Sports editors
August 22, 1994
For immediate release
HEPBURN WILL ATTEMPT TO SHATTER WORLD RECORDS
Doug Hepburn, once known as the World's Strongest Man, and the only member of the Commonwealth to win a heavyweight world championship, is confident that he can break several world Masters Weightlifting records. The sixty-eight-year-old Hepburn will make his world record attempts on 7:00 p.m. on Thursday, August 25, 1994 at his gym at 38 East Fourth Avenue in Vancouver. Everyone is welcome to attend.

As with my July 7, 1980 demonstration, I performed it before a running video camera and used calibrated Olympic weights so that there could be no doubt as to the exact poundages. I also imposed on myself a forty-five-minute time limit and broke six Masters records and one Open record as follows:

LIFT	WORLD RECORD	MY LIFT
Bench press	215 lbs. (masters)	280 lbs.
Two-handed curl	154 lbs. (masters)	180 lbs.
Military press	181 lbs. (masters)	210 lbs.
One-arm dumbbell press	84 lbs. (masters) 110 lbs. (open)	100 lbs.
Bench press (close grip)	197 lbs. (masters) 230 lbs. (open)	215 lbs.
Press-behind-neck	143 lbs. (masters) 160 lbs. (open)	180 lbs.

Once again, public reaction was mixed. Some were impressed. A Vancouver newspaper reporter wrote an article on it a couple of days later:

> Forty years ago, Douglas Ivan Hepburn was the strongest man in the world. He would qualify that claim now to read: The strongest 68-year-old-man in the world. To prove it, he hoists a 100 pound dumbbell over his head in a one-armed military lift for the benefit of Ian Lindsay and myself. He has just set a world record for over-65, and with any effort at all, he could have beaten the open record of 110 pounds.
>
> (Archie McDonald, "Still Going Strong,"
> *Vancouver Sun,* August 27, 1994)

Although a few others pooh-poohed it, the facts could not be ignored. Slowly but surely, people took notice and I began receiving calls from around the globe from individuals wanting advice on training, nutrition and meditation. They also ordered my courses, protein powder and gym equipment, and within a very short time I was the "man to see" for the development of safe, natural, super strength that lasted well into the later years.

But there was still a lot left to do to increase public awareness, and I wondered how it would all eventually end. As I leaned back in my easy chair with my eyes closed and the world tuned out, I imagined how it might feel to be a living Master of Strength: a guru sent from the highest level of his existence to guide physically and spiritually needy weightlifters through their earthly cycles.

It was such a satisfying feeling that I dwelt upon it for quite a while.

CHAPTER 11

CHALLENGE TO
THE WORLD

Conceive, believe, work and achieve.

— DOUG HEPBURN
(Author communication, June 15, 1996)

As my reputation as a "Builder of Ageless Strength" increased, people from all walks of life continued to seek my advice. Although some were famous, like American bodybuilder Bill Pearl, most were older gentlemen inquiring about diet, training routines and ways to maintain a positive outlook while aging. As a result, I made many enjoyable acquaintances and felt a growing satisfaction that I was helping these people lead a fuller, healthier life.

One elderly gentleman in his late seventies, Mel May from Sherman Oaks, California, phoned me at least once a week and was soon referring to me as his strength doctor. As he learned more about my views and background, he decided that both fame and fortune were to be made by promoting me as the World's Strongest Drug-free Senior and suggested the launching of a weekly television series called *Search for the World's Strongest Drug-free Man.* The search would be open to all males able to prove themselves lifetime drug-free (by a professionally administered lie detector test) and able to match or surpass some or all of my world record lifts and feats. Those who qualified would become the program contestants and would lift against each other for cash, prizes and the title.

There was already a popular television series on the air called *The World's Strongest Man Competition,* where athletes from all parts of the globe competed for points in a series of strength tests. When he told me that he planned to launch the program in the United States I saw it as a lost cause. America had its own strength heroes and wasn't about to endorse a foreigner.

Mel disagreed, staunchly averring that the contest's "drug-free angle" was strong enough to make the show a hit in any country. After providing me with recent correspondence between himself and some of the television moguls from the three main networks, he then set about presenting the idea to networks, cable companies and talk shows. As I suspected, none was interested and although Mel turned every stone at least twice, he was eventually forced to give up.

Health and strength enthusiasts continued to solicit my counsel, however, and a couple of weeks later, I received a visit from a fortyish gentleman and his seventeen-year-old son, whom I shall refer to as Jim and Derek, respectively. Derek was a tall, lanky hockey player who, according to both his father and his coach, had the potential to make it big in the professional ranks *if* he could increase his muscular size and strength without reducing his skating speed and maneuverability. Since both father and son made it clear that they would happily do whatever it took to make these changes, I agreed to act as Derek's strength mentor — free of financial charge — *if* they gave me three promises in return. First, Derek would follow *exactly* and without question every program that I drew up for him. Second, he would never resort to drug use of any kind to accelerate results. Third, once Derek attained his desired size and strength, both he and his father would spread the word to friends and peers, thereby initiating an anti-drug campaign that would probably save a lot of careers as well as lives. They agreed, and Derek began training the next day.

He was a good student and progressed quickly. Within a few months, he had added inches to his arms, legs and chest and had made equal gains in skating speed and dexterity. He then began regular meditation techniques to help reduce his stress level during games and practices. Within a short time it was obvious to everyone who watched him on the ice that he was destined for a lengthy professional career.

Then, without warning, Derek quit my training sessions and rebuffed all my attempts to discover why. I later discovered from his father and coach that he had exchanged my safe and natural workout for a steroid-based workout that some of his teammates had been using and had suffered a major knee injury as a consequence. The steroids had caused his muscles to strengthen faster than his supporting tendons and ligaments, and his knee joint had buckled under the strain.

That night, after my regimen of music, meditation and exercise, I logged onto the internet and pulled up the latest information on steroid abuse, *Psychological and Behaviourial Effects of Endogenous Anabolic-Androgenic Steroids Among Males,* by M.S. Bahrke, C.E. Yesalis and J.E. Wright. I was shocked to learn that the problem was rampant in most types of competitive and non-competitive athletics right down to the junior high school level. The report, gleaned from a series of strictly monitored national surveys, stated that in most sports throughout North America requiring strength and endurance (which includes most, if not all of them) 4 to 9 percent of the athletes involved take a combined steroid dose of four to eight times the recommended medical limit; use more than one anabolic-androgenic steroid at a time; combine the use of injectable and oral anabolic-androgenic steroids; and use the drugs frequently, usually in cycles, with an episode of use lasting from six to twelve weeks or more. For those

requiring directions on purchasing, implementing and camou-
flaging the effects of these dangerous substances, "how-to" web-
sites on the internet were but a keystroke away. These "dispensers
of disaster" not only provided precise dosages and brand names,
they offered them in the guise of diet and exercise programs so
that the unsuspecting would think that they had been medically
approved.

In an attempt to prove once and for all that athletes do not
need drugs to become successful in sports, I established my own
website (www.doughepburn.com) and challenged the world to
match or beat the many world strength records and feats that I
had set without drugs:

> Canada's Doug Hepburn, former World's Strongest Man and pres-
> ent World's Strongest Senior, CHALLENGES THE WORLD! Beat
> or match five of his world records in either division with no drugs,
> belts or support gear of any kind and win a chance to compete with
> other qualified lifters for cash, prizes and the title of World's
> Strongest Natural Man or World's Strongest Natural Senior!

As with Mel May's search concept, all competitors were required to
take a lie-detector test to prove that they had never used steroids
or any other strength-enhancing drugs. Once passed, they were
required to submit a high-quality VHS video tape of themselves
performing five qualifying lifts. Calibrated bars and plates were
required to verify the poundages used, and competitors for the
senior division needed to submit a government-issued birth certificate. (Refer to Appendix 7 for the details of both challenges.)

Although I submitted a copy of my challenge to a number of
popular strength magazines in both Canada and the United States,
few were willing to run it. Their excuse was that they were in the
business of providing articles and training information, not issu-
ing challenges. My opinion, however, was that they were afraid of
offending the many pro-drug companies and individuals who regularly purchased their magazines and advertising space.

Not to be dissuaded, I forwarded a copy of my challenge, along
with a video tape of me performing the qualifying lifts for my sev-

enty-and-over age group, to the media and strength associations
of over 65 countries.

Shortly after, a Vancouver newspaper reporter showed up on
my Fourth Avenue doorstep to ask me why I was doing this. Taking a determined breath, I explained that I wanted to prove that
steroids aren't necessary:

> The human body can out-perform any drug if it has the right stuff.
> It exceeds the strength of steroids. In the so-called "pre-steroid
> era," I knew that it was a man that I was lifting against. Now I don't
> know if it is a man or a drugstore. What does it say about the evo-
> lution of sports when we have a pre-steroid era?
>
> (Kerry Gold, Vancouver *Courier,* August 16, 1996, p. 13)

I further explained that while young people are daily bombarded
(via television, movies, magazines and other media) with the false
message that drugs are the only way to ensure success in sports, I
was living, breathing *proof* that it wasn't true. If no one could match
my accomplishments — and I was certain that no drug-free lifter
could — then perhaps I could help give these impressionable
young people and future athletes another way to measure success.
As I indicated to a second Vancouver newspaper reporter:

> I'm not making this point for self-aggrandizement. I am the *one* per-
> son in the world who has the credibility to influence young people
> to stop taking drugs because they can see that getting super strong
> is possible without them. I feel that my mission at this point in life
> is to save the lives of many thousands of people.
>
> (Bob Mackin, Vancouver *Courier,* September 27, 1998)

The lifting community, however, did not share my enthusiasm.
Months passed without a single response. Rewriting my challenge
to include a $10,000 cash prize that I did not have and had no way
of getting, I was still ignored. When I changed my seniors' challenge to include those lifters who were *on* drugs as well as those
who were not and still drew a blank, I knew that I was wasting my
time.

I kept running my challenge, in hopes that a staff sports writer
or reporter would grow curious why the world was passing on an

"easy ten grand," but it never happened. My phone remained silent and friends and customers eventually quit expressing interest. It was as if my challenge had never been issued.

There were, however, always a few crack-pots showing up — good comic relief, if nothing else. One early afternoon, while I was doing paperwork at my desk, the door flew open and a dishevelled, sixtyish man with a wild look in his eyes burst in and ran right up to me.

"You Hepburn?" he snorted.

"I am he," I said, not quite sure what to expect.

"Can you levitate?"

I eyed him, wondering if I was being put on.

"Levitate!" the man said, scowling at my lack of response. "Lift yourself in the damn air with just your mind. Can you or can't you?"

His flushed face and vibrating neck veins told me that he was serious, so I replied, "I'm sorry, no. The most I can manage is levity."

"What the hell good is that!" the man snorted, and bolted away as quickly as he had arrived.

I wanted to yell out, "Try the airport!" but I was afraid that he would barrel back in.

Another time, while I was lifting weights in the rear area of my closed shop my telephone rang. I usually unplugged the phone to prevent interruption but on this occasion I had forgotten and it rang until I was forced to answer. An articulate, male voice of indeterminate age informed me that he had to meet with me in person — both our futures depended on it. Less than ten minutes later, a tall, balding man clutching a heavily taped shoe box appeared at my door. As I cracked the door to shoo him away, something about the way he guarded the box piqued my curiosity.

As we seated ourselves at my desk, he introduced himself as Wallace Clooney of no fixed address (no relation to the singer Rosemary Clooney) and carefully positioned his package between us. "I received the idea by studying an African tribe renowned for their heavily stretched ears," he said in a low voice. "So it's no fly-by-nighter!"

With that, he opened the box and extracted an egg-sized lead weight that was attached to one end of a six-inch length of surgical tubing. The opposite end of the tubing was attached to a three-inch strip of velcro. The idea, he very carefully explained, was to suspend the weight from the end of the penis via the velcro strip, to gain penis length from the stretching and sexual strength and endurance from the body's inner muscles straining to keep the penis from popping out of its fleshy socket. He also produced a complicated array of straps and thin, metal rods designed to keep the suspended weight stationary while being worn, and assured me that a mere twenty minutes a day produced remarkable results.

Before I could ask how he knew, he produced a hand-written contract that would have made us equal partners on the deal — his manufacturing and marketing skills in exchange for my exclusive endorsement — and offered me a pen. Resisting an urge to ask for a practical demonstration (I was afraid that he would give me one), I calmly said, "Anyone who would endorse or employ such a foolish and dangerous contraption would have to have a screw loose — no pun intended!" Mr. Clooney curtly repackaged his invention and left without a word. I wanted to shout after him, "If he was still able to screw, that is!" But I locked the door and pulled the blinds.

For the next couple of months, my life went on quite uneventfully. Friends, customers and strength enthusiasts appeared on a regular basis, and I continued to lift, meditate and take long bicycle rides to keep my stress levels in check. My desire to get my anti-drug message to the world was never forgotten, however, and as people picked my brain for health and lifting tips, I picked theirs for a solution to my problem.

In late May of 1997 my efforts were rewarded. A middle-aged gentleman who had entered my shop to purchase some protein powder looked up at me and asked, "Why does it have to be in a big way? Wouldn't a little of something be better than a lot of nothing?" After wrestling all night with the comment, I set about initiating a local challenge. I had little money and no experience at promoting strength shows but I had desire, and that would have to do.

My first step was to construct a workable format. Since there was little use in advertising for drug-free lifters able to match or beat my career lifts (if they weren't interested in doing it for money, they certainly wouldn't be interested in doing it for free), I geared the contest more towards fun than financial gain. I would begin the event by breaking a series of world records in my age group, thereby making my point that natural strength far outlasted drug-initiated strength. Then I would invite men, women and children from the audience to try the lifts themselves.

Scheduling the event for 1:00 p.m. to 5:00 p.m. on July 13, 1997, at the Plaza of Nations Building (located near the B.C. Sports Hall of Fame and Museum), I hired a young, fit Master of Ceremonies to guide the event and a couple of assistants to help with the changing of weight and transporting of equipment. I then sat back and tried to convince myself that I had everything under control. In my heart and soul I was certain that I was doing the right thing and that the stars would watch over my endeavours as a consequence. But the night before the event I had a hard time sleeping. What if no one showed up? What if those who showed up grew bored and left?

To my relief, the event was a success. Over four hundred men, women and children attended, all intrigued that I was still super strong and healthy at the age of seventy-one. Each time I broke a record, everyone clapped and cheered. Long-time friend, Syd Brunt, snapped photographs, and many members of the audience formed a line to attempt the lift or to test the weight of the barbells and dumbbells. The moments that gave me the most satisfaction were when children as young as ten years old shook my hand and asked how they might one day perform similar feats. I gave them free copies of my six strength courses, and had a stack of one hundred disappear within minutes. When older spectators clamoured for a more detailed account of my strength routines and over-all views on health and muscle maintenance, I returned to my Fourth Avenue storefront and, later that evening, sowed the seeds for a book about my life to be written by my friend Tom Thurston.

About this time, I chanced upon a television broadcast of a local arm-wrestling contest. As I watched the contestants straining and concentrating — much the way weightlifters strained and concentrated through their routines — I realized that here was an easy, popular sport in which anyone could participate.

Then a thought: what if I taught these athletes how to achieve maximum strength, endurance and pulling power to the point of developing a national team to represent Canada in world competition? One of the truths of arm wrestling is that the strength and endurance required is not restricted to the arm and shoulder. Since all muscles, ligaments and tendons work in unison, the simple act of grasping an opponent's arm and attempting to twist it to the table brings many other muscle groups into play: the feet and legs for balance; the back and stomach for providing a solid twisting base; and the neck and shoulders for stabilizing the head.

Although I quickly assembled a system of exercises that would strengthen the body in the required manner, I soon realized that what was needed was a machine that would not only simulate an actual one-on-one match, but would allow the athlete progressively to increase the tension of the pulling arm as he or she became stronger. As luck would have it, a neighbouring engineering company assured me that such a machine could be constructed using the same friction principle as my Dynatron. If I wished, a money slot and timer could be attached. Although I hadn't considered a pay machine, the more I visualized the idea the more I realized that "pay as you play" was probably the most financially feasible route for a man with a large dream and a small bank account.

For a total cost of $1,400 plus tax, I had a prototype constructed with a four-foot-high base, a handle attached to a thick metallic lever, a vinyl elbow rest and a "disqualification light" that flashed when the wrestler's elbow left the rest. I personally tested the machine and was elated by its smooth efficiency: you set the dial for the required tension, dropped a "loonie" into the slot and had thirty seconds to wrestle the lever to the "win" position.

After demonstrating the machine to a couple of customers, I was struck with an ingenious plan for promoting it to the public. I would have all current world champions (both male and female) wrestle the machine and note their tension strengths. Then, I would list these strengths on a large chart and challenge all comers to beat the champion of his or her division. Those who qualified would win an opportunity to wrestle other qualifiers, with the winners of these confrontations receiving a face-to-face shot at a world title. Christening the concept "Beat the Champ," I dubbed the machine the Powermaster 3, drew up a set of rules and regulations and formed the World Invitational Arm Wrestling Federation. I then got permission to place the Powermaster 3 in the Fraser Arms Hotel and I sat back to see how it fared.

At first, it was a huge hit, with everyone clamouring for a chance to "beat the champ!" As time and alcohol took its effect, however, the machine became the focus of so much arguing and fighting that the management ordered it removed. Searching out an establishment where the clientele seemed less aggressive, I placed it in the Century Plaza Hotel in downtown Vancouver. Similar problems arose there too, however, and I was again asked to remove the machine.

Not to be dissuaded, I looked for another venue, one that would stimulate healthy competition instead of drunken antagonism, and came up with Fitness Vacation, a health club located at 180–13040 Number 2 Road in Richmond. The machine did so well there that I placed a second machine in Gator's Gym at 12320 Trites Road in Richmond. This also did well — as evidenced by Gator's Gym manager Mark Lentsch's comments to a Richmond newspaper reporter:

> Everyone's trying to beat the heavyweight champion. You get all types doing it. Arm-wrestling is a popular test of strength between

people, and what better place to gauge one's power than in a gym?
(Martin van der Hemel, *Richmond Review*, October 21, 1998)

As I further explained to Mr. van der Hemel: "The strongman is symbolic of the strength of a nation. At one point, during Canada's heyday in the 1940s, Canada was the stronghold of strongmen in the world. But in recent times, Canada has tumbled from the world stage in athletics, losing most of its top athletes, in sports like hockey, to the United States. If not for 100-metre world record holder, Donovan Bailey, Canada would be all but absent from the athletic stage. The Powermaster 3 could restore some athletic pride to Canada because anyone can arm-wrestle."

Spurred on by the success of the first two machines, I placed a third machine in the B.C. Sports Hall of Fame and Museum and made plans to place enough of them throughout the city to launch my "Beat the Champ" contest in a big way. I wasn't making much profit — the recouped loonies barely funded the construction of new machines — but because I wasn't doing it strictly for money, I was satisfied. After seventy-two years, I was finally on the verge of making the difference to the world that I had been struggling to achieve since childhood.

Then, in early December of 1999, as if to punish my good luck, my landlord, the owner of Mount Pleasant Furniture, informed me that they needed my space to expand their operations. Although affordable accommodation in the area was scarce, I managed to secure a small, one-room flat in a commercial building owned by an engineering company at 55 East Fifth Avenue. There was little room for anything other than living and storing my possessions, but since I had no other option, I made do. When I launched my "Beat the Champ" contests, everything would change and I would be able to move to a more suitable location.

Life, it seemed, had other ideas. The novelty of the machines soon wore off, leaving me financially unable to construct more, and my dreams of expansion were put on hold. The machines already in use remained in their locations, earning a feeble trickle of loonies, and I returned to my lifting, meditating and waiting.

I remained at my cramped, one-room abode for almost ten months. During this time friends such as Professor Tuck Wong of Simon Fraser University and one of my relatives, Mark Hepburn, would drop by regularly. So did fellow lifters such as Paul Bjarnason, Stan Gibson, Ernie Fulton, Leo Aquino and Gerry McGourlick. And Dennis Wong was training with me all through this period, using my patented drug-free program. Still, I knew that if I didn't soon find a place where I could move, think and breathe, I would die of a broken heart like poor Bernard in his Cloverdale pen so many years ago. It was obvious from rising rents and land values that I wasn't likely to secure a new place as spacious or conveniently located as my Fourth Avenue store even with my government pension and I took a long walk into Stanley Park to think.

As so often in the past, I ended up at Lost Lagoon watching the waterfowl. As I felt the serenity around me, it struck me how much I had always wanted to live in a place that overlooked the park. I studied the nearby highrises that seemed to be studying me back and was struck with an idea: why not go the whole route and move into a top floor where I could look out over both the park and the ocean? I wouldn't be able to construct gym equipment, of course, but it wasn't likely to cost me much more than I had been paying for commercial space and I would still have my protein sales, strength booklets, singing tapes, arm-wrestling loonies and old age pension to get by on. With more room in which to think and create, who knows what other ideas I might come up with?

I immediately rented the penthouse atop the Harbour View: a concrete highrise located at 1920 Alberni Street, for $1,000 a month, and moved in on October 1, 2000. Taking only what I needed — kitchen utensils, furniture, singing equipment and the master copies of my six strength courses — I locked the rest in a nearby storage facility, notified friends and customers of my new location and took a silent vow to make the very best of my remaining time on my earthly plane. I placed a small table and chair on the east side of my apartment so that I could watch the sun rise every morning, and a second table and chair on the west side so that I could watch it set every night. Then I sat back to see what the future would bring.

Later that evening, as I sat staring down on the rest of the starlit world, I marvelled that my life had changed so much in some areas, yet had remained so static in others. Countless times throughout my life, I had found myself at Lost Lagoon staring at the waterfowl and wondering how my future would play out. Here I still was — a little higher and less apprehensive, perhaps — but still wondering the same thing.

I was certain of one thing, however. Whatever was fated for me *would* come to pass as long as I kept to my barbells and didn't give up. People were beginning to listen. I just had to come up with a plan to voice my message in a big way — if not through my "Beat the Champ" competitions, feats of strength or world lifting records, then by some other means.

AFTERWORD

ON NOVEMBER 22, 2000, Douglas Ivan Hepburn, winner of gold medals and possessor of a platinum heart and spirit, died of a perforated stomach ulcer at the age of seventy-four. Dennis Wong, a long-time friend and protégé who discovered the body, remembers the events leading up to it with extreme sadness. "Doug had been suffering from stomach pains for some months. He was having difficulty eating and he had lost a lot of weight. I suggested many times that he make an appointment with a doctor but he was reluctant to do so, saying that 'the pains just come and go.' Finally when he was quite weak and the pain had increased, he agreed. I don't know what he told the doc but I am pretty sure that he minimized the pain he was feeling. That was Doug. At any rate, the doctor assumed the situation was minor and sent him away. Things seemed to go on as normal for a time but in our last phone call, just before he hung up, he thanked me for always being there for him—as though he sensed what was coming. When next I tried calling, I found his phone continually busy, and so I arranged to enter his Stanley Park apartment with the building manager. We found Doug lying on the floor with the telephone receiver beside him, suggesting that he had attempted to call for help. He had been unable to complete the call."

His memorial service, held at 3 p.m. on December 9, 2000 at the Hamilton-Harron Funeral Centre on Fraser Street in Vancouver, British Columbia, bore testimony to his accomplishments and to the relationships he treasured throughout his life. Two hours after the service began, the room was still filled to capacity with wet-eyed friends and well wishers taking to the podium to bid "Mighty Doug" God-speed and to share how his presence had enriched and inspired their lives. This show of respect was not confined to his memorial service. Vancouver mayor Philip Owen, called for a moment of silence during the December 5, 2000 regular city council meeting, and Doug's internet address was flooded with letters of condolence from power and weightlifting associations around the globe. The B.C. Weightlifting Association has formed a "Doug Hepburn Division" for young lifters, and the 2003 World Weightlifting Championships are being held in Vancouver (November 15 to 22) in honour of his 1953 gold medal win in Sweden. Also, a drive is under way to place a bronze statue of Doug inside the B.C. Sports Hall of Fame and Museum, and a movie script of his life and accomplishments, entitled *Strongman: The Doug Hepburn Story*, is making the rounds. Although slow to be fully recognized in his hometown and country, Doug was eventually heralded by virtually all world strength authorities and historians as the strongest drug-free weightlifter, powerlifter and all-around strongman.

But Doug was more than just an athlete. He was a philosopher, wrestler, inventor, avid reader, singer, strength-dietician, fitness consultant and, according to veteran *Vancouver Sun* reporter Archie McDonald, who had interviewed him countless times, a "living legend." Doug was a strong and eloquent advocate of drug-free sports and a writer of songs and poetry that glorified life, freedom and one of the places that he loved most — Stanley Park. Although physically strong and perhaps intimidating to the average observer, he hated violence to the point of shunning the daily media — the television and newspapers — to spare himself the anguish of dealing with the disasters that are their stock in trade. "I know what's wrong with the world," he quipped, "I don't need to know the details." Most of all, he was an honest and loyal friend who always had time for anyone who stopped in to see him. A quick visit with Doug was never possible, no matter how short the visit was intended to be. One of his good-natured jokes or anecdotes would lead to many and the time would quickly be eaten away by echoing laughter.

Towards the end of his life, Doug made it clear to me and many of his friends that he had only two remaining desires: to have his complete training principles and procedures made available to anyone who wished to utilize them, and to publish his life story in a way that would show the world who he was and what he had been trying to accomplish with his life. It is my hope this book will help at least a little.

— Tom Thurston
July 2003

MY COMPLETE DRUG-FREE STRENGTH-BUILDING SYSTEM

*If a man's temperament is suited to it,
I believe he will make better progress in weightlifting
by training for strength first and for style second.*

— DOUG HEPBURN
(Communication with author, May 27, 1999)

THIS CHAPTER CONTAINS all the information that you will need to make yourself as strong as you wish to become. The product of over sixty years of study, experimentation and training, it is easy to understand and employ, works equally well for either sex and produces regular and continuous gains that are precise enough to last months, possibly years, into the future. Since there are no tricks or drugs involved, the strength that results is real and will last well into later life.

The first step is to decide how many times a week you will be able to train. For best results, the minimum is two times and the maximum is six times per week. Less than twice will not allow the body enough exertion to realize its potential in either size or power; more than six will not give the body enough time fully to recuperate between workouts — especially if the workouts are rigorous.

The second step is to choose the exercises that you feel will most efficiently work the muscle groups that you wish to strengthen, and to organize these routines into a weekly schedule that never exceeds more than three exercises per workout, never work the same muscle group more than three times per week, and *if you are working out more than three times a week,* never include upper and lower body exercises in the same workout. Failure to follow these rules can over-tax the body within a few months, or even weeks, into your training. (Refer to Appendix 9 for a detailed explanation.)

If you desire a total body workout but can train only two or three times a week, you should choose the three exercises that will most effectively work the three largest muscle groups. My experience has shown these exercises to be the full squat for the legs, the bench press for the chest and the deadlift for the back. (Refer to Appendix 8 for a detailed explanation.)

If you desire a total body workout and can train four to six times a week, you should choose six exercises. Three are those mentioned above. The other three should target muscle groups that complement the first three. For best results, I would suggest arm biceps curls for the front of the arm, since the bench press thoroughly strengthens the back of the arm; leg biceps curls for the back of the leg, since the squat thoroughly strengthens the front of the leg; high pulls for the upper back, since deadlifts thoroughly strengthen the lower back. (Refer to Appendix 8 for a detailed explanation.)

If you want to strengthen a specific muscle or muscle group rather than the body as a whole, feel free to employ any exercises that fulfil the requirement. Take care, however, that you give equal attention to opposing muscle groups. Failure to do so can throw the body out of muscular balance and, as a consequence, make it more susceptible to injury. Two common failures are doing bench presses without doing opposing rowing or high pulls; doing arm biceps curls without doing opposing arm triceps extensions.

Once you have organized your exercises into a workable schedule, your final step is to choose an appropriate training program for *each* exercise. While scheduling establishes *what* you want to do, programming outlines *how* you will do it, by giving precise starting poundages, poundage increases and repetition increases for each exercise. For the purpose of developing maximum size and power in the shortest time possible, my "A" and "B" programs have yet to be beaten.

The "A" program, although the less rigorous of the two, has been designed to increase the lifting capacity of any large muscle group (pectoral or thigh, for example) 120 pounds per year and any small muscle group (biceps or triceps, for example) 60 pounds per year. It is composed of two routines: a power routine for developing maximum strength in the muscles, tendons and ligaments, and a pump routine for developing maximum muscle size and endurance. The power routine is always completed first. To begin the "A" power routine, pick a poundage that you can lift eight times in a row without resting (eight continuous repetitions) but not nine. For your first workout, perform eight sets of two repetitions with this weight, which is written in weightlifting shorthand as: 8 x 2. A set is one group of continuous repetitions (in this case, one group of two) and you always take a two to three minute rest after each set. For your second workout, add one repetition to what you did in your first workout to get seven sets of two repetitions plus one set of three repetitions, or 7 x 2 and 1 x 3. For your third workout do 6 x 2 and 2 x 3 and keep increasing repetitions in this manner until you can do eight sets of three repetitions, or 8 x 3. At this point, increase your training poundage no more than ten pounds for large muscle groups and five pounds for small muscle groups and return to the 8 x 2 formula. (Refer to Appendix 10 for a detailed explanation.)

Once the above-noted power routine has been completed, take a five minute rest and begin your "A" pump routine. Reduce your training poundages by about twenty percent and, for your first workout, do three sets of six repetitions, or 3 x 6. For your second workout, do 2 x 6 and 1 x 7 and keep adding repetitions in this manner until you can do 3 x 8. At this point, increase your exercising poundage five to ten pounds and return to the 3 x 6 format. (Refer to Appendix 10 for a detailed explanation).

Once you have employed the above-noted "A" program for at least one full year and wish to embark on a more rigorous training schedule, the "B" program is the ultimate for developing both power and size. Like the "A" program, it is composed of both a power routine and a pump routine — with the power always performed first. It differs from the "A" program in that it incorporates "heavy singles," where the athlete lifts a weight only once before resting. The advantage of this procedure is that it allows you to employ the heaviest poundages possible during your workout, thereby allowing you the fastest strength gains. Be aware, however, that because the poundages used are considerably heavier than those in the A routine, there is more danger of injury or overtaxing.

To begin the "B" power routine, choose a warm-up poundage that you can *easily* lift once. Take a three to five minute rest and increase the poundage to a weight that you can *comfortably* lift once. After a three to five minute rest, increase your poundage to a weight that you can do for three continuous repetitions but not four, and this will be your training poundage. For your first workout, do five sets of one repetition, or 5 x 1, making sure to take a three to five minute rest after each heavy single. For your second workout, do 6 x 1 and keep adding one repetition per workout until you can do 8 x 1. At this point, increase your training poundage by five to ten pounds and return to the 5 x 1 format. (Refer to Appendix 10 for a detailed explanation).

After completing the power routine, take a ten to fifteen minute rest and do the "B" pump routine. Decreasing your training poundage to a weight that you can comfortably lift for eight but not nine consecutive repetitions, perform six sets of three repetitions, or 6 x 3. For your second workout, do 5 x 3 and 1 x 4 and keep adding repetitions in this manner until you can do 6 x 5. At this point, increase your training poundage by five to ten pounds and go back to 6 x 3. (Refer to Appendix 10 for a detailed explanation).

To obtain maximum benefit from these two programs, adhere to the following rules: always keep as relaxed and at peace with yourself as you can; always follow a power routine with its indicated pump routine; never miss a workout, repetition increase or poundage increase; never attempt to accelerate your progress by taking drugs or altering the program.

Above all, never "over-train." In other words, *never push your body faster than it can physically withstand.* This is probably the main reason why lifters fail (notice that I said lifters and not programs) and most lifters are guilty of it at least once in their lives. Sadly, many lifters over-train on a regular basis, but remain unaware that they are doing it. Look at it this way: when a lifter arbitrarily decides to increase his or her training weight ten pounds a week, he or she is really saying 520 pounds a year or 1,040 pounds in two years — a completely unrealistic and unattainable goal. Unable to keep up with such a rigorous schedule, the body will quickly "stagnate" — a weightlifting term that means become unable to lift past a certain poundage due to muscle fatigue. Although all programs will probably result in stagnation if followed long enough, it has been my experience that faithfully following the two rules about repetition and poundage given above will produce constant and predictable gains for at least one year — quite probably two to three. What's more, you will never feel that you're struggling. As friend, protégé and twice Canadian weightlifting champion Paul Bjarnason explains it:

> You never seem to be working that hard. You go through your regular, relaxing workout, making your regular relaxing increases as indicated, yet a few months later you are lifting all this weight that you never dreamed that you would be able to lift.

Should muscle stagnation occur, there is a simple cure. Eliminate the power routine for two to three weeks and continue the pump routine. If the problem persists, drop the power routine for another two weeks. If the problem is still present and you are adhering to the "no more than one repetition increase per workout" rule, then your training poundage needs to be reduced. You have either started with too heavy a weight or are adding weight too quickly. For best results, a good rule is "*never* expend your full lifting capability while working out." Occasionally, you can load up your barbell or dumbbell for a maximum lift to gauge your progress. But do this no more than twice a month — and only after your regular workout, followed by a fifteen to twenty minute rest.

If a five- to ten-pound resistance increase becomes too much for your body to handle during *any* of the aforementioned programs or routines, feel free to reduce the amount of your increases to whatever you feel comfortable with. Since every person gains strength at a slightly different rate — depending on a variety of hereditary factors — it is just a matter of finding what works best for you. Also, be aware that when a person begins a strength program, he or she will usually gain fairly quickly because the muscles will be relatively fresh and quick to respond to the stimulation. As the program continues, however, progress will usually slow as the body begins to feel the effects of the extra work you are putting on it, and you might need to reduce slightly your rate of increase to compensate. Listen to your body as you exercise and you will know exactly when and how much. As long as you regularly increase your training poundages to *some* degree, your strength will increase in direct proportion. In this case, "slowly but surely" is the only rule to follow.

Another common reason why athletes fail in their strength aspirations is because they embark on a program that they do not have the time to maintain. Outside obligations and distractions invariably get in the way until the athlete either skips workouts (thereby destroying the program's long-term effectiveness) or quits altogether. It is imperative, therefore, that you examine thoroughly your social obligations *before* you schedule your training. Better a moderately rigorous schedule that you can stick to, than a super-rigorous schedule that you can't. This is particularly relevant if you plan to compete, because every pound that you are unable to lift due to irregular training is one more opportunity that you give your opponents to beat you.

Once you have a specific goal firmly fixed in your mind, whether it is a future meet that you wish to win or a certain amount of weight that you wish to lift by a certain date, spend time meditating on it while you perform your workouts. The more you can visualize yourself succeeding at your goals, the more likely you will be to succeed for real when the opportunity arises. Seven-time World Weightlifting Champion John Davis of the United States once confided to me that he *never* attempted a lift — either in training or in competition — that he wasn't absolutely certain that he could complete. Former World and Olympic Champions, Paul Anderson, of the United States, Yuri Vlasov of the Soviet Union and Vasili Alexeyev of the Soviet Union also adhered to this philosophy.

Visualizing yourself succeeding during your non-training hours also enhances your lifting ability. Many times, while I was preparing either to enter a contest or to attempt a maximum lift, I would spend the entire day before the event not just "watching" myself complete the lift but actually "experiencing" myself completing it — over and over until it felt as though I had performed it hundreds of times. When the time to perform came, I was so "hyped up" I literally exploded with power and confidence.

Another mandatory and too often overlooked requirement for maximum size and strength gains is the maintenance of a proper diet. If you wish to gain a lot, you must eat a lot. In preceding chapters, I have referred to the massive amount of food that I consumed during my training (over 10,000 calories a day). If your goal is to compete on a world-class level, you must do the same. If your goal is to get strong for the sake of getting strong, then listen to your body and feed it well every time it asks for food. Just as some athletes find it impossible to realize that the body needs time to recuperate after a heavy workout, so others seem unable to comprehend that it also needs to be adequately fuelled after hard exertion. On numerous occasions I have watched enthusiastic athletes undergo a lengthy training session only to sit down to a meal that wouldn't sustain a field mouse. They then wonder why they failed to gain more strength or size. When forcing your body to handle ever-increasing poundages, your food intake must be ever-increasing as well.

Your diet must never be random. For maximum strength gains, it must be balanced and high in vitamins, minerals, complex carbohydrates and complete amino acid-based protein. Dietary information has increased dramatically since the '50s, so do some research. Read books and talk to professionals for a program that is compatible with your goals. Once you begin training, weigh yourself daily (in the nude for accuracy) and keep a lifting journal. If you don't experience substantial increases in both strength and body weight, re-evaluate your lifting program and food intake.

Also emphasize *liquid* calories and nutrients. Shakes made from milk, juices, eggs, protein powder and honey are digested more easily than solid foods. Liquids also let the body assimilate more food in less time, accelerating progress.

I also recommend milk, juices, shakes and other liquids during the actual training session. I have, on many occasions, consumed as many as three quarts of milk during a single session, with no ill effects. As a result, I have actually gained weight during my workouts. The only solid foods that can be consumed during a workout are easily digestible high-energy foods such as dates, figs, raisins and honey. But they should be taken in small doses only. This rule also applies to all cold liquids, including water.

One of the best ways to obtain quick energy during a lifting session is to drink a mixture of coffee and honey. Since coffee contains caffeine, however, it is recommended that you follow this practice only when you are competing, demonstrating or attempting a maximum lift.

Once you have established an effective diet and training program, it is crucial that you receive regular sleep and relaxation to offset your physical exertions. As previously noted, heavy barbell exercise temporarily depletes the body's energy reserves and the only time that the body can replace this energy is when it is at rest away from the gym. At least one hour of extra sleep a day is recommended if you are following the "A" program, and two hours if you are following the more rigorous "B" program.

Perhaps even more important than getting enough physical sleep every twenty-four hours is getting enough mental relaxation. Regular meditation will allow the mind, which is constantly racing to keep up with the hectic pace of the world around it, to slow down and relax. Tensions will melt away and you will soon be better able to distinguish those aspects of your daily life that deserve concerned attention and those that do not. During important competitions or public demonstrations, I made it a habit never to stand when I could sit, and never to sit when I could lie on my back with my eyes closed. A lot of athletes and spectators perceived this to be laziness, but it was a simple technique that many world class lifters of the time employed. The great American lifter John Davis, had so conditioned himself in this method that he was able to sleep immediately prior to competing and had to be awakened when it was his turn to lift.

As important as it is, at times, to be able to blot out everything around you except lifting and thoughts of lifting, it is equally important to be able to blot out all thoughts of competing and training. Life is more than just exercise; in order to be truly happy, you have to know how to give equal time and attention to such endeavours as family, career, hobbies and relaxation. As philosopher Paul Brunton once said: "We must be selective and take no more from the world than we need to attain our goal. Many may laugh at this belief, but they produce nothing extraordinary." Be aware, also, that by faithfully following the above-noted programs, you will discover more of yourself. What you accomplish, you accomplish on your own because you have the faith, honesty, courage and determination to delve into yourself and discern your exact capabilities. While dishonest lifters struggle to create an illusion, you tear illusion away and, as a consequence, build a strength of spirit that no dishonest lifter can come close to, and no amount of aging can destroy.

Before my conception and implementation of these training principles, the general state of weightlifting was at a standstill. No one in the world, for example, had been able to bench press 500 pounds (which is why it was referred to as the "500-pound barrier"), and most world strength authorities considered it impossible. Not only was I the first man on the planet to do so (completely drug free), I added another eighty-five pounds to my world record within a few months.

My methods were emulated following my gold medal win at Stockholm. The Russian and Bulgarian lifting teams began studying and adopting my principles and training procedures — to the point of following me from competition to competition. This is because they were able to realize early that the total poundage that an athlete lifts over a long and controlled time period is infinitely more beneficial than a series of maximum or near-maximum lifts performed over a shorter, more sporadic time period.

What you *must* understand if you are to get the most from your training, is that these principles will work as well fifty years from now as they did fifty years ago because the timing of the routines has been synchronized, as far as possible, with the body's inherent rate of response to training with heavy weight. Athletes and other so-called experts in the field have resorted to drug use because they have been unable to accelerate the effectiveness of these programs and routines in any other way.

In conclusion, let me re-affirm the promise that I made at the beginning: this information is all that you will need to become as strong as you wish to become on all three levels of your existence.

The rest is up to you. Good luck and good training.

DOUG HEPBURN'S LIFTING HISTORY

(drug free)

ALTHOUGH FAR FROM complete, the following list shows the degree to which Doug was able to set and maintain world records in a variety of lifts throughout his career and life.

1948
- broke local records (too numerous to list)
- set unofficial Canadian clean/press record of 230 lbs.
- Canadian record rejected by CAAU weightlifting headquarters in Montreal, Quebec.

1949
- broke local records (too numerous to list)
- set unofficial Canadian clean/press record of 300 lbs.
- Canadian record rejected by CAAU weightlifting headquarters in Montreal.

1950, May 28
- won B.C. Open Championships, Canada.
- set unofficial world record clean/press of 339½ lbs.
- world record rejected by CAAU weightlifting headquarters in Montreal.

1950, November 19
- gave lifting exhibition at Western Club Gym
- set unofficial world clean/press record of 341 lbs.
- world record rejected by CAAU weightlifting headquarters in Montreal because it was set on a Sunday. (Al Horton, *Vancouver News-Herald,* April, 1951).

1951, January 9
- won U.S. Open Weightlifting Championships, White Plains, New York, beating out a young Paul Anderson.
- set official world clean/press record of 330 lbs.
- world record accepted by U.S.

1951, March 23
- New Westminster YMCA Show, Canada.
- set unofficial world clean/press record of 343½ lbs.
- set unofficial world bench press record of 420 lbs.
- world records *twice* rejected by CAAU weightlifting headquarters in Montreal.

1951, April 17
- set unofficial world clean/press record of 345 lbs. at the Western Sports Centre, Vancouver, Canada.
- world record rejected by CAAU weightlifting headquarters in Montreal because it was set on a Sunday. (Al Horton, *Vancouver News-Herald,* April, 1951)

1951, June 19
- went to Senior Nationals, Los Angeles, California and came second to America's John Davis who won on total points.
- set world clean/press record of 345½ lbs. which beat John Davis' clean/press of 337½ lbs.
- world record accepted by the U.S.
- went to Venice Beach and broke every strength record on its record board.

1951, December 5
- went to Greatest Physical Show of the Year in Manhattan, New York.

– set world two-handed curl record of 220 lbs.

– set world bench press record of 456 lbs.

– set world squat record of 600 lbs. to hold four simultaneous official world records, counting his clean/press of 345½ lbs.

1952, July 5

– declined the Olympic Games in Helsinki, Finland because the CAAU weightlifting headquarters in Montreal refused to accept his records.

1952, August 7

– gave exhibition at Kitsilano pool in Vancouver, Canada

– set unofficial world clean/press record of 353½ lbs.

– set unofficial Canadian snatch record of 269 lbs.

– set unofficial Canadian clean/jerk record of 348½ lbs.

– All three records rejected by the CAAU weightlifting headquarters in Montreal because they were set on a Sunday. NOTE: above-noted three-lift total (press, jerk, snatch) of 971 lbs. was 46 lbs. *more* than the 925 Helsinki Olympics total of Noranda Quebec's Dave Baillie, the lifter the Montreal CAAU elected to send to Helsinki after Doug declined — 8.5 lbs. more than the 962½ total of American James Bradford, the lifter who won Helsinki silver.

1952, November 5

– gave demonstration at the Canadian Junior Weightlifting Championships in Vancouver.

– set world assisted press record of 430 lbs.

– set world clean/press record of 360 lbs.

1952, November 10

– won the Pacific Coast Weightlifting Championships in Portland, Oregon.

– set official world clean/press record of 361 lbs.

– set official world push-press record of 420 lbs.

– both world records accepted by the U.S.

– became one of only three lifters in the world (Doug Hepburn, Steve Stanko and John Davis) to total over 1000 lbs. in the three competition lifts: 361 press, 290 snatch, 360 jerk).

1953, May 14

– won Junior Nationals Weightlifting Championships in Cleveland, Ohio.

– broke three Junior National records (clean/jerk of 360 lbs., clean/press of 366½, snatch of 291¼), Doug's three-lift total of 1016½ beating out Paul Anderson's total of 940.

– set world clean/press record of 366½.

– four records accepted by the U.S.

1953, June 30

– first man to officially bench press 500 lbs. (Western Sports Centre, Vancouver).

1953, August 1

– gave a demonstration at the Alma Academy in Vancouver to raise money for his trip to the Stockholm Olympics.

– broke *three* British Commonwealth records (clean/press of 372 lbs., clean/jerk of 372 lbs., snatch of 302 lbs.)

– set world clean/press record of 372 lbs.

– all *four* records rejected by the CAAU weightlifting headquarters in Montreal.

– three-lift total of 1046 lbs., just 16 lbs. below John Davis' world record total of 1062 lbs.

1953, August 30

– won World Weightlifting Championships at Stockholm, Sweden with an injured right ankle (clean/press of 371¼ lbs., snatch of 297½ lbs., clean/jerk of 363¾ lbs.) — on a *Sunday.*

– set world clean/press record of 371¼ lbs.

1953, November 2

– gave a demonstration at the B.C. Seniors Weightlifting Championships at Vancouver.

– set world assisted press record of 440 lbs.

– set world two-hand curl record of 255 lbs.

1953, November 4

– made a guest appearance on the Art Linkletter's House-party television show in the U.S.

– strict-pressed Art, who was well over 200 lbs.

1953, November 11

– gave a demonstration at Ed Yarick's *Big Show* in Oakland, California.

– squatted 665 lbs. to break Paul Anderson's world record of 660 lbs.

– pressed pair of 160 lb. dumbbells.

– right hand military pressed 170 lb. dumbbell.

– did pedestal handstand at weight of 270 lbs.

- pressed 260 lbs.
- cleaned 90 lbs. with little finger.

1953, December 10
- gave a demonstration at the 2nd Annual Strength and Health Show in Vancouver, Canada.
- set world bench press record of 502 lbs., first lifter in history to break the 500 lb. bench press barrier.

1954, May 10
- won the Western Canadian Weightlifting Championships in Vancouver (clean/press of 381 lbs., clean/jerk of 350 lbs., snatch of 270 lbs.).
- set world clean/press record of 381 lbs.

1954, July 1
- gave a demonstration at the Horseshoe Bay Dominion Day Celebration in Vancouver, duplicating his May 10, 1954 total to prove it wasn't luck.

1954, August 7
- won the British Empire Games in Vancouver with an injured right knee, the only B.C. athlete to win gold (clean/press of 370 lbs., snatch of 300 lbs., clean/jerk of 370 lbs.) in any BEG event.
- set Games clean/press record of 370 lbs., 30 lbs. more than Quebec lifter Dave Baillie's 340 lbs.

1954, October
- toured eastern Canada, giving lifting exhibitions and performing strong man stunts: bending spikes, ripping license plates and crushing cans of oil with his bare hands.

1954, November 21
- set three world records at the Montreal Forum: 505 lb. bench press, 460 lb. push-press-off-rack and 167 lb. one-arm military press.

1956, December 8
- passed over for the Melbourne Olympics in Australia because CAAU weightlifting headquarters in Montreal stated that they were sending no lifters that year, even though Doug was heavily favoured to win.

1959, November 19
- gave an exhibition in Vancouver to promote his return to wrestling (assisted push press of 420 lbs., two-hand curl of 225 lbs.).

1963, July 17
- made a comeback as a world-class strong man by pressing 420 lbs. in perfect form, 7 lbs. greater than the official world record at the time held by Yuri Vlasov of Russia.

1973, November 3
- set a world one-arm military press record of 170 lbs. in Vancouver, B.C., destroying Dennis Hillman of Great Britain's record of 147.7 lbs.

1988
- all Doug's official lifting records were discarded by the CAAU and the BCWA when a new weight division system was employed.

1996
- Doug issued a "Challenge to the World" to beat his lift records drug free for a prize of $10,000. No one accepted.

An article by Eric J. Murray in the March 1997 edition of *Milo* Magazine outlined Doug's 1980 comeback feats (at age 54) as:

1. Squatted 600 lbs. for 8 reps.
2. Push pressed 390 lbs. off-the-rack.
3. Two-hand curled 230 lbs.
4. Right-hand military pressed 170 lbs.

A December, 2000 *Vancouver Sun* article by former Canadian Weightlifting Champion and Olympian, Paul Bjarnason, of Vancouver, Canada, lists Doug's lifting *"firsts"* as:

1. First to military press 400 lbs. overhead.
2. First to push press 500 lbs. overhead.
3. First to bench press 500 lbs.
4. First to two-hand curl 250 lbs.
5. First to perform a crucifix with two 100 lb. dumbbells.
6. First to military press a 200 lb. dumbbell with one hand.

DOUG HEPBURN'S AWARDS AND ACKNOWLEDGEMENTS

IN 1953, AFTER WINNING gold in the World Weightlifting Championships in Stockholm, Sweden, Doug was

1. Met at the airport by Mayor Hume and driven through the city as a hero.
2. Voted B.C. Athlete of the Year by a poll of the Vancouver *Sun* newspaper subscribers.
3. Voted B.C. Athlete of the Year by a poll of the Vancouver *Province* newspaper subscribers.
4. Selected as Canada's Outstanding Amateur Athlete by the Amateur Athletic Union of Canada.
5. Awarded the Lou Marsh Memorial Trophy as Canada's outstanding athlete.
6. Voted Athlete of the Year by a poll of the Canadian Press and Radio Sports Writers and Broadcasters.

7. Voted British Columbian of the Year by a poll of the Newsman's Club of B.C.
8. Given the Vancouver City Council's Civic Merit Award, the highest honour the city can pay its champions.
9. The first athlete to bring a world gold medal in any sport to Vancouver since Percy Williams' Olympic run in 1928.

In 1954, after winning gold in the British Empire Games in Vancouver, Canada, Doug was

1. The only B.C. athlete to win a gold medal in the Games.
2. Congratulated by Lord Alexander of Tunis.
3. Written up in *Time, Maclean's* and *Life* magazines.
4. On the cover of the July 1954 edition of *Life* magazine.
5. Inducted into the Canadian Sports Hall of Fame (June 10, 1955).
6. Inducted into the B.C. Sports Hall of Fame (July 7, 1966), where his lifts and the Landy/Bannister run are the two most popular exhibits.
7. The subject of a CBC Times documentary (1967) entitled *The Strength of Giants.*
8. The subject of two movie scripts: *The Magnificent Journey,* by Barry Whittaker and *Strongman: The Doug Hepburn Story,* by Tom Thurston.

OFFICIAL 1952 AND 1956 OLYMPIC WEIGHTLIFTING RESULTS

(in pounds)

HELSINKI, FINLAND — JULY 5, 1952

	PRESS	SNATCH	JERK	TOTAL
1. J. DAVIS, U.S.	330.0	319.0	363.0	1012.0
2. J. BRADFORD, U.S.	308.0	291.5	363.0	962.5
3. H. SELVETTI, ARGEN.	330.0	264.0	357.5	951.5
4. H. SCHATTNER, GER.	286.0	286.0	357.5	929.5
5. D. BAILLIE, CAN.	319.0	269.5	335.5	924.0

MELBOURNE, AUSTRALIA — DECEMBER 8, 1956

	PRESS	SNATCH	JERK	TOTAL
1. P. ANDERSON, U.S.	368.5	319.0	412.5	1100.0
2. H. SELVETTI, ARGEN.	385.0	319.0	396.0	1100.0
3. A. PIGAIANI, ITALY	330.0	286.0	379.5	994.4
4. F. PEJHAN, IRAN	324.5	291.5	374.0	990.0
5. E. MAKINEN, FIN.	280.5	302.5	368.5	951.5
6. D. BAILLIE, CAN.	324.5	269.5	357.5	951.5

Given Doug Hepburn's three best official lifts of 1952 (set during a competition outlined in Appendix 2) it is fair to say that he would probably have won a medal for Canada at the Helsinki Olympics — quite possibly gold. Yet the weightlifting division of the Canadian Amateur Athletics Union in Quebec, Canada elected to send fellow Quebecer, Dave Baillie, a lifter who had never beaten Doug in any of the three Olympic lifts and who only placed fifth at Helsinki.

DOUG HEPBURN'S THREE BEST OFFICIAL LIFTS FOR 1952
(Pacific Coast Weightlifting Championships,
Portland, Oregon — officially accepted by the U.S.)

	PRESS	SNATCH	JERK	TOTAL
D. HEPBURN, CANADA	361.0	290.0	360.0	1011.0

Even using his official 1954 total set at the British Empire Games two years before the Melbourne Olympics, it is clear that he could have won gold in Melbourne if he had trained the extra two years. His total of 1040 would certainly have placed — a second lost medal for Canada.

DOUG HEPBURN'S THREE BEST OFFICIAL LIFTS OF 1954
(British Empire Games, Vancouver, B.C. — officially
accepted by Canada)

	PRESS	SNATCH	JERK	TOTAL
D. HEPBURN, CANADA	370.0	300.0	370.0	1040.0

APPENDIX 5

DOUG'S EXACT 1953
WORLD CHAMPIONSHIP
TRAINING PROGRAM

DOUG HEPBURN'S SIMPLE but profound principle for building super strength without drugs, wraps or aids of any kind is to "lift heavy weights for low repetitions." It earned him the title of "Grandfather of Modern Powerlifting" and allowed him huge gains in strength that were unforced and controlled.

Since training for the Olympic clean-and-press, the Olympic snatch and the Olympic clean-and-jerk requires lifting technique as well as power, Doug employed five exercises to develop both:

1. SNATCH — the snatch is performed in one continuous movement, so it must be practised regularly to ensure proper balance and coordination.
2. CLEAN (from floor) — since the clean-and-jerk and the clean-and-press are performed in two movements, practising cleans alone allows the lifter to employ maximum weight.

3. CLEAN (from hang) — cleaning a second time without allowing the weight to touch the floor requires more brute power than a regular clean, even though the weight on the bar remains the same.

4. BENCH PRESS — guarantees maximum shoulder power for pressing and jerking.

5. FULL SQUAT — guarantees maximum leg power for all three competitive lifts.

To prevent injuries and muscle stagnation due to over-training, Doug trained three times a week with three of the above five exercises per session:

1. MONDAY — clean
           — bench press
           — full squat
2. WEDNESDAY — snatch
              — bench press
              — full squat.
3. FRIDAY   — clean
           — bench press
           — full squat

Doug's repetitions, sets and training poundages were as follows:

1. MONDAY:
    A. CLEAN — 280 lbs. for 2 repetitions (first repetition from floor, second repetition from hang).
           — 300 lbs. for 2 repetitions (first from floor, second from hang).
           — 320 lbs. for 2 repetitions (first from floor, second from hang).
           — 320 lbs. for 2 repetitions (first from floor, second from hang).
           — 320 lbs. for 2 repetitions (first from floor, second from hang).
           — 320 lbs. for 2 repetitions (first from floor, second from hang).

— 320 lbs. for 2 repetitions
(first from floor, second from hang).
— 320 lbs. for 2 repetitions
(first from floor, second from hang).
— 320 lbs. for 2 repetitions
(first from floor, second from hang).
— 320 lbs. for 2 repetitions
(first from floor, second from hang).

B. BENCH PRESS — 350 lbs. for 5 repetitions.
— 400 lbs. for 2.
— 450 lbs. for 2.
— 450 lbs. for 2.
— 450 lbs. for 2.
— 450 lbs. for 2.
— 450 lbs. for 2.

C. FULL SQUAT — 475 lbs. for 5 repetitions.
— 520 lbs. for 3.
— 550 lbs. for 3.
— 550 lbs. for 3.
— 550 lbs. for 3.
— 550 lbs. for 3.
— 550 lbs. for 3.

2. WEDNESDAY:
A. SNATCH — 200 lbs. for 3 repetitions.
— 240 lbs. for 2.
— 260 lbs. for 2.
— 260 lbs. for 2.
— 260 lbs. for 2.
— 260 lbs. for 2.
— 260 lbs. for 2.
— 260 lbs. for 2.
— 260 lbs. for 2.
— 260 lbs. for 2.

B. BENCH PRESS — same as Monday's workout.
C. FULL SQUAT — same as Monday's workout.

3. FRIDAY:
   A. CLEAN — same as Monday's workout.
   B. BENCH PRESS — same as Monday's workout.
   C. FULL SQUAT — same as Monday's workout.

During each training session, Doug drank copious amounts of milk and spent his rest time visualizing how he would win at the Stockholm competition. Doug firmly believed that mental and emotional conditioning are as important as the physical.

DOUG'S EXACT 1954 BRITISH EMPIRE GAMES TRAINING PROGRAM

DOUG CONSTRUCTED a completely new training routine for the British Empire Games. While training for any event, he always concentrated on the muscles and lifting techniques that he felt needed the most attention at the time. Since his abilities and strong-points had changed since 1953, he adapted his 1954 program to suit.

Doug employed seven exercises simultaneously to develop power and technique. Working out three times a week, he performed two of the seven exercises each workout day, and followed this routine for approximately twelve weeks:

FIRST WEEK
    1. MONDAY — press-off-rack
                — snatch

   2. WEDNESDAY — bench press
                   — squat
   3. FRIDAY   — press-off-rack
                   — snatch

SECOND WEEK
   1. MONDAY   — press-off-rack
                   — high pull
   2. WEDNESDAY — bench press
                   — squat
   3. FRIDAY   — press-off-rack
                   — high pull

THIRD WEEK
   1. MONDAY   — press-off-rack
                   — snatch
   2. WEDNESDAY — bench press
                   — squat
   3. FRIDAY   — press-off-rack
                   — snatch

FOURTH WEEK
   1. MONDAY   — press-off-rack
                   — high pull
   2. WEDNESDAY — bench press
                   — squat
   3. FRIDAY   — press-off-rack
                   — clean-and-jerk

After the fourth week, he returned to the first week's routine and began the cycle again.

When Doug badly injured his thigh approximately two weeks before the BEG competition (as noted in Chapter 4), he dropped the above routine and performed only the three Olympic lifts. He was careful to do no lift more than twice a week:

   1. MONDAY   — snatch
                   — clean-and-press
   2. WEDNESDAY — snatch
                   — clean-and-jerk

3. FRIDAY   — clean-and-press

                     — clean-and-jerk

Doug employed the following poundages, sets and repetitions for his entire BEG training:

1. PRESS-OFF-THE-RACK

                300 lbs. for 3 repetitions.

                350 lbs. for 2.

                390 lbs. for 3

                390 lbs. for 3.

                390 lbs. for 3.

                390 lbs. for 3.

                390 lbs. for 3.

                390 lbs. for 3.

                390 lbs. for 3.

                390 lbs. for 3.

2. SNATCH

                210 lbs. for 3 repetitions.

                250 lbs. for 3.

                270 lbs. for 3.

                270 lbs. for 3.

                270 lbs. for 3.

                270 lbs. for 3.

                270 lbs. for 3.

                270 lbs. for 3.

                270 lbs. for 3.

                270 lbs. for 3.

3. BENCH PRESS

                360 lbs. for 5 repetitions.

                410 lbs. for 2.

                450 lbs. for 3.

                450 lbs. for 3.

                450 lbs. for 3.

                450 lbs. for 3.

                450 lbs. for 3.

                450 lbs. for 3.

450 lbs. for 3.

450 lbs. for 3.

4. DEEP SQUAT

480 lbs. for 5 repetitions.

525 lbs. for 3.

550 lbs. for 6.

550 lbs. for 6.

550 lbs. for 6.

550 lbs. for 6.

550 lbs. for 6.

550 lbs. for 6.

550 lbs. for 6.

550 lbs. for 6.

5. HIGH PULLS

410 lbs. for 5 repetitions.

450 lbs. for 2.

490 lbs. for 3.

490 lbs. for 3.

490 lbs. for 3.

490 lbs. for 3.

490 lbs. for 3.

490 lbs. for 3.

490 lbs. for 3.

490 lbs. for 3.

6. CLEAN-AND-JERK

300 lbs. for 3 repetitions.

320 lbs. for 2.

340 lbs. for 3.

340 lbs. for 3.

340 lbs. for 3.

340 lbs. for 3.

340 lbs. for 3.

340 lbs. for 3.

340 lbs. for 3.

340 lbs. for 3.

7. CLEAN-AND-PRESS

300 lbs. for 3 repetitions.
320 lbs. for 2.
340 lbs. for 3.
340 lbs. for 3.
340 lbs. for 3.
340 lbs. for 3.
340 lbs. for 3.
340 lbs. for 3.
340 lbs. for 3.
340 lbs. for 3.

Once again, Doug drank copious amounts of milk throughout his workout and continually visualized himself winning the BEG competition.

DOUG CHALLENGES
THE WORLD

DOUG ISSUED TWO CHALLENGES to the world (see the next two pages). The first was to "all ages" and was to duplicate or best his five *verified* lifts — life-time drug free. The second was to people aged "seventy and over," and was to duplicate or beat 30 lifts that he could do at age seventy — life-time drug free.

WORLD ELITE WEIGHTLIFTING ASSOCIATION

PHONE 604 873 3684

HEPBURN CHALLENGES THE WORLD

Canadian Doug Hepburn challenges · · · · · · · · ·
· · · worldwide to an invitational series of **5** all round strength lifts in defence of his title of world's strongest. · · · · His challenge is presented under the auspices of the World Elite Weightlifting Association.

5 LIFT SERIES QUALIFYING POUNDAGE:

1 one arm dumbell press **200**LBS
2 squat **800**LBS
3 two arm curl **260**LBS
4 press off rack **450**LBS
5 hold out at side **110**LBS

All contestants are requested to comply to the following terms — No belt, or wraps, loose fitting sweatsuit only to be worn. Must be lifetime drug free. Polygraph requested as arranged by W.E.W.A. upon acceptance of entry form. Birth certificate required. VHS video documentation of the above **5** qualifying lifts endorsed by 3 witnesses presented with entry form. All qualifying lifts to be performed with internationally accepted calibrated bars and plates.

Entry form with rules available at
WORLD ELITE WEIGHT LIFTING ASSOCIATION
40 East 4th Avenue, Vancouver, BC Canada V5T 1E8

PRESIDENT

CENTRAL DIVISION 40 EAST 4th AVENUE   VANCOUVER BRITISH COLUMBIA CANADA V5T 1E8

HEPBURN CHALLENGES THE WORLD

Canadian Doug Hepburn challenges seniors 70 and over worldwide to an invitational series of 30 all round strength lifts in defence of his title of world's strongest senior. His challenge is presented under the auspices of the World Elite Weightlifting Association.

30 LIFT SERIES QUALIFYING POUNDAGE:

LIFT	LBS	KILOS	LIFT	LBS	KILOS	LIFT	LBS	KILOS
1. Military Press (Dumbell) Rt. Arm	106	48	11. Military Press (Off Rack)	220	100	21. Crucifix (Dumbells)	85	38.5
2. Military Press (Dumbell) Lft. Arm	90	41	12. Press Behind Neck (Off Rack)	180	82	22. Hold Out in Front (Barbell)	80	36
3. Clean & Jerk (Dumbell) Rt. Arm	115	52	13. Jerk (Off Rack)	240	109	23. Press Behind Neck (Seated)	165	75
4. Clean & Jerk (Dumbell) Lft. Arm	95	43	14. Cheat Curl (Dumbell LH)	70	32	24. Seated Press	180	82
5. Squat (Heels 12" Apart)	400	181.5	15. Cheat Curl (Dumbell RH)	70	32	25. T.N. Snatch (Barbell)	150	68
6. Deadlift (Heels 12" Apart)	400	181.5	16. Cheat Curl (Barbell)	170	77	26. T.N. Anyhow (Dumbells)	170	77
7. Bench Press (Hands Together)	225	102	17. Strict Curl (Barbell)	160	72.5	27. Clean & Jerk (Dumbell)	190	86
8. Bench Press (Feet in the Air)	300	136	18. Clean Press (Barbells)	190	86	28. Dumbell Swing RH	90	41
9. Rt. Arm Snatch (Dumbell)	90	41	19. Clean & Jerk (Barbell)	190	86	29. Dumbell Swing LH	70	32
10. Lft. Arm Snatch (Dumbell)	80	36	20. Clean & Press (Barbells)	180	82	30. Clean & Jerk (Dumbells)	190	86

All contestants are requested to comply to the following terms — No belt, or wraps, loose fitting sweatsuit only to be worn. Must be lifetime drug free. Polygraph requested as arranged by W.E.W.A. upon acceptance of entry form. Birth certificate required. VHS video documentation of the above 30 qualifying lifts endorsed by 3 witnesses presented with entry form. All qualifying lifts to be performed with internationally accepted calibrated bars and plates.

Entry form with rules available at
WORLD ELITE WEIGHT LIFTING ASSOCIATION
40 East 4th Avenue, Vancouver, BC Canada V5T 1E8

CHOOSING YOUR STRENGTH EXERCISES

THE FOLLOWING EXERCISES have proven to be extremely effective for working the larger muscles of the body. To receive the maximum strength and size from your training effort, perform them exactly as explained and pay particular attention to the cautionary tips provided.

FULL SQUAT (DEEP KNEE BEND)

To prepare for the exercise, place the bar on lifting stands so that you would have to bend your knees slightly (no more than three to four inches) if you were to stand underneath the bar with it snug against the *back* of your shoulders and as far away from your neck joint as possible. Load the bar to the desired poundage, face the lifting stands and stand underneath the bar as described above. To avoid discomfort, place a pad or folded towel between the bar and your shoulder muscles. To avoid unnecessary back strain from the body leaning too far forward during the upward portion of the movement, grip the bar with both hands and employ as wide a grip as possible.

To perform the exercise, lift the bar from the stands by straightening the legs and carefully move three to four feet backwards. Keeping your heels and your shoulders parallel (your right shoulder above your right heel and your left shoulder above your left heel), position your feet approximately eighteen inches apart with your toes pointing outwards. Keeping your feet flat on the floor, take a deep breath and hold it as you squat down to the point where the leg biceps touch the leg calves. At this point, still holding your breath, start back up to a standing position, taking care *not* to expel your breath until your knee joint angle (formed by the articulation of the femur and tibia bones) is greater than ninety degrees. Keep your body properly balanced throughout the movement by holding your back flat and your line of vision angled upwards at about forty-five degrees. Once standing, take three deep breaths. If you are doing heavy singles, place the bar back on the stands and take your required rest, as indicated by your heavy singles program. If you are doing repetitions, take a fourth deep breath, hold it and repeat the movement. Never squat with an elevated platform under your heels or while using elevated shoes, since it will diminish the efficiency of the exercise and increase strain on the lower back. If you are unable to keep the heels flat on the floor during the entire squatting movement, warm and stretch the Achilles tendon at the back of the heel before you squat.

HIGH PULL MOVEMENT

Place the bar on the floor, load to the desired poundage and stand facing the middle of the bar so that your shins almost touch the steel. Positioning your feet about twelve to fourteen inches apart with your toes pointing outwards, grasp the bar with both hands using a "regular thumbs around the bar" grip, where both palms are on the same side of the bar and the thumbs are pointing towards each other. The distance between the gripped hands should be exactly shoulder width or the exercise's efficiency will be lost. Bending your legs slightly, maintain a flat back (neither arched nor rounded), and make certain that your arms are completely straight. Elevate your chin to a forty-five degree angle and hold in this position throughout the exercise movement.

To perform the movement, take a deep breath and pull the barbell as high as you can by bending your arms and straightening your back and legs. At the completion of the exercise, you should be standing erect with the barbell pulled up your body at *least* past your belt level. When this is not possible, a lighter poundage must be employed. Since this is a training exercise for the "cleaning" portion of Olympic style weightlifting as well as an extremely effective power builder for the upper and lower back, it must always be performed in a swift but *controlled* manner. Never jerk the barbell from the floor and never begin the exercise with your arms bent or you will vastly reduce the efficiency of the exercise. Hold your breath until you are standing erect at the completion of the exercise movement, then expel and take a couple of deep breaths. If you are doing heavy singles, place the barbell back on the floor and take your required rest. If you are doing repetitions, place the bar back on the floor and repeat the movement.

TWO-HAND DEADLIFT

To prepare for the exercise, place the bar on the floor, load it to the desired poundage and stand facing the bar so that your shins almost touch the steel. Positioning your feet about twelve to fourteen inches apart with your toes pointing outwards, grasp the bar with both hands using a "reverse thumbs around the bar" grip so that the palms are on opposite sides of the bar and the thumbs are pointing in the same direction — either both pointing to the left, or both pointing to the right. This grip will allow you to hold the bar more securely (thereby allowing you to employ the heaviest weights possible) and will prevent the bar from rolling out of your hands while lifting. The legs should be bent, the back should be flat and the distance between your gripping hands should be exactly shoulder width. The head should be angled upwards at about forty-five degrees and should remain so throughout the movement.

To perform the exercise, take a deep breath and hold it as you *smoothly* straighten your legs and back until you are standing erect. Never jerk the bar during any stage of the lift or you could suffer severe muscle damage. Unlike the high pull movement, the arms remain straight throughout the exercise and the emphasis is on straightening the back and legs rather than "arm-pulling" the weight as high as possible. Once erect, exhale and take a couple of deep breaths. If you are doing heavy singles, place the bar back on the floor and take your required rest. If you are doing repetitions, place the bar back on the floor and repeat the movement.

BENCH PRESS

To prepare for the exercise, place the bar on the arm supports of your bench press machine and adjust their height so that you will not have to lift the bar more than one inch to assume the full weight. Load the bar to the desired poundage and make sure that the collars that prevent the plates from sliding from the bar are tight. When lying on the bench, be sure that your neck is between the supports and your shoulders are almost touching them. The back and hips must be flat against the bench and must remain so throughout the entire exercise. The legs must be fully extended with your heels resting on the floor and must remain so throughout the entire exercise. It is important to keep the back, hips and legs in this position so that they cannot "assist" the chest muscles with the lift. When gripping the bar, make sure that you have the correct width between your hands by ensuring that each of your extended arms forms a forty-five degree angle with the horizontal bar. Make sure, also, that you employ a "regular thumbs around the bar" grip, where both your palms are facing away from the support arms and your thumbs are pointing towards each other.

To perform the exercise, take the deepest breath possible and hold it as you *smoothly* and in a controlled manner assume the weight from the support arms, lower it to the chest (a point just below the nipples) and push it back up until the arms are fully extended. For maximum results, do not expel your breath until the weight has risen past the most difficult or "sticking" stage of the upward press. For your own safety, make sure that the bar is equally supported by each arm before lowering it to your chest. If you are doing heavy singles, place the bar back on the support arms after your first press and take your required rest. If you are doing repetitions, take a deep breath and repeat the exercise.

OLYMPIC PRESS

To prepare for the exercise, place the bar on a pair of squat stands and load it to the desired poundage. Adjust the height of the stands so that you can face the bar with your legs slightly bent and grip it with both hands as though you had just completed an Olympic clean to the shoulders. If the height is correct, the bar will be horizontal across the upper chest and you will be able to easily assume the weight from the stands by straightening your legs. Once this is completed, move backwards about two to three feet and position your feet fourteen to eighteen inches apart.

To perform the exercise, keep your legs completely straight, take the deepest breath possible and hold it as you quickly but smoothly push the barbell above your head until your arms are fully extended. For maximum results, exhale as the barbell moves upwards past the most difficult phase of the exercise, which will be approximately level with the top of your head. Never use another part of your body to "help" you get the weight up during any phase of the movement, as this will greatly reduce the effectiveness of the exercise. If you are doing heavy singles, place the barbell back on the stands and take your required rest. If you are doing repetitions, take another deep breath (either when the weight is fully extended above the head or as it is being lowered) and repeat the exercise.

TWO-ARM BICEPS CURL

To begin the exercise, place the bar on the floor, load it to the desired poundage and face it with your shins almost touching the steel. Positioning the feet twelve to fourteen inches apart, grasp the bar with both hands using a "regular thumbs around" grip, where both palms are on the same side of the bar and the thumbs are pointing away from each other. Keeping the arms straight and the elbows snug against the body, stand as erect as possible with the bar held horizontal against the top of the thighs.

To perform the exercise, take a deep breath and hold it as you smoothly curl the barbell to the top portion of your chest. Strive to keep the elbows snug against the body throughout the entire movement and never attempt to "throw" the weight up with your arms, hips or legs. If you are doing heavy singles, exhale as you lower the weight to the floor and take your required rest. If you are doing repetitions, exhale as you lower the weight down to where your arms are completely straight and repeat the exercise. To prevent the development of a "shortened biceps" (where the arm can no longer be fully straightened by the triceps), it is imperative that you never begin the curl until both arms are *completely* straight.

TWO-LEG BICEPS CURL

To begin the exercise, load the leg-curl machine to the desired poundage. Lying chest down on the bench, grip the padded curling bar with the heels and lower calves of both legs and grip the sides of the bench with both hands for support. There is no mandatory leg or heel spacing because the curling bar can only be employed one way.

To perform the exercise, take a deep breath and hold it as you smoothly curl your heels towards your upper leg biceps. As with the two-arm curl, always begin with the legs *completely* extended to prevent a "shortened biceps" problem, as previously described. Strive to keep the front of your body flat against the bench throughout the curling movement and never try to "throw" the weight up with the hips or any other part of your body. If you are doing heavy singles, exhale as you lower the curling bar to the start position. If you are doing repetitions, exhale as you lower the bar to the start position and repeat the exercise.

TWO-LEG CALF-RAISES

To prepare for the exercise, decide whether your goal is to stretch out your Achilles tendon so that you will be able properly to perform full squats (as outlined above), or to develop maximum power and size in the calf muscles. If you wish to do both, do your power routine first and follow it with your stretching while the muscles are still warm.

To prepare for the power routine, place the bar on the lifting stands, load it to the desired poundage and assume the weight on your shoulders as described in the full squat exercise.

To perform the exercise, carefully move three to four feet backwards and position your feet shoulder width apart and parallel. With your knees slightly bent (no more than two to three inches), take a deep breath and hold it as you *smoothly* raise your heels from the floor as high as you can. Expel as you reach your maximum height. It is extremely important always to perform this exercise in a controlled manner so that you do not lose your balance. Never try to "throw" yourself up or the effectiveness of the exercise will be lost. Since the calf muscle responds only to *high repetition* exercise (one of the few muscles of the body that does) heavy singles and heavy low repetitions are never used in either the power or the pump routine. The normal and most effective procedure is to do three to five sets per workout, using fifteen to twenty repetitions per set.

After you have completed your power routine, place the bar back on the lifting stands and take a couple of deep breaths. Once relaxed and breathing normally, place a three foot length of wood (four inches thick by twelve inches wide) on the floor in front of you so that your toes are touching one side. Using the wall, a lifting stand or your training partner for support, stand on the wood so that the balls of your feet are supporting your weight and your heels are jutting out over the side. Bending your knees slightly, allow your heels to drop towards the floor. Concentrate on the stretching sensation that you will feel in your calves and try to help the process by relaxing those muscles as much as you can. Do ten sets of stretching and hold each stretch for a minimum of ten seconds. Breathe normally during each stretch and walk around for a few seconds after each stretching set. Stretch both calves at once or do them separately. Stretching them separately allows you to place more of your body weight on the calf.

SCHEDULING YOUR STRENGTH WORKOUT

IF YOU DESIRE a total body workout but can only afford two or three times a week, you will get the best results by exercising the body's three largest muscle groups (chest, legs and back) with the three following exercises.

1. Two times a week:
   TUESDAY — bench press, squat, deadlift.
   THURSDAY — bench press, squat, deadlift.
2. Three times a week:
   MONDAY — bench press, squat, deadlift.
   WEDNESDAY — Olympic press, squat, high pulls.
   FRIDAY — bench press, squat, deadlift.

If you desire a total body workout and can afford four or six days a week, you will need to work your upper and lower body on alternate days. You should also employ three more exercises to make your workouts more rigorous.

1. Four times a week:
    MONDAY — bench press, deadlift, arm biceps curls.
    TUESDAY — squat, leg biceps curl, calf raises.
    THURSDAY — bench press, high pulls, arm biceps curls.
    FRIDAY — squat, leg biceps curl, calf raises.
2. Six times a week:
    MONDAY — bench press, deadlift, arm biceps curls.
    TUESDAY — squat, leg biceps curls, calf raises.
    WEDNESDAY — Olympic press, high pulls, arm biceps curls.
    THURSDAY — squat, leg biceps curls, calf raises.
    FRIDAY — bench press, deadlift, arm biceps curls.
    SATURDAY — squat, leg biceps curls, calf raises.

With the three, four and six times a week schedules, you will notice that on some training days the bench press and the dead-lift have been replaced with the Olympic press and high pulls. This is because they work more or less the same muscles as the bench press and the deadlift, but are not quite as taxing. If you prefer to employ the more strenuous bench press and the deadlift in place of the Olympic press and high pulls (respectively) this will be fine. Just be aware that in doing so, because you are working each muscle group three times a week, you increase your chances of encountering muscle stagnation. Conversely, if you adhere strictly to the aforementioned training rule of never exerting your maximum lifting ability during training, muscle stagnation should not become a problem.

EXACT POUNDAGE AND REPETITION INCREASES FOR DOUG'S "A" AND "B" PROGRAMS

PROGRAM "A"

1. Power:

   Pick a weight that you can lift eight but not nine times in a row and do the following power routine as indicated, making sure to take a two- to three-minute rest after each set of repetitions:

8 x 2	first workout
7 x 2 and 1 x 3	second workout
6 x 2 and 2 x 3	third workout
5 x 2 and 3 x 3	fourth workout
4 x 2 and 4 x 3	fifth workout
3 x 2 and 5 x 3	sixth workout
2 x 2 and 6 x 3	seventh workout
1 x 2 and 7 x 3	eighth workout
8 x 3	ninth workout

(increase the weight no more than 10 lbs. for large muscle groups and 5 lbs. for small ones — less if you feel the need — and return to 8 x 2)

2. Pump:

   After the power routine, reduce your training weight approximately 20 percent and perform the following, making sure to take a three- to five-minute rest after each set of repetitions:

3 x 6	first workout
2 x 6 and 1 x 7	second workout
1 x 6 and 2 x 7	third workout
3 x 7	fourth workout
2 x 7 and 1 x 8	fifth workout
1 x 7 and 2 x 8	sixth workout
3 x 8	seventh workout

   (increase the weight no more than 10 lbs. for large muscle groups and 5 lbs. for small ones — less if you feel the need — and return to 3 x 6)

PROGRAM "B"

1. Power:

   Pick a poundage that you can *easily* lift once and rest for three to five minutes. Increase your weight to a poundage that you can *comfortably* lift once and rest for three to five minutes. Increase the weight to a poundage that you can lift three continuous times with but not four and use this weight for your heavy singles, still making sure that you take a three to five-minute rest after each single lift:

5 x 1	first workout
6 x 1	second workout
7 x 1	third workout
8 x 1	fourth workout

   (increase the weight no more than 10 lbs. for large muscle groups and 5 lbs. for small ones — less if you feel the need — and return to 5 x 1)

2. Pump:

   After the "heavy singles" power routine, take a fifteen- to twenty-minute rest, reduce your weight to a poundage that you can

lift for eight consecutive repetitions but not nine and do the following, making sure that you take a three- to five-minute rest
after each set of repetitions:

6 x 3	first workout
5 x 3 and 1 x 4	second workout
4 x 3 and 2 x 4	third workout
3 x 3 and 3 x 4	fourth workout
2 x 3 and 4 x 4	fifth workout
1 x 3 and 5 x 4	sixth workout
6 x 4	seventh workout
5 x 4 and 1 x 5	eight workout
4 x 4 and 2 x 5	ninth workout
3 x 4 and 3 x 5	tenth workout
2 x 4 and 4 x 5	eleventh workout
1 x 4 and 5 x 5	twelfth workout
6 x 5	thirteenth workout

(increase the weight no more than 10 lbs. for large muscle
groups and 5 lbs. for small ones — less if you feel the need —
and return to 6 x 3)

To begin either the "A" or the "B" program, do the first power
workout and the first pump workout together on the first training
day, the second power workout and the second pump workout
together on the second training day, and so on. For example, if
you are starting the "B" program, your first workout would be
5 x 1 from the power routine followed by 6 x 3 from the "B" pump
routine; your second workout would be 6 x 1 from the power routine followed by 5 x 3 and 1 x 4 from the pump routine. If you are
beginning the "A" program, your first workout would be 8 x 2
from the "A" power routine followed by 3 x 6 from the "A" pump
routine; your second workout would be 7 x 2 and 1 x 3 from the
power routine followed by 2 x 6 and 1 x 7 from the pump routine.

Since the number of workout days in the power routines are
different from the number of days in the pump routines (9 workout days in the "A" power routine compared to 7 workout days in
the "A" pump routine; 4 workout days in the "B" power routine
compared with 13 workout days in the "B" pump routine), it is

extremely important that, when you reach the end of either a power or pump routine in either program and are directed by that routine to return to its beginning sets and repetitions, you do not automatically return to the beginning of its corresponding routine at the same time. Each routine must be completed as *written,* or you will overtax your body by increasing your repetitions and training poundages too quickly. Follow the directions of each routine separately and the programs will take care of themselves.

INDEX